The Space Jar

Lucas
Trance

Volume One

ISBN-13: 978-1724845047
booksofprospero@gmail.com

Library of Congress Cataloging-in-Publication Data
Ray, Sandip
The Space Jar
ISBN-13: 978-1724845047
ISBN-10: 1724845047
Genetic Engineering

Illustrative Abstract

While it may be difficult to paint a picture, describe a painting, or worse, attempt to write a book about the space jar, a simple imaginative rendering may be of a sailing ship inside a clear glass bottle. Endymion's saga opens with wondering how the hull and the mastheads could possibly have been assembled and affixed inside a bottle. The quantum calculus is a subject of calculus without limits and deals with a set of non-differentiable functions. The quantum operators are widely used in mathematic fields such as hypergeometric series, complex analysis, orthogonal polynomials, combinatorics, hypergeometric functions, and the calculus of variations. The first problem is a Riemann-Liouville fractional Fermat Space boundary value problem for fractional Fermat integro-difference equations. The second is a fractional Hahn integral boundary value problem for Caputo fractional Fermat difference equations. The Banach fixed-point theorem and the Schauder fixed-point theorem are used as tools to prove the existence and uniqueness of solution of the problems. The author also studies the existence and uniqueness of solution for the initial value problems for Fermat difference equations by employing the method of successive approximations; in addition, they proved Fibonacci and Bernoulli's inequalities with respect to the Fermat difference operator and investigated the mean value theorems for this calculus. To further a genuine fastidious nature to the discrete, Endymion's saga opens with a definition of an observatory, defined as a place, a particular position or point in space, a portion of space available or designated for or being used by someone- the observer, Endymion, where the autobiographical discrete space are calculated as semi-classical Newtonian in style, rather than type, demonstrating how synchrotrons think, compared to physiologists in clinical practice, both of which has changed since the birth of Lenin, in how we think about biochemistry, and cell biology. Gravitational wave (GW) astronomy has come to revolutionize our understanding of astrophysics, cosmology and fundamental physics. GWs from binary black-hole (BH) mergers allow us to learn about the population of BHs, their origin and their role through the history of the universe. If these BHs have a primordial origin and are abundant enough, they could comprise a large fraction of the Dark Matter (DM). As a case of study, I will present the primordial black-hole production in Critical Higgs Inflation, a particle physics motivated model in which the SM Higgs is both responsible of inflation and DM, and discuss its GWs signatures. Moreover, GWs detected with an associated counterpart can probe the evolution of the universe and Dark Energy (DE). The recent measurement of the GW speed following GW170817 is an excellent example of the immense potential available to GWs tests of gravity. I will present the conditions for anomalous GW speed and classify the theories for DE that remain viable after GW170817. Finally, I will discuss how other propagation effects could also shed light on the quest for the nature of DE.

Liner Prospective

Relax and lean back, this could take a while, perhaps four and half generations in the development of the average Pentium load capacitance, without the smell of Shinigami cheese melt. Mathematics is based on a certain set of assumptions, well known assumptions; does not fare well with too-quick-to-respond. When the quill becomes emptied of its ink, we can compare how any particular assumption may be different from their subsequent assay. While most fuck heads tend towards being oblate, several fuck heads are mutinous. Begun in 1982 as a collaborative enterprise with AAAS Science and Nature, code encryption comprising such buoyance matter as learning to read and learning to look, ahead of experimentation, hypothesis, and observation, while keeping the conclusions impermeable to interpretations is what we call nasty business. Eating during travel is an essential, as various relegations may appear quixotic – *remember the snow monkey.* There were some who had come to doubt their existence, and long before the invention of the Pentium, they had turned into Xerox photo copiers for slap happy pedantics. Perhaps not that long, but rather quickly after the invention of Pulsars, with Quasars lagging in facilitating their promise to the Holy Roman Empire due to the dearth in Albigeois terrace landings worthy of, the resistors melted down as sheet metal for reading papers. *Contes a Ninon* could be good place to start unless you're averse to faqs or allergic to personality; look up space centric earth model.

An introduction to transcription of Xenopus 5S RNA gene in an oocyte nuclear extract depends on the presence of an intact control region in the center of the gene could be seen as deletion clone 61 in poly-acrylamide – while the protection assays were consistent for clone 83 in a 0.03% xylene cyanol and 0.03% bromophenol blue – the syllabus offered, in Les Lappin Agile, before the copyright could be mounted on the chicken feathers in 1983. *You've got to remember the snow monkey*, I would remind myself ever since I came to know there were snow monkeys – or you'll end up like them, resistors melted down for reading paper. The completely fraudulent publication of the Human Genome (Nature volume 409, pages 860–921 (15 February 2001) is an immeasurable atrocity to the creative existence of human beings on the planet, beginning from the age of exploration. Our analysis of the enterprise 155.40 LH Oct. 27, 2017, suggests that the market position is a platform for 3D gaming. Our analysis of Pi Eri 176.26 LH Jan 22, 2018 suggests, high-level development of multi-server on-line games. Our analysis of Gamma Hyi 164.74 March 26, 2018 suggests a new methodology of design and development for serious games. As a result, in our search since 2000, we've made changes as an attempt to prevent catastrophes, which we suspected as originating at Bleak House, Fall of the House of Usher, and a third possibility, the French novel Le Père Goriot, 1032.00 Nippon Sheet Glass Company Dec. 27, 2017, where we have implemented programs for empirical risk management of severe accidents at Fukushima, while leaving open the possibility of interrelationships between climatic and ecological determinants anywhere in the fifty states and Puerto Rico 11,834.77 GDAXI 5:00PM March 23, 2018.

No sooner was my interest in reels of gun caps aligned with slime that grow on hydrogenated soybean oil in search of components for migratory escapades, than did the Cancer Ward open up to ISL/ZAR 3.35 at 166.24 Deere & Co. Feb. 23, 2018 with ISK/GMD 0.48 at 73.41 Dell March 1PM 23, 2018. Like a famous first novel retrieved from the garbage dump, this much is at least true, when *"Kostoglotov realizes that the imbrication was provocative; that there can be no surmise, now that Stalin has gone. As with cancer, there may be periods of observation but no completeness."*

The effectuals – par lequel je compte impliquer, les valeurs familiales qui constituent les objectifs de nos systèmes natifs – have to sufficiently be congruous within component structures to exert their influence over Time in order for "Immigration" to be authenticated. Le contraire est noté, rather flimsily, as "savages." *Une luxuriance ivre, violée par trois moche Mexicains à la pointe d'un fusil dans une voiture de Lee Morris à New York, n'est pas une valeur de famille.* That was an abandoned car for the filming of Haathi Mere Saathi (1971), for the movie Shakespeare Wallah (1965). Where is Denebola now, the nebula, made famous by the Michaelangelo of da Vinci, born at the third hour of the night, on 23 April, might be a stretch for the imagination in as much as the disappearance of Ursa Minor. Trends in Immunology, Molecular Medicine, and Cancer leaves the

Genetics a bit in awe of how they came about the fax papers for Chie*ff* Calculations, 780, 50∘2', Dystrophy, and Banach.

Comment la masse de la congrégation du Aryl-sulfonase 4N, et IL-4 Methotrexate pourrait répondre à une telle diaspora est un itinéraire provisoire. For the same reason Hiesos and Molesworth may be perceived as interference in foreign governments by Sean Hayes. While prior experience by my agency to broker an artifice between an arbitrator and a firewall had expectedly descended into a rocky hill and could not be quelled due to the lack of a regularized annuities program unforeseen for fair value trade market options on commodities, such as BHP, HBV (new), THB, SGD and other terms used by network computers in designated areas of space, say between 1326.50 Sky April 10, 2018 and 48.57 Sony 48.57 April 9, 2018 to compute stock trades for NASDAQ, Dow Jones, FTSE do exist- there does not seem to be insufficient interest for such exchanges through the Buenos Aires Exchange (ARS/USD) Nikkei (BP/Shillings) and IPC Mexico (MXN/BRL) for NASDAQ (EUR/AUD), Dow Jones futures (Commercial Papers) – as alternatives to BitCoins (FTSE), where benzodiazepine marsh-mellow sticks with glutons would have been the outcome savior faire for financial arbitrage against NZX (GBP/EUR) or AORD (CAD/AUD).

Luigi, have you seen this on the menu item at the space bar, might'nt be the proper way to introduce ourselves, though -2.5456E22 does express our empathy for getting laundry mixed-up with London, in as much as say vacuuming mixed-up with Hoover. Terms and conditions, as they say in Kashmir, are not as interchangeable as Sandip Ray and Emannuel Macron, or for that matter interposed as Kaj Blennow and Lennart and Minthon.

L'escapade migratoire, calculated as 2.54446E22 seemed to have at least three feasible inclinations for Pulsar-Quasar habituation, possible fourth deutéronome for manifolds, as explanation for, do the English who carry an umbrella have questions about the weather. Mon contact, Claith Beast, a présenté au moins les segmentations pour les photos, logos, et plus from the new testament of extensible galleria, as preparation for arrest and detention of U.S citizens without warrant anywhere in Europe, on suspicion of money laundering from the period convening 1 December, 2017; once the period had well passed its authorship for the Prisoners of Azkaban, with "personifications" of Chatterbox, and Foulmouth, with Ismail tailing off our Halley Plotter, USD/TTD 6.74 44.48 Oracle 1PM, April 6, 2018. He, the oracle of Delphi, belly, belly, flamous, aplears as the tlibune Flavius in Slakesplare's bioglapical play Julius Sleezer.

The new hierarchies USD/DZD 114.36 50.28 AAL 3:15PM April 6, 2018, USD/CLP 604.80 55.12 LUV 3:25PM, are a geo-synchronous orbit of the entirety, coded as earth centric space model. That was the only possible mechanism we could find to support "non-arbitrary" Mexican arbitrage for determination of residual value of the GBP, when kilos

became pertinent. For the same reason the safety and
security of American tourists visiting anywhere in the United
Kingdom (GDAXI) cannot be guaranteed sell-waivers without
proper documentation (i.e. source code) reservations a year in
advance, and non-refundable British-Australian Treasury
Security Commons in (CLP/Newtons) calculated as
7.560419304E26 should provide a context for the illustration
in space for the jar, in the Swiss tradition of making
chocolate, for des lapins de paques toutes les formes.
Whereas, our friendly staff are always open to new business
opportunities in (USD/AUD) at the Paris Exchange, as long
as you have a utility with you, preferably electric.

Diedra could probably fill you in our plan for Dr. Hookah
where the calculations seem to point at 2.25551829
E2518834 bytes as the compositional matter for conjectural
space in-scape landscape where, if you are a trader of gas
subsidies (BSESN) the LSE is probably your one stop shop
for commodities and commercial papers. No, the post– war
economic enterprises are not lacking in the rise of Artificial
Intelligence, as two of the largest open banks for commercial
papers would say, the Amsterdam Exchange is well worth a
vist for Grand Unified Models. And, if you are like me, a
British Commoner without the closures of celebrity, and
neither are you keen to read or memorize plays by
Shakespeare, then the Madrid Exchange could show how the
space jar is shaping up at the ship; and though I have never
been to Jakarta, I've heard that the beaches are endless,
where once in a while an Ophelia wanders by as in a whim of

eternal sunshine asking of hilal, halvmåne, yarimoy, ilargierdi.

A lift with swingline options being contemporaneous with second order Dirac equations leaves one to wonder to what extent the Heisenberg uncertainty principals effect the delineation for any one arrondismont. Does Anne Hidalgo require tuition re-imbursement from Édouard Philippe for Chancellerie des Universités de Paris, need qualifiers for the argument that third order Jungian derivative forms are imaginaries, are intrinsic to the British Empire, where the motivations for questions of a cosmological construct are ascertainable 8442.01 NZX50 Jan. 31, 2018 moveable, 25.81 Twitter Jan. 31, 2018, searchable 31.91 March 26, 2018, re-produceable 8508.12 NZX50 March 27, 2018, negotiable 41.28 BBL 3:40PM April 12, 2018, latitudinal 17.24 11:20AM April 12, 2018 GLYC and incontrovertible 59.97 Alaska Air Group 1:35PM April 12, 2018. Further, one would have to intermediate the cause celebre for Maxwell-Thompson in designing robots with a scapegoat. Given the apparent rate of inflation in human evolution we have to wonder when *Faggy Lil' Goldblatt's Dyke Bar of Horrors with Adjuvant Therapy for Hollywood Girls* were to completely fall off the radar, how the succeeding exchange rate could be supported by a disen-franchised federation of underwriters limited in order to qualify for actuarial provisions in the absence of European risk management. Developing a comptrolling interest in markets can be used to observe phylogenetic traits of Sinn Fein compared to Fianna Fail where the teams are (x1x0, x3x0) compared to (x2y0, x2x0) for determination of sickle cell as percent plays in public equity markets April 3, 2018 (864.80/6896.12) 3i/Nasdaq compared to percent plays in commodities markets (859.60/ 23861.91) 3i/Dow Jones compared to percent plays in securities markets (865.20/ 327.89) 3i/BA compared to percent traded in health insurance plans (860.60/5844.70) 3i/AORD compared to buys for health insurance protection (857.60/5868.7) 3i/ AORD compared to SFIT budget (858.00/8673.17) 3i/SSMI on a daily basis, where we limit the commodities for calculating mathematical biosciences to ILS, DKK, BND and CHF as the organizing principals for sickle cell, while for the stars i-Cen r-Vel SEC/NOK 0.93 NOK/CHF 0.12 are intermediaries for calculating synchrotron science, Trieste, Grenoble, and Brugg at 7212.63 FTSE 2:55 PM April 6, 2018, when the introduction to transcription of Xenopus 5S RNA gene in an oocyte nuclear extract purveyed intact control region in the center of the gene where we were born, came into existence, became known, as Iskergod. The measures of our existence or non-existence therefore, depends on workers compensation for work-time 7128.17 FTSE 12:05PM April 5, 2018, hazard scoring for quantum relativities with maple leaf syrup 7191.90 FTSE 4:10PM, genetic risk factor associated with European markets in Oceania 7118.18 FTSE 8:25AM, Likelihood scores for Higgs-Bosons 7125.26 FTSE 9:45AM.

Information is seldom thought of as having food value; however, in the mountains of Santiago, Chile, where food groups consist of such imaginary matter as accruals, quarries, and acquisitions, food value tends to be obliquely ephemeral. Understanding that where we are is intrinsically based on food value, much as it is true in Wein and Venice, or Shanghai and Beijing, to differentiate the nature of the cosmopolitan from with metropolitan, some sequences may be of relative importance based on how they are contrived into the theme, which has its ups and downs due in part to ideas, which are managed by two interests, 5284.26 FCHI 1PM April 11, 2018. How do fractal aggregates of Mercury differ from Saturn, and to what extent are they harmonious; the nature of harmony being aardvark to defining an ontologically substituent code encompassing mechanical properties, rules we may be unfamiliar with, functions we may never have heard of, attributions we may never know. The weed does not grow on trees, as far as we know.

A neutron star is non-Archimedean. Neutrino inferences which could be dialectic are essentially our passage towards the ominous, much as our reflections on Liner Notes, as a way to preserve our process memory, while developing inductive traits. Scum, we need understand, is moisture, whereas Bahadur Shah is impregnate. Let our risk be beauty, where fallacy is which we define as incongruent. Then matter is how we examine theory as a scope for finding a lace bottom dress by Isaac Mizrahi, wherefore name is illuminated, and naughty is seasonal, since dystopia is either impaired or heavenly. We keep the synchrotron at some distance to excavate the affects imbroglio, without imposing the rule of conjecture, to keep with discrete by signing for Lucifer.

What we know about Gamma-neutron is that it is computationally expensive 3874.14 BFX 5PM March 29, 2018. The engineering department made sure to develop a program that is semi-lateral with random observations of a magnetic dipole, and then gesticulated with passengers on a train about the nature of his observations. The engineer then made fun of his observations as "Trolius of Cressida." To quote freely from Proserpina's Legate, owner of copyrights, logos, and transcriptions for the Home Ministry of the United Kingdom, the play is believed to have been written around 1602, shortly after the completion of Hamlet. It was published in quarto in two separate editions, both in 1609. It is not known whether the play was ever performed in its own time, because the two editions contradict each other: one announces on the title page that the play had been recently performed on stage; the other claims in a preface that it is a new play that has never been staged. The play was entered into the Register of the Stationers Company on 7 February 1603, by the bookseller and printer James Roberts, with a mention that the play was acted by the Lord Chamberlain's Men, Shakespeare's company. No publication followed, however, until 1609; the stationers Richard Bonian and Henry Walley re-registered the play on 28 Jan. 1609, and later that year issued the first quarto, but in two "states". The first says the play was "acted by the King's Majesty's servants at the Globe;" the second version omits the mention of the Globe Theatre, and prefaces the play with a long Epistle that claims that Troilus of Cressida is "a new play, never staled with the stage, never clapper-clawed with the palms of the vulgar."

Unsatisfied with the unexpected outcomes of his play, the engineer then made fun of his observations as functionally perverse and circumstantial as if on a train, for the creation of a paramagnetic dipole as "Cymbeline." To quote freely from Sosostris' Legate, owner of copyrights, logos, and transcriptions for the Prime Minister of the United Kingdom, the play is believed to have been written in 1609, Cymbeline is generally regarded as a comedy, although it also has elements of tragedy and romance. Cymbeline is the King of Britain and he has three children, a daughter, Imogen, and two sons, Guiderius and Aviragus. The two boys have been missing for a long time and appear in disguise as Polydore and Cadwal. They have been raised in the woods by Balarius, a banished lord, who has kidnapped them and educated them into gentlemen. The Queen is Cymbeline's second wife, a power-hungry and scheming woman who wants Imogen to be killed so that she can get her hands on her inheritance for her son, Cloten. Cloten is a cloddish, nasty young man, who wants to marry Imogen so that he can inherit the throne. However Imogen has other plans. She falls in love with Posthumus Leonatus, a noble young man, and marries him in secret. Their love is tested, betrayed and finally redeemed. The play's themes of truth triumphing over falsehood, good over evil, are exemplified in the life of the heroine, Imogen. Appearance and reality infuses the play - there is magic and mischief and nothing is as it seems.

Oliver Cromwell isn't well known in the United Kingdom and this is largely due to the history of the English. While protestant mass consists of what we describe as tables which altercate with chairs, catholic mass consists of harbors. To quote freely from the physician Ovid, owner of copyrights, logos, and transcriptions for the Foreign Ministry of the United Kingdom, Cromwell's hostility to the Irish was religious as well as political. He was passionately opposed to the Catholic Church, which he saw as denying the primacy of the Bible in favour of papal and clerical authority, and which he blamed for suspected tyranny and persecution of Protestants in Europe. Cromwell's association of Catholicism with persecution was deepened by Irish Rebellion of 1641. This rebellion, although intended to be bloodless, was marked by massacres of English and Scottish Protestant settlers by Irish ("Gaels") for working paper. To the extent the arrangement is co-operative with Westminster Abbey is quite unknown, and possibly preposterous. There are some known circumstances when a incubation mixture of 66 mM KPO_3, pH 7.7 10mM $MgCl_2$, 10 mM DTT, and 150uM dNTP could be used to create a basc transversions was communicated by Har Gobind Khorana, the Urdu stylist then living at Babcock Towers, specializing in droughty French novellas called "skank-wanker." Their, as a primer on some of these differences between atomic theory, which is to say infinitely small spaces, we set the stage for showing the differences between classical Newtonian mechanics, and semi-classical Newtonian mechanics, which do not apply to atomic physics, such as quantum relativity, or sub-atomic scales such as electron spin radiuses. The tokamak produced the expected result for the calculation for torque speed of the expanding universe 663.60 Fujitsu 10:10 AM April 13, 2018, from which instant velocity of space was calculated as 1126.00 Nissan 1:55 PM April 13, 2018, for the nearest approximation of radius in space where the work-time function, and genetic algorithms for European markets in Oceania could be applied 128.87 Toyota 1:45PM April 13, 2018, to accommodate this semi-classical Newtonian notion for impedance, different from the Canadian healthcare system, and the English healthcare system 787.20 Hitachi 1:55PM April 13, 2018, for an understanding of the function of speed in buoyance matter 11.34 Ford 10:05 AM April 13, 2018. Besides clarifying the distinction for how a compressor-repressor functions in Newtonian space, which is different from an air conditioner, Scottish bagpiper with tartans standing on a hillside, doves flying out of flag poles, the motives here were to continue to develop an understanding for which Artificials could occlude.

Louis MacNeice is probably a forgotten omen of the Kildare for swims in the river of life. Not much for small talk, chit-chat and formalities. Major poets, like trick-or-treaters, tend to arrive in pairs or small groups (whether this is a matter of fate or academic convenience may be debated). And yet from roughly 1930 to 1950, British and Irish poetry seemed to fall under the sway of a single writer: W. H. Auden. Auden was hardly a solitary figure, of course — his compatriots included Louis MacNeice. Yet MacNeice is effortlessly, almost ridiculously articulate — he seems capable (again like Auden) of writing about nearly anything, and in nearly any form. The 800 or so pages here include tiny poems (the nine-line "Upon This Beach"); book-length poems ("Autumn Journal," which helped make his reputation); book-length poems in terza rima ("Autumn Sequel," which nearly undid it); virtuoso deployment of nearly all forms of rhyme ("London Rain" rhymes a word with itself in every stanza is probably one his most gorgeous poems); and a vocabulary that suavely extends from "Tom or Dick or Harry" and "trams" to "ochred" and -"archaize, " to quote some passages from Free Range. As a parliamentary figure with rights and entitlements to copyrights, logos, and transcriptions for the Government of Australia, his first speech acknowledged the role of women in his election success. He distanced himself from Tony Abbott's social conservatism, saying "I reject the assumption that merit is more located in the brains of men than women." Surely a poet of loneliness should do a little more stammering. What we most want, MacNeice suggests, is simply to "know each other better," but that possibility depends on laboring blindly through darkness to stumble upon the radio, using binoculars five meters away to look through a stereo-microscope at a nebula. The Bodleian Library, where from Louis MacNeice emerged as a Fellow of the Royal College, around the age of twenty one, provided his thesis as -1.690645727, for which the integral of $0.026611602x/4\pi$ where $x = n$ to $2^n - 1$ provides Louis MacNeice's keynotes for Oxford thesis, thesis from other UK Universities, thesis from universities in the U.S., and thesis from universities elsewhere in the world, and a thesis for thesis finding aids 54.44 SGEN 2:40PM March 5, 2018. Consider "Meeting Point," which is about the fiction writer Eleanor Clark, one of MacNeice's many, many paramours, 53.66 SGEN 10:40AM March 5, 2018, as we hasten towards *Benign-Malignant Tumors: Case Studies of Patient Duplication on HYW 101* . Though he would go on to distinguish himself at Oxford, meet and befriend many of the great literary figures of his day and travel the world as a writer for the BBC and a widely recognized poet, there is always a sense that the isolated boy described in the conclusion to "Autobiography" has a hand on the pen of the grown-up MacNeice, *Benign-Malignant Tumors: Case Studies of Cluster Populations Associated with the English Channel* 53.96 SGEN 1:10M March 5, 2018. But it wasn't a relationship of equals: the MacSpaunday poets were usually considered notable not because of how closely they resembled one another, by how much the other three looked like Auden, *Rhode Pizza on Commonwealth Avenue: Undemented Cluster Populations of Malignant Tumors* 53.91 SGEN 11:20 AM March 5, 2018. As a simplified rate function for understanding the population migration from malignant to benign, the calculations were set forth as an example of a hemotaxis model (erythrocytic lineage, where) if: $y = (-0.00470217)(-0.00625) - 0.000689583$, or $y = -0.000660194$; then $t = 1.044685462 - (- 0.000660194)$, or $t = 1.045345657$, for which the survival curve for onset collateral for undemented cluster populations for HBV, HPV, and Anemia are cluster-populations in Italy, Slovakia, and the Czech Republic.

While observation of these cases, suggested extremely high (3X) counts of plasminogen activation factors for Italy, extremely low (-40X) counts of plasminogen activation factors for Slovakia, and a benign state of affairs for the Czech Republic (0.8X), Virginia Woolf took Hardy's phrase as a key to the occasions of heightened intensity that gave meaning to life: "the year is marked by moments of great intensity," where a patient informed of the condition may at first aggressively reject the clinical diagnosis before admitting to committing suicide with over the counter medications just as as aggressively at a Hague tribunal (Slobodan Praljak, 2017).

If only Hardy's 'moments of vision had been to drive around in a Ferrari, instead of a Lamborghini, then the glow worm in Proust's early life as Swann might have been spared. Works in progress are often the condition statement for many writers – though none more than Hardy. Depression, we could surmise requires multi-tasking as an ally. Rage is least often seen amidst incompetent cinderblocks as insufficient knowledge base, where the inability to communicate may lead to disdain 262.15 Biogen 12:55 PM, April 9, 2018. Whereas most number theorists tend to be dry, Hardy's work tends to be ascertainable 262.88 Biogen 12:05PM. As a poet provocateur, in Return of the Native, when Hardy stoops beneath his wit and wisdom to remark, "Dominos, DeLuise is the measure of success for survival," he asserts a kind of indoctrination seldom to be found among pulsars and quasars, 263.63 Biogen 12:20PM April 9, meaning he tends to be very specific of his distaste. It hurts the ear to hear

"Hiatus," only to the extent that we can wonder if, my hope is you plummet in a watery grave might have sounded like for chumpy school friends at St. Xavier's yard.

Southern Baptists might do well to remember who Pascal is - at the same time - for knocking the cross from the wall, and leaving behind balloon mortgage payments for Navaho Indians of New Mexico, USA 70.88 STI 3:05PM Feb 23, 2018 as the top down classification with native American populations clusters suffering from Jägermeister Syndrome (knock-out 9hrs, 3000), Boddington's Leishmania (knock-out 4hrs, 15000), and Bombay Dry Gin Apnea (knock-out 6hrs, 400), for automobile insurance. In the case of the data dredging Pascal tested maltose anaerobes for executive function of the pre-frontal lobes at 16,000/23500, compared with galactose anaerobes 20,000/ 23000, and barley anaerobes 17,500/23000 for the newspaper headline *Traffic Plays Spoilspo* Times of India Oct. 14, 2010, where 23500 is the average measure of executive function of pre-frontal lobes for college graduates, meaning at least a B.Comm, B.Tech, B.A., B.Sc or B.Eng. "Besides the Pensees, Pascal is known for communist views, becoming a member of the Communist Party of Great Britain, and his early poetry was marked by didacticism and a preoccupation with social themes 259.46 Biogen 10:30 AM April 9, 2018. He edited The Mind in Chains: Socialism and the Cultural Revolution, from where Blake left off. In the introduction, he supported a popular front against a "Capitalism that has no further use for culture," 257.15 Biogen 9:45 April 9, 2018. He explains that the title refers to Prometheus bound by his chains, quotes Shelley's preface, Prometheus Unbound and says the contributors believe that "the Promethean fire of enlightenment, which should be given for the benefit of mankind at large." As compatriots of anti-Americanism, they do well together for classical Newtonian Mechanics, in making England proud of its contempt for greed, egotism, and compounding interest in fiscal affairs where neighboring states are concerned. As a long term strategy, for owner of copyrights, logos, and transcriptions for the Prime Minister of Australia, where security matters are crucial for float, Hardy and Pascal can be interpreted as Real Analysts, with Rational Objectives. In England, that leaves us to fathom the nature of how a pulsar functions with a quasar, and the kinship between a neutrino to a gamma-neutron through the façade of endangered earth, where the happy few live - to testify for the new adventures in death valley.

1. Spines were frequently synchronized in spontaneously active networks, thereby forming dendritic foci that received locally convergent inputs from presynaptic cell assemblies, of Herge's Calculas Affair, NASDAQ 6926.27 11:30AM, April 4, 2018.

2. In all pairs, we measured dynamic changes in the postsynaptic response to a 20 Hz train of presynaptic action potential, from the Australian Utilities Project NASDAQ 7052.89 10:30AM April 10, 2018.

3. Subsequent action potential electrogenesis and probably propagation from sensory neurons innervating cold tissues depends upon the presence of Na(v)1.8, the sole voltage-gated

sodium channel that fails to inactivate at low temperatures, for <u>Circuit Bioscience of SGEN 50.86 1:40 PM, April 6, 2018.</u>

4. Spike timings of bursts continue to change cyclically or irregularly during propagation depending on intrinsic properties of the neurons and the coupling strength of the network for <u>Gulliver's Travels 24275.68 Dow Jones 10:00AM April 10, 2018.</u>

5. We show that such aperiodic synchronization arises naturally under a simple set of plausible assumptions, depending crucially on heterogeneous cell properties, for <u>Kaiser-Permanente of California SGEN 51.31 12:15PM April 6, 2018.</u>

41. The model predicts gamma-ray bursts to be anti-correlated with their gravitational wave emissions *as a function of depth of field with greater than expected empiricism with mean of osteopathic inference for 39.75 Spirit Airlines on Aug 19, 2016 emerging as 48.24 where the STDEV in edge space is 48.67 with a trans-sectional value for Salesforce of 109.05, compared with a Universal delineation at 110.16, against a mean planar of 110.36, which yields the non-Cartesian value as 109.46 for the actual wave emission as 109.89.*

39. A major limitation of current technologies is the relatively slow scan rates along the z direction compared to the kHz rates obtainable in the x and y directions, *where the calculated nuclear magnetic resonance (NMR) for the Y-intercept is Oracle 50.00 and the calculated NMR for the X-distance is Oracle 49.58 and the jolt-value of Mass Spectroscopy (MS) is Cypress Semiconductor 17.11.*

60. Gamma-ray bursts are known to come in two duration classes, separated at approximately 2 s, *where the maximum resonance fit for a disaster of the scale of Tohoku's 54,000 death toll March 11, 2011 is Arena 33.99 and the minimum stochastic fit for delay amplitude modulation (DAM) in purposeful endangerment of very large-area populations is Arena 33.29 and the net casualty-function for tidal is hazarded at 34.00 for property insurance management claims, and the risk to overcoming Black Body Radiation is hazarded*

at Arena 33.59, with the operating risk of a tsunami in the N.E. hazarded at 33.46, where we specifically based our calculation for a flow-through cache flow model for Princeton-Cranbury, N.J, as the attributions for commercial, and property-casualty losses in winter weather, Dec. 6, 2017 the Thomas Fires of in the northern greater Los Angeles 230,500 acres; the Rhea Fire in Western Oklahoma, 241,280 acres, April 15, 2018. Hurricane Maria, Sept. 20, 2017 Puerto Rico, 70,000 homes destroyed in twelve hours.

9. Serotonin blocks repetitive large inhibitory postsynaptic potentials evoked in hippocampal neurons by topical application of 4-aminopyridine, in <u>Lettres du System Industrial et Leurs Partisan LSE 4206 April 6, 12:00 2018.</u>

31. Cocaine produced a rapid increase in absolute theta, alpha, and beta power over the prefrontal cortex lasting up to 25 min after dosing.

32. A ten minute infusion of Estrogen reversibly increased fast excitatory postsynaptic potential and promoted theta burst-induced LTP within adult hippocampal slices.

8. This result indicates that spontaneous rhythmic synchronous events are not a direct reflection of tissue epileptogenicity, for new <u>ATLAS Mountains NASDAQ 7079.62 2:00PM April 10, 2018.</u>

61. The brevity of the flares implies that the gamma rays were emitted via synchrotron radiation from peta-electron-volt or 10^{15} electron volts in a region smaller than 1.4×10^{-2} parsecs.

65. We examine the implications of the recent Milagro gamma-ray Observatory detection of extended, multi-TeV gamma-ray emission from Geminga, finding that this reveals the existence of an ancient, powerful cosmic-ray accelerator that can plausibly account for the multi-GeV positron excess that has evaded explanation.

63. The Geminga pulsar has long been one of the most intriguing MeV-GeV gamma-ray point sources.

62. Our observations challenge standard models of nebular emission and require power-law acceleration by shock-driven plasma wave turbulence within an approximately 1-day time scale. Kappa Peg 2602.00 9AM April 16, 7.68 RBS 3:30 April 12, 48.20 FGEN April 11, 2018.

10. Single axon excitatory postsynaptic potentials evoked in the non-pyramidal neuron by action potentials in the pyramidal neuron were large and fast and demonstrated large fluctuations in amplitude, with coefficients of variation between 0.1 and 1.25.

20. We found that glutamatergic neurons in medial septum and diagonal band of Broca (MS-DBB) as a population display a highly heterogeneous set of firing patterns including fast, cluster, burst, and slow firing.

40. The resonant excitation of neutron star (NS) modes by tides is investigated as a source of short gamma-ray burst (SGRB) precursors.

18. Some gamma-aminobutyric acid containing interneurons fire phase-locked to theta oscillations (4-8 Hz) or to sharp-wave-associated ripple oscillations (120-200 Hz), which represent different behavioral states.

7. A second set of connections is activated by a spontaneous burst of activity in a group of closely coupled interneurons which are excitatory to some of the motor cells and inhibitory to the others, of the Niagara Utility Project, famous in Gary Oldman movies for rapid one liners such as, "Will, you did a good job," NASDAQ 7056.63 12:00, April 9, 2018.

11. In both layer one neurons and layer two and three pyramidal neurons, changes in membrane potential did not greatly alter action potential properties.

6. We found that dendritic inhibition is the primary regulator of input-output transformations in mouse hippocampal CA1 pyramidal cells, and acts by gating the dendritic electro-genesis driving burst spiking, of Circuit Bioscience for SGEN 50.99 11:15AM 2018.

12. Furthermore, comparisons of high versus low confidence judgments revealed modulation of neural activity in the hippocampus, cingulate and other limbic regions, previously described as the Circuit of Papez.

13. Sampling techniques revealed an average of 42% of all neurons within the anterior thalamus were glutamic acid decarboxylase immune-reactive, one of the highest reported percentages of local circuit neurons in the mammalian thalamus.

14. Here we demonstrate in the rat that neuronal activity exhibiting strong state-dependent synchrony with rhythmic hippocampal electroencephalogram is present also at the brainstem level, specifically in the relatively small tegmental nuclei of Gudden intimately connected with the limbic forebrain.

15. It has recently been shown that cells of mammillary body fire rhythmically in bursts synchronous with the theta rhythm of the hippocampus.

16. At the same time, the majority of interneurons consistently display synaptic gamma oscillations.

17. Field theta oscillations were co-expressed with pyramidal distal apical dendritic burst spiking and were temporally related to trains of inhibitory postsynaptic potential with slow kinetics.

19. Two gamma generators were identified, one in the dentate gyrus and another in the CA3-CA1 regions.

21. The reversal point for the potential change was about 5 mV greater than the resting membrane potential of 75 mV.

22. Namely, a network of neurons bursting through a Ca(2+)-dependent mechanism exhibited sharp transitions between synchronous and asynchronous firing states when the neurons exchanged the bursting mode between singlet, doublet and so on.

23. Much evidence indicates that synchronized gamma-

frequency 20-70 Hz oscillation plays a significant functional role in the neocortex and hippocampus.

24. Gamma-aminobutyric acid currents in interneurons is close to their mean membrane potential -56.5 mV.
25. Additionally, the phase of posteromedial cortex theta oscillations modulated the amplitude of ongoing high gamma (70-180Hz) activity during the resting state.

26. We link early synchronisation of anterior theta and beta oscillations to regional activation of right and central frontal cortices, reflecting retrieval and integration of information.

27. The alpha-rhythm becomes less pronounced everywhere in parallel to the decrease in synchronism of its fluctuations in different zones; at the same time low-frequency activity (delta-theta) increases both by the amplitude of oscillations and the capacity for its unidirectional shifts over the whole cortex.

26. An enhancement of theta- and alpha-oscillations has been found in such conditions which becomes less pronounced to 9-10 years.

27. It has been shown that the envelope of both theta and alpha activities oscillates at 0.04 Hz and 0.07 Hz in the healthy subject and at 0.03 Hz and 0.06 Hz in a patient with Alzheimer's disease.

28. With respect to topography in the antero-posterior direction, sources of alpha and beta activity shifted more anteriorly in Alzheimer's patients.

29. In contrast to the intrinsic theta rhythm in stellate cells with one dominant peak frequency at approximately 7 Hz, the synaptically mediated oscillation induced by carbachol showed three characteristic peaks in the theta and gamma frequency range at approximately 11, 23 and 40 Hz.

30. Disruption of septo-hippocampal connections completely abolished theta-rhythm in EEG and in neuronal activity of the hippocampus.

33. Furthermore, MEC medial entorhinal cortex grid cells increase the scale of their periodic spatial firing patterns along the dorsoventral axis, corresponding to the increasing size of place fields along the septotemporal axis of the hippocampus.

34. As to pharmaco-EEG investigations, seroquel caused a moderate increase of the absolute power in the alpha, theta, and beta frequency bands, paralleled by a decrease of delta activity.

35. Using whole-cell patch-clamp recordings from CA1 pyramidal cells in vitro with dynamic clamp to simulate theta-frequency oscillation (5 Hz), we show that gamma-aminobutyric acid-A receptor-mediated inhibitory postsynaptic potentials can not only delay but also advance the postsynaptic spike depending on the timing of the inhibition relative to the oscillation.

36. A set of gamma-aminobutyric acid containing hippocampal interneurons located in stratum oriens displayed the pattern of axonal arborization characteristic of axo-axonic cells with radially aligned rows of boutons making synapses exclusively on axon initial segments of pyramidal cells, as shown by electron microscopy.

37. Perisomatic inhibitory interneurons fired at high frequency (18.1 +/- 2.7 Hz), shortly after the negative peak (1.97 +/- 0.95 msec) and were strongly phase-coupled.

38. Since the net potential at a point reflects the sum of currents flowing into and out of the point, a zero change in potential could reflect either the absence of current sinks and sources, or a zero sum of sinks and sources.

42. Here we present the discovery of the X-ray afterglow of a short-hard burst, GRB 050709, whose accurate position allows us to associate it unambiguously with a star-forming galaxy at redshift z = 0.160, and whose optical lightcurve definitively excludes a supernova association.

43. Here we report the discovery of a short-hard burst whose accurate localization has led to follow-up observations that

have identified the X-ray afterglow and (for the first time) the optical afterglow of a short-hard burst; this in turn led to the identification of the host galaxy of the burst as a late-type galaxy at $z = 0.16$.

44. The energy release probably occurred during a catastrophic reconfiguration of the neutron star's magnetic field.

45. To create this nebula, at least 4×10^{43} ergs of energy must have been emitted by the giant flare in the form of magnetic fields and relativistic particles.

46. Near and within the Io plasma torus the instrument detected high-frequency electrostatic waves, strong whistler mode turbulence, and discrete whistlers, apparently associated with lightning.

47. Near closest approach, the plasma wave instrument detected broadband electrostatic noise and a changing pattern of weak electron plasma oscillations that yielded a density profile for the outer layers of the cold plasma tail.

48. Indeed, one of the first mechanisms invoked to produce strong gamma-ray emission involved accretion of comets onto neutron stars in our Galaxy.

49. At a density of rho approximately 10^{12}-10^{14} g/cm^3, the conductivity due to superfluid phonons is significantly larger than that due to lattice phonons and is comparable to electron conductivity when the temperature is approximately 10^8 K.

50. The detection of polarized x-rays from neutron stars can provide a direct probe of strong-field quantum electrodynamics and constrain the neutron star magnetic field and geometry.

51. We describe a new instability that may trigger the global unpinning of vortices in a spinning neutron star, leading to the transfer of angular momentum from the superfluid component to the star's crust.

52. Rotation-powered radio pulsars are born with inferred initial rotation periods of order 300 ms (some as short as 20 ms) in core-collapse supernovae.

53. The estimated mass of the disk is of the order of 10 Earth masses, and its infinite lifetime significantly exceeds the spin-down age of the pulsar, supporting a supernova fallback origin.

54. It orbits the star with a period of 3.56 days at 0.04 au, inside the inner rim of the disk.

55. Here we report the detection of burst oscillations at the known spin frequency of an accreting millisecond pulsar, and we show that these oscillations always have the same rotational phase.

56. Here, I report binary stellar evolution calculations that show that the braking torque acting on a neutron star, when the companion star decouples from its Roche lobe, is able to dissipate >50% of the rotational energy of the pulsar.

57. The results show that, irrespective of the value of the pairing gap, only interstitial pinning takes place all along the inner crust.

58. A large shear modulus also strengthens the case for starquakes as an explanation for frequent pulsar glitches.

59. We estimate the effect of a solid crust on their viscous damping rate and show that the dissipation rate in the viscous boundary layer between the oscillating fluid and the nearly static crust is more than 105 times higher than that from the shear throughout the interior.

64. The 7 year data set of the Milagro TeV observatory contains 2.2 x 10(11) events of which most are due to hadronic cosmic rays.

66. We show that for six pulsars the timing noise is correlated with changes in the pulse shape.

67. The bursts were accompanied by a sudden flux increase and an unprecedented change in timing behavior.

68. We analyzed archival survey data and found a 30-jansky dispersed burst, less than 5 milliseconds in duration, located 3 degrees from the Small Magellanic Cloud.

1. Issue – Where Endymion creates junk furniture for babysitting daughters with the boy back at headquarters- to avoid decode diaspora – worries for drowning in sorrows – worries for Manichaean stalls – and worries for wild gambits of kingdom – with a foothold in Agincourt – for the Dutchess of Longchamps - ainsi, en calculant Amartya Sen de te C-compilateur, le programmmateur est capable de développer un diagramme de scatchard des vecteurs – confesses to liking tarts and slags, as way for Theresa May to *enoncer* which difference betwixt the words policy and police she may be inculpable of, in persuading Jeremy Corbyn that jealousies do not abound – where peremptorily had the claims been shiitaked, as an anticipatory conjecture for wavy gravy prize – with as many cigarette boxes for pause – to transfer with equanimity of the Aegean from quantum on, for pilbara and renegades, with exception for Twinning the breakfast tea, who receives the ohsumi for proceeding on a few of merry old soul's novelties in edition, to study effects of such gothic romance novels.

Development, deployment and, cryptographic engineering of Astrobiological Data Systems began in 1986: while most of the field had been operable as a parameterized induction of field densities in a planar gradient of co-poles, where homomorphic segments could be scatchard plotted as averages for co-ordinate texture of unsolvable surfaces as assimilates of silicon wafers on a balloon surface, a problem became apparent when the determination of exact latitudes for nonplaner earth objects became invisible. Methods to exploit such problems for the development, deployment, and cryptographic engineering from astrobiological data systems to a Mathematical *Biologic Data Systems* led to the adaptation of indexes from cluster computing to batch computing with gap-frame solutions from within context reference of mainframes, 55.95 HAL 1:35PM Jan. 24, 2018 transistors with mobile relay switches and resistance pads 35.79 SNN 11:35AM Jan 24, 2018, field coils, and electron beam transfer regulators 0.27 SDRL 12:25PM Jan 24, 2018, along with solaris prototype studies of a Cartesian coordinate system for branched leaf segmentation pattering of x-ray 7425.37 NASDAQ 1:55PM Jan. 24, 2018.

The fundamental economic emergence is a coherence facsimile of earth as biosphere (éclature diversity) without a magnetic diode, an acceleration induced hyper-loop of in-scape non-space, cosmically induced quantum gravity fields for forecasting substantive parc 13.31 UA Jan. 25, 2018 Exon-4 5' AX4, neutron spacers 66.08 UAL Jan. 25 2018 Exon-6 5' AX3, a branched forked conservation of spatial equilibrium with modular cost function analysis 110.15 TXN Jan 25, 2018 Exon-6 5' AX3, five delayed field diopters in edge space with in-scape landscape potentiation 15,555.43 TSX 2:20PM March 6, 2018, and a topo-isomeric bending of gamma neutron-positron in a covalently bound real-space of rational ordinaries with irrational functions which tend towards zero 6066.70 AORD 2:00PM March 1, 2018, demonstrated November 10, 2017 2:45PM Morris Plains, West Virginia -- appears very distinguished over a parsec 16.79 MRC 12:00 PM March 2, 2018. If we were to hypothesize, that the ORF for sickle cell anemia was 15.56812Kb TSX 10:00 AM March 6, 2018, then how would we answer the following questions a) why is sickle cell non-autosomal dominant b) why is anemia autosomal recessive c) are multiple mylomas fragile-x d) what is the load variance of Rh-/A compared to Rh-/AB and what are the allelic copy number requirements for sickle cell anemia in a Rh+/AB background – as fulfilment objectives for fellowships, and before choosing therapeutic intervention strategy away from sauvignon, and cabernet, where we have to first consider the twin studies data David Wu, et. al. 2007, Ann. Neurol. 62(6): 609-617 for Wt(m), Ts(f), and autosomal recombinant twins (m,f) of the Wt(m), where the mother has thrombocytopenia, as a way of analogizing with the populations of Northern and Southern Ireland, where the 0.17 fold difference in hematopoietic background becomes a difference of 3 fold after five passages in tissue culture, as a way of avoiding terrorist activities in Anglaise, where neither population would be expected to respond as well as the autosomal recombinant twins, and the response could be less than the twin-sibling.

In a Mexican population the questions were different, because amyolateral sclerosis occurs in 1.8 per 100,000 people, which is what we call an incidence rate, or a 2-fold difference in hematopoietic differentiation with Wt(m), where three loci, 18q21, 16q12, and 20ptel-p13 for typical autosomal dominance exist, as with autosomal recombinant twins, as we discovered with J. Goldbloom in *Benign-Malignant Tumors: Case Studies of Patient Duplication on HYW 101,* compared with twin-sibling with autosomal recessive for 2q33, and 15q15.1. Due to the limitations of

Artificial Intelligence, the development of Thinking Machines begun in 2015 to solve problems based on core operating system of machines, which is common among a majority of shareholders. Parallel processors taken from a single array were used to develop two network monitor. In the final phase of the development heightened reality nanorods were used to create panel transformers for Creative Thinking, miniaturized cyberspace sensory networks operated by JPL, Air France, and British Airways, respectively. THM-1 operates from Chicago O'Hare Airport, and THM-2 operates from San Francisco International Airport under NASA. A third monitor TMN-1 operates from Tokyo Haneda International Airport, and a fourth monitor TMN-2 operates from Amsterdam Airport Schiphol, which are a part of the grand unification of time network. Two additional monitors LYS-1 and LYS-2 operate between Calcutta International Airport and Heathrow International. The operating principals demonstrated feasibility for Cartesian phenomenologicals defined as extensa, which are different from res cogitans. Inference, thus, in field deployment of Thinking Machines in 2017, provided computable solutions for objectification of the Fermi atom, insofar as could be shown that the Fermi atom consists of variable mass, with an implied molecular dynamic of atomic orbitals, 287.33 Biogen 1:55PM Feb 22, 2018, where we assume the orbitals to be expressed circumstantially, as luciferase expression in firefly, and jelly fish, but residually expressed in moths, and dragonfly. Second, provided computational segmentations of the Oppenheimer atom 290.62 Biogen 11:15PM Feb 22, 2018 where the luciferase expression is rotational from moth, to jellyfish, to dragonfly, to firefly, in as much as an evolutionary system of splicing functions in environmental adaptation to luciferase, 183.99 Amgen, 11:00PM Feb 22, 2018 as a study of high-density neutrons, with molecular modeling of high-energy particles to demonstrate how neutrons move, are docile, demonstrated November 17, 2017, 1:41PM Morris Plains, West Virginia, incorporating momentum, similar to batch computing, where the functionality is variegated in broad segments and substantiated in short segments.

Third, provided an exomorphic periocular decomposition of charged particles in a tunneling microscope of gamma radiation sources, with compensating sources of pulsars and quasars, 22,198.92 Nikkei 225 Feb. 26, 2018, after being in exile somewhere in the tip of the pelt, without a map of the world. It's actually quite frightening, if you were to imagine, flying on a spaceship with Norwegian Securities collections, church-offerings for the most part, tron-chronicles of the last ninety years, the Betamax which could become a valuable technology if the Russians ever get their hands on it, and the Motorola whose deployment in the thesis for cargo could be seen as a sit situation similar to, "but I didn't order a book shelf; or vow, you know, we got all this cauliflower and what not sent to us from panama, and the Egyptians people, they said to keep it." There was a storm coming. The Princeton Plasma Physics Laboratory had probably not figured out yet that once benign tumors have been identified, in most instances, people have five to fifteen years to live, Yep, et. al. Am J Manag Care. 2004 Aug;10(8):553-60. *Interventions to improve quality of care: the Kaiser Permanente-Alzheimer's Association Dementia Care Project.* The calculated hazards of buying polyneuropathy insurance was 95.22 SREN 4:24PM April 16, 2018, and the calculated hazards of buying post-mortem-autopsy insurance was 95.14 SREN 1:10PM April 16, 2018. As we questioned the nature of purchases in polyneuropathy insurance, to understanding our client's needs, for instance – was Kentucky Fried Chicken, low on the supply of chicken breasts, or was Kentucky Fried Chicken running low in their inventory- we had to wonder exactly what their daily income from chicken breasts at Kentucky Fried Chicken was, compared to chicken patty sandwiches.

Let me correct you on a couple of things, OK, Yep began crunching numbers. Aristotle is not Belgian, and the central message of Buddhism is every man for himself. Fourth, provided the dialectical basis for electrons of a Bohr atom, exclusive of Wolfgang Pauli, October 2017, which demonstrated the feasibility of free falling in non-Euclidian space - similar to a roller coaster, only faster 13.83 BBRY Jan 5. 2018. Fifth, examined a stereotype of Feynman's electrostatic field theory in a hyper-axiomatic electron dense background, June 2017, where the space defined as Euclidian – similar to threading a space needle, only stranger then a stranger, appearing exo-facto at 2:40PM on November 20, 2017 as Hooks Bay, Australia with a companion drought as Kangaroo Island, giving the dimensionality of Higgs Boson toujours as between 3962.24 January 10, 2017 and 4043.49 November 20, 2017. That's probably the most noteworthy configuration of dimensionality which could be described, where the attributions are apparent.

Sixth, provided a view of an atom in unified space-time 154.99 Apple June 8, 2017 where the atom is a made of atomic mass, but does not possess charge; as a single neutron. Seventh, provided two objective conclusions for Jean Paul Satire's philosophical blogs on "the thing in itself" and "the thing of itself" to improve the drag co-efficient in romantic literature (Cheswick field surveys, of Cheswickshire lowlands latitude of 52°22'48.17"N longitude of 1°48'43.32"W or 52.380046 and, Wawona field surveys of Wownaminya, Yalgoo, Western Australia latitude S 28° 27' 0" longitude: E 116° 49' 59") – for the Europeans of Henry James' novels with flawed atmospheric undertones in cinematic translates, whereas fiscal limitations and aircraft unavailability impose restrictions on asymmetric tempro-textual, physiological ensambles of lost in time complementarity, which is a rather unique repressor-free-innate 4N expression (severity) 3963.00 LSE 10:50AM Feb 5, 2018, where virtually three tectonic plates merged into one creating a gravity free strata for super-fast jet travels.

The conception of an Earth centric space model was launched with *Functional Groups in Theory* in 2013, which initially included homo-topologies to the Indus-Chenab Delta, the Volta-Aveyime, the Benares-Narayanpur Pump Canal,

Todd River run-off near Alice Springs, Lozhou-Wangye Tea House, and Karaiskaki-Mpoumpoulinas, developed from indexes for International Standards (Singapore), Linear Hadron (Lisbon), and Archimedes (Milan). The *New Theory of Groups* in 2017, consisted of FTSE HSI elements as a temporal ordering of DJI and NASDAQ classes, before the introduction of grand unified time, which allowed for rapid development of methodologies within NASDAQ Dow Jones for homo-topologies, where the Indus-Chenab Delta was adapted into a metricized linear regression for higher order pairs, the Volta-Aveyime was evolved into a rotating latitude, the Benares-Narayanpur Pump Canal was cast into a probabilistic angular distribution among Euclidian distances from Todd River run-off near Alice Springs, Lozhou-Wangye Tea House was developed as a multi-parity format, and the Karaiskaki-Mpoumpoulinas was developed into a business model for FCHI with force vectors in Theory, where the days between June 3, 2013 to April 24, 2017 constitutes an Earth revolution – where 95.46 SREN 3:00 PM April 16, 2018 is the average probability density for the "Local Likelihood" of 95.28 SREN 10:50AM April 6, 2018 for encountering 365 daisies in the jar.

Implicit to the context of an Earth centric space model is the Euro, discovered in 2000 by Guy Fillmore, where longitudinal divergence functions from the pro-region to the caudal region to Theory region to the Sum were integrated into the Dow Jones for risk assessment of fish habitats, the Equator 6991.89 FTSE 11:20AM March 22, 2018, the Tropic of

Cancer 6941.88 FTSE 1:05PM March 22, 2018, the Tropic of Capricorn 6932.40 FTSE 3:25 PM March 22, 2018, and the Grand Meridian 6927.85 FTSE 4:00PM March 22, 2018. While their composition is segmented as components for formal analysis vector function of multivariate definite integrals as vector function of Newtonian-paramagnetic dipole, formal analysis vector function of in-situ, vector function of in-vitro, vector function of helicoid, vector function of discrete space, vector function of in-space no-space, vector function of discrete Pascals, vector function of discrete Calvins, vector function of Arctaurus, vector function of gravitational collapse in subspace, ERG function of Haline, Cosmic degree mapping in-field inductions, Milky Way galaxy function, gravitational collapse in space function, gravitational collapse on galaxy Sirius function, gravitational collapse on galaxy Sirius in subspace function, Newton EURSEK function, Newton AUDUSD function, Newton Theory period function, these functions superimpose functions associated with twelve indefinite integrals for AUD/USD with subset indefinite integrals for Casa Lupita, which approximate 12.34 months for rotation as of 01:30PM November 17, 2017, which is a fortuitously different from 30.26 days per month, accounted for on November 10, 2017- improved from a drug rehab clinic figured as 29.45 days per month on October 25, 2017, due in large part to 14.69 days gained as of November 3, 2017 from dredging the Ob River. There is a lesson in feminine hygiene for the developing world, Asiatics and Orientalists alike, on that note for understanding orbital-mass for Sirius Galaxy policy chocotuers.

Though much of references are intended to appear as facsimiles of a regime ancien, the disingenuous nature of allotments would point to a Homotopy as disfigured as Julia Roberts' film Wonder. It became necessary due to the number of different venues of Cod Fish offered by theoretical physics to develop a query language between 2016 and 2017 to interface the Chicago Mercantile Exchange and Toronto Stock Exchange for futures due to the positional influence of their information in series dilators for international currency. The options board for notes from the New Zealand Exchange would be a late stage development to understand power structures associated with FTSE circuits. Until then the query language, Number Theory (MAT) developed as a collaboration between the International Standards of SGX and OSEAX for the Thinking Machines Portal, issued data base certifications by SUN Microsystems, connectivity to N225, NASDAQ, Dow Jones, NYSE, LSE, AORD, HSI, and experimental data displays to Google and Yahoo, as a fast and easy re-entry towards the Chrysalis- Earth's shell space as a function of the galaxy known as Ursa Minor before the Big Bang of 2012, where we *took heed*, of *Two Broke Girls*.

Though the facilities are not as posh as French Prime Minister Edouard Phillipe's quarters in Rue des Beaux Arts staring at a diaper rash in the middle of nowhere, the latitudes and homo-topographies include Pristaniste Varna Zapad, Eyton, Anthy sur Leman, and Vanersborg, which are well known for fisheries such as the Thames, Volga, Drina, Pek, Weser, Po, Arno, and Godavari. For generalized risk assessment models Microsoft certificate standards for Resonance Fits, Poisson Distributions, Pascal's Laws, Drag's Law, and Discretized Sets, with high yield bonds through J.P Morgan Chase produce high quality arbitrage for actuarial assets. Rules of Inference require data base theory for risk arbitration, risk capitalization, risk capital amortization, provided by Swiss Light Source. Intel Capital provides certificates for U.S. regional municipal bonds at risk of association with U.S. treasury notes and at risk of dilution with Pounds and Euros, through NASDAQ, DJI, and GSPC. We of the Laboure Party, LH, JASRI, JKSI, and Trieste, nuclear plants of humanity's sober reconnaissance in service to much less than a billion folktales, developed a firm understanding and, overcame attenuated gated signal damping. A general conclusion is that signal damping occurs due to the absence of transmitter gates, and a more specific understanding is that gate attenuation has to be modulated. The scenario is similar to channel induced coverage of amplitude selection in noisy environments and voltage gating the channel in a low order conditional period. If the degree of freedom in a low order conditional period is high then the need for computational ram options are exponential, whereas if the degrees of freedom in a high order conditional period are low then the rom options are logarithmic.

The suggested technology for therapeutic intervention in cases indicated as 95.22 SREN 4:24PM April 16, 2018, operates in much the same way, where the first challenge is to identify a volume of plasma which constitutes Plasminogen

Activation Inhibitor 18.52 HPE 1PM March 1, 2018, to calculate a theoretical outcome 23.91HPE Jan. 26, 2018, then calculate a deterministic model of the theoretical outcome for antibiotics which could be tolerated in milligram quantities (pediatric dosage) – as we are speaking of cancer care for a U.S. population (black, white, asian, hispanic) 23.30 HPE Feb 1, 2018, for controlling the top three hypoglycemic components 18.91 HPE 10:30 AM Feb 27, 2018 as a way to defer decision for isolating 3/74 survivors over a 5 year period due to the nature of the cancer types.

The strategies taken in the instance of rotational periods in higher dimensional space, were to abbreviate the number of algebraic lie computations with the development of co-linear integration networks and linear co-efficient integrals, unified field theories and their applications, gravitational field theory in real space, and specialization in broad market strategies with multi-cultural backgrounds for geo-products and EM interference.

2. Issue – Quite literally, where Endymion stepped on deck of the Mayfaire – the Argentines were recording tango's – the Aegean's were bathed in bright distinguished hues – among the Persephone, a quizzical gaze fell upon Ovid -

For what it's worth, super-indexing Mayfaire may as well be regarded as a dystopic utopia of disillusionment and despair where the journeys are divided as "the believers" and "the non-believers." For their part, neither party know with any certainty if the super-index is legitimate, or authentic with respect to autobiographical references of the Mayfaire. The journeys are a composition of various processes and languages which progress as a Slovakian lullaby.

The journeys, begins with an apostolic apocalypse of *"Permanent U.S. Government Hiatus,"* and soon follows an armageddon which can only be described as *"I hate you the more,"* 17.89 USG Jan 29, 2016. Among "the believers" the talk is rarely of any such mesmerizing spells as would be described as proverbs, although their adverbial proclivities are known to be comminglingly suitable for our comedians, felicitous charmers as they are risen from savages, 39.14 USG Jan 19, 2018. Among "the non-believers," their faith are tested by fragmented memories of long ago and far away, hallucinations, dream paradoxes, and shady curriculum vitae 31.37 USG April 21, 2017. Half-way into the saga the barren landscapes emerge as a reminder of the dead, and the dead thereafter 32.42 USG Feb 28, 2018. By the end, we come to recognize as in a less obvious perspective how failure subverts knowledge, where at the most obvious cocktail parties of breaking confidentiality, prognosis is observed of as a casual statement to clean houses, reverse mortgage, or count the days left on social security payments.

As pumping of chemical into the stem failed, forest officials are infusing the chemical solution drop by drop using saline bottles similar to a saline drip given to patients in the hospital. Termites had affected almost entire tree due to which parts of it are fallen, and it closed for tourists in December 2017, the report from Hyderabad, Times of India, April 16, 2018 read. The world's second largest Banyan tree in Pillalamarri of Mahabubnagar district in Telangana is on 'saline drip' now as part of the rejuvenation of the tree that is almost dying. The 700-year-old ficus tree is now given treatment by injecting a diluted chemical to kill termite population that infested the tree. The tourists damaged the proper roots. These roots are also given artificial strength using pillars and pipes. Interestingly no enquiry is conducted into the negligence of the officials in protecting the tree heritage.

During a surprise inspection of Osmania General Hospital (OGH) mortuary, the Health Minister said that all mortuaries in the State will be modernised.to improve infrastructure and streamline the process of handling bodies in mortuaries at teaching hospitals, authorities are set to introduce a new mortuary policy in Telangana. On Monday, Health Minister Dr. C Laxma Reddy said that the policy will not only be aimed at improving infrastructure in mortuaries but also streamline the entire process of conducting post-mortems in the State.

As with most complex biological systems such as sea paramecium, lake euglena, river fish, and ocean turtles, circuits have been shown to coincide with space. A recent example of continental drift for instance, developed entirely on principals of such organisms showed that continental drift isn't only localized to *Dope Shit Crack Ass Niggas* (DSCAN) from Arizona, but occurs within a much wider context of *Niggas* and *Crack*. Though a circuit of this type is technically blind in functional origin, their component are architectural in USD/AUD space, and provide capital allocation of DSCAN *in transit*. Described initially as *"To me, came one gun core, high as sun,"* and later translated into Pascal's Calculas, the circuit demonstrates the motility of a continent in geological scape concurrent with interstellar space – or, gravitational collapse as described in Plato's Phaedo. These high-minded movements weren't plucked from thin air, read the Boston Globe, April 14, 2018. Instead, much of what scholars call the American Renaissance originated from Boston's streets: a crooked, cramped, vice-ridden urban labyrinth, piled high with "night soil," and riven by the same inequality that haunts us today.

Boston's elites placed an outsize blame for their political woes on the urban landscape. In sermons and pamphlets, reformers argued that a claustrophobic and unsanitary urban environment corroded popular judgment. According many ministers, visual exposure to "innumerable indulgencies and gratifications," from luxurious carpet shops to seedy oyster bars, deprived urban spectators of their capacity to think and behave properly, making good New Englanders into drunkards, sensualists, adherents of feverish religious revivals.

De organisatie verwacht onder de deelnemers veel hardlopers uit Alkmaar, De kinderkopjes op de Munnikenweg, de molens, het Kippenbruggetje; de klassieke bezienswaar-digheden van Oudorp zijn allemaal verweven in de run. Wij hopen natuurlijk dat de deelnemers nog tijd hebben om tijdens het rennen om zich heen te kijken en van al het moois te genieten. Waar de route langs de huizen leidt hebben we de inwoners van Oudorp gevraagd de renners vooral hard aan te moedigen en de route gezellig te maken. Het geeft je als renner echt een 'boost' als je ziet dat iedereen om je heen daar voor jou staat. Samen coachen we iedereen naar de finishlijn, Door Redactie op Donderdag 12 April 2018.

Posthumous circuits for reasons thereof consider relative integrations as the subsistent metamorphosis of space-time equilibrium elements as a temporal ordering. The architect of the Maserati circuit, built on a reverse induction platform, showed the turning point for the radius, as fag ash blew from the tip of his dendritic splines. The scope of the circuit was to establish the core technology of any functional circuit, the series dilator, within a neologism of load capacitor, thermoresistor, or thermostable decoupler. Darwin's data showed feasibility of the platform for development as a load capacitor with speciation distributions and encouragingly non-positive hertz fields of non-prime. Here, our own Vidyasagar Surajprasad Naipaul, much accomplished for tomes as Million Mutinies Now compared with A House for Mr. Biswas could be quoted as writing in the Guardian 10 March, 2007, "I had to be true to my own world. It was more fluid, harder to pin down and present to a reader in any accepted, 19th-century way. Every simple statement I could make about myself or my family or background had to be qualified in some way." Based on isometric inductions in interstellar space, the Sham circuit provides a standard reference for geo-position, non-collateral substituents, non-cosmic hyper-looping, tight junction asymmetry, and the subsequent to gravitational collapse with partial hertz fields – and tenable functions of origin, 48.20 FGEN, April 11, 2018. Again we can include, our own Vidyasagar Surajprasad Naipaul in writing about Million Mutinies Now, "The book was dedicated to a further idea: that India was, in the simplest way, on the move; that all over the vast country, men and women had moved out of the cramped ways and expectations of their parents and grandparents, and were expecting more. This was the "million mutinies" of the title; it was not guerrilla wars all round."

While many war correspondents, have trouble understanding how "Subject," "Object," and "Predicate" operate in spoken English, films such as Salvador directed by Oliver Stone, present a metamorphosis of spoken English to French dialects covering Africa, and South-East Asia, in such films as Whiskey Tango Foxtrot directed by Glenn Ficarra, as custodian to public knowledge. Correspondent to Light Distance Mass Acceleration (LDMA) the Memetic circuit phases as a tube light with an oscillator and a diopter bridge, is more of an infantile fantasy for how things work while braving the winds in the background, and the mayflies. Before going further, one could say, I bet you wouldn't be able to identify correctly the subject, object, and predicate of the previous thread. Or, as if I refuse to bet - you know who's quite good at managing such debaucheries; who else, Gypsum Moss, partner to the firm of Barack Obama.

In Sienna, I would be dazzled, my mind organizing, who came first, the chicken or the egg. Unresolved issues with Lata Mangeshkar need to be addressed to the Department of OEM, as the ferrule, for line-intercepts- for load, for velocity, and for cognate. Such is the nature of autonomy; auto-taxis behavior can either mesmer or meander, as a hyperbole to the planarian. Say then, here's a question for people in your line of business: while most of the Australian Utilities, in Australia, which is a continental shelf, serving a population of 24.13 million residents in an area of 2.97 million square miles, what would be the stoichiometric equivalence for day and night in price, per KWH.

Based on a working model of cache flow for velocity function the circuit is an actualized anisotropic wave guidance birefringence with determinants to plate tectonics, defines the Cathode circuit. Based on the nature of exchange Joules and Chilean Joules of the International Monetary Fund to provide missing Biri-Biris for the scientifically illiterate, defines the Thermo-resistance circuit. Based on several archeological expeditions in Antarctica, based on facts rather than delusional and dissociative personality disorders of the U.S. population, the Focus circuit provides the basis for the Joyce Corporation's probabilistic distributions for class segregation and mass alignment of the Solar system in Walla-Walla.

Jonathan Swift's Gulliver's Travels is perhaps one of the least known of circuits, though Jonathan Swift is better known as the mother board to various circuit components or circuit breakers with unknown circuits. The nature of various previews of the noir film genera, *Clueless, Walkabout, Calcutta, Wannui, Le Mepris, and Eurovision* made by J-P. Goddard *as seen in movie theaters*, is to allow the observer to think about movies which are already in studios or in production. Previews in themselves have no plot references to the movie being shown at the theatre. Given that the prior probability of randomly assigning positions in a circuit is 1/10,000,000,000,000 what would be the nature of a systematic method for performing a circuit survey – as a way of discovering more about the various previews of the noir film genera – such as the *cost allocation process of the circuit*, the *amortization scheme of the circuit*, and most importantly *the demento negro por la loco Americano*. In other words, the draftsman developed several blueprints from the remote recesses of her imagination and left the civil service chaps to accept/reject and/or re-define any component wither through financial means or technical erudition. Hemispheric bias, to be construed as Focus, by the time resistors could be burned down on high quality bond paper was unexpected to the extent that thrust angle associated with momentum would have to be irresolute in picking fruits from the garden of eden. A reference for remanence is to observe how graphene glides across the surface of arcs created by x(sqrt(x − 0.085) for 0.01 to 0.1 compared with x(sqrt(x − 0.065) for the same limitation. What we want to understand is their difference. But I didn't want to run the raft in the daytime without anybody aboard to answer questions but me; so I didn't want the plan to begin working till pretty late tonight.

3. Issue – where Endymion tries to establish what is expected to happen – size what he has learned from a year before – attribute a recalcitrance – from the sarcophagus of the Dubliners, which for the better part is interpolated as the Dead by Sir Clive Lytton – as remarkable, the deductions of a young boy looking upon the dead to surmise the way of the spy – in so far as how we become who we are – from prone to fits of amnesia to what are you doing here – as Endymion in felicitous rapture for whorl of lump, stole, and swagger-

Mayfaire tares Zed and Lorenz evolves Ismail's Madness might describe the foyer for an introduction to a thermostable decouple circuit where several principals are observed as new DJIA 24,778.94,1:36PM May 16, 2018. Fifteen components of the Ptashnea genetic switch died on the streets of Tokyo with a Darwin G value of -6.02E18. Three components of Ptashnea genetic switch drowned in the ocean with a Darwin G value of -5E17. Two components of the Ptashnea genetic switch died on the streets of Buffalo with a Darwin G value of -1.34E16 with cross-reactivity values unknown, leaving American trade agreements, and U.S. trade agreements at an all time low 0.00027/UGS. Commercial insurance, Swiss Re reported nine months 2017 loss of USD468 million after large insurance claims from recent natural catastrophic events. Could Zero-trade be the future of Plato's Phaedo in one rotation?

Imagine that you've failed to gain entrance into the world of sociology due to such as it is, what's it they call it amortization schemes. The stream of ancient philosophy in the Alexandrian and Roman times widens into a lake or sea, and then disappears underground to reappear after many ages in underground to reappear ages in a distant land. It begins to flow again under new conditions, at first confined between high and narrow banks, but finally spreading over the continent of Europe NASDAQ 7412.89, 3:02PM May 16, 2018. It is and is not the same with Plato's Phaedo FTSE 7707.04 12:20PM May 14, 2018. There is a great deal in modern philosophy which is inspired by ancient. For what appears to be engaging is quite remarkably dialectic, from the perspective of several perimeters that defy definitions. The mojo ward seems to be a designers paradise with a seamstress 7.68 RBS 3:30PM, April 12, 2018. The coastal communities from the Great Barrier Reef to the Coast of Brunei play a provocative role in betwixt. The imperatives among foreign substances rolling out of cache registers as receipts are cross-eyed and silhouetted against a far off sea of mesmerizing spells of self in these vitae, where Hiesos is acknowledgement rarer than awkward, as it happens, 2602.00 ABF 12:00PM April 16, 2018.

The stag films of impresario, Bill Shorten, may well be a good rounding off point in the outback, considering his career, was well observed. A thin crescent appears late, and disappears quickly, very late. Over the succeeding quadrilles, the crest appears earlier and is slow to disappear, until finally the crest becomes a Muon, a Bohr atom in plain English even though you have zero ability to script in JAVA, because your computerwalla encrypted the language in a combination of assembler and S , even earlier into the daybreak of FTSE

7696.46 2:44PM May 14, 2018. For Phaedo, when Margaret Thatcher was Prime Minister, there were scarcely any tutors available to the experience of the "silenscieux," it would seem. The said objective, Free Body Motion; was income-prehensible; a letdown; an embarrassment; a double post-hoc stupefied notion as colorful as granny Dana Elcar's September 1968 production of "Fear I to Fall," from a nursing home in Pasture Institute, University Hospital. As a linear function, or as a bias angle variance, binary differential equations are not for the faint of heart, where Laurent spaces can be challenging, with Joyceans lurking in the background. For the most part we try to find the earth through the maze. A maze implies labyrinth. When John Major was Prime Minister, the avocation could therefore scarcely have been known - that means elucidated somewhere, where people could point to and say, their. The laments of style were a contemplation of Tony Blair's government, in so far as the epic scenes of Harry Potter from Bloomsbury's rap activism foreshadow. The references herein might have been a conspiracy, a deterministic model for provocative styles, a proposal. Construction and characterization of extrachr-omosomal probes for mutagenesis by carcinogens: site-specific incorporation of O6-methylguanine into viral and plasmid genomes. Cloning and mapping of the replication of origin Escherichia Coli. Their flippancy takes several days, often two weeks to develop a rapport; surveys begin to emerge in two months; co-homologies flicker. Here is how we move in the space jar.

That leaves the utilities experiments of Gordon Brown to decide the unison of previous administration for the role of Teresa May as comedian, not in the least as might expected of watching re-runs of *Fry and Laurie*, but as masterful as the *Paul Hogan Show* at their best. Isn't it familiarity which breeds contempt or is it the other way around? A legacy of betrayals certainly illuminate the Malcom Turnbull government as excelling in areas known to fans of Perth as sketchy details, anagrams and analogies, and the interest folder. Indeed, if a Claith Beast were old enough to pen such a vocation it would be called, Cod. The Fish itself is quite a bit as flakey. The rapper cometh tapped and bi-layered, for scaling such heights as might be of some interest to blurry eyed number theorists and for archeologists in search of the archaeopteryx. Extracting the fish, as much as the rapper, are a sampling of ensembles, voters, constituencies, and computing time. Welcome to Vasco da Gama, where astrophysics and cosmology meet. English is of consequence and the farce, mustardy, with a face book emotion of Stephen Biko's also passion, in wake of cry freedom.

Likewise, inaction during an annexation can be mutinous. Faculty members with personal contacts at Starlings were contacted with procedural specifications for local utilities to avert a State of New Jersey. There were inevitables. Diffraction and NMR studies of proteins, an uneasy alliance, veering off into "subsequently, it was found that EDTA bound to RNase affected only the titration curve-" is thought to have been a novel pursuit at the time, with different experimental models, including the fabrication of nylon, with free energy simulations for acyl group and electron pair relay systems as a network of interacting lipoyl moieties in the pyruvate and ketoglutarate dehydrogenase complexes from Escherichia coli, where the psychoanalytical gambit for Endymion was to have been, can I correctly differentiate between indoor socks and outdoor socks. Trieste the hi-throughput software conceived by Pasta Fresca Bongusto, famous for trite one-liners as "frailty thy name is woman" in the Fontana Candida of Retired Punk Rockers Talking About Recording Contracts, then superseded the nomenclature with his own "Dumb shit USA," for a meld of Bill Shorten's parliamentary elegiacs; while wandering in Athens, reported the dunce relocating from an expensive villa in France to a museum in Russia, where the former life of Keats could be seen for what it really was, or "what gibbs," as they say in native American vernacular, for which a travaller from remote Baluchistan presented the awkward pause for "no one lives their anymore." The wind was cool and crisp, refreshing, lamentably an endless breeze, and the endangered art bellowed through the hall of their geographic.

There was worse adumbrations to come. The nomads had writ their own fate for maleficence to good. The nomads hardly ever understood at all. The nomads had been chaliced for the difference between 5779.00 AORD and 5769.70 AORD on September 19th, 2017. A trippy helical estuary of emerging economies could hardly have been surmised from ownership documents pertaining to the management of indexes, and as with any licensing agreements, the licensors were expected to pay royalty fees from each licensee as maintenance cost fulfillment for source conduct, whereas scaling the space jar for tripe would be foreshadowed as – wacky, by professors of pre-cambrian periods. In quick haste, the arbors of barbarian indecisiveness were finally disengaged from Neolithic periods as an apt metaphor of CERN.

Circuit integration, which implies post analytical implementation of circuit components of known function, whether Nadja's Foreword, or Alexander Dumas, much like a mouth which is used to eat, and associated with a tongue is used to speak, can present various challenges from the perspective of cattle. Just as most electrical appliances such as the toaster used for toasting eggo waffles and the electric pencil sharpener used for sharpening pencils, the radio used for listening to music, the space bar used to create space, and the rechargeable battery pack used in fuel cells operate on livestock, so do most livestock in astronomical space.

By most we mean to exclude the possibility of marsupials as livestock along with golfing vacations in Cornwall, as would be suitable for midsomer outings in a Lincoln continental for Blaxploitation films. As typically good read on livestock, the Italian novelist Italo Calvino perhaps renders some of the best vistas of waves, in as much as the American novelist Mark Twain parries over a river. Within these paintings the oft wanderer of Athens might view a freighter, a cruise ship, Jesus walking on water, certainly various surfers with singing talent – "that means the ability to sing for a recording contract. Making marble rye, isn't quite the same as Miley Cyrus intoning the range of Jimi Hendrix Stratocaster, or Brittney Spears intoning the notes of Johnny Lee Hooker's fender – which is say, there isn't anything vastly imprecise with auditions and their outcomes at Aristophanes' – implying, yes, for the format where we are labile.

It may not seem as obvious, as we leave the franchise for others to develop, the sound stage has been our ulterior motive, which concerts do provide as a venue, in a very noisy wafer where the idealization of the artist-performers resonate as drowning in bathwater with soap suds for income. Extensibly, it can be stated that our business began with film-in-music as a genera, when music-in-film consisted of drums and cymbals, with a few exceptions, where sound is used to illuminate the subject, such as Persona, Easy Rider, Five Easy Pieces, Roshoman, Life is Sweet, and 8 ½ as an illustration of how sound film integrates, where the ordeal is to be able to navigate the viewer through scenery by evoking a sense of taste – which is to say, palatable, or considerate of food diversity and sauces subtleties – which allows the viewer of "experience the film" instead of "creating an impression on the viewer." The last thing any actor of self-worth wants to do is go up to Ms. Random Memorandom at three in the morning and say, "Hey, did you see my movie?" in large part because, an actor has to overcome Japanese masks, self-imposed, or otherwise, to be able to break through the light in film. A Kabuki theatre, such as Gosford Park, in that sense, attempts at the development of the un-movie, or positional effects within a sound stage, while in a movie, the Cheetah Children, the kabuki in-and-of-itself becomes a movie of positional effects within a sound stage 96.06 SREN 2:04PM April 17, 2018. Whereas, A Night of Earth explores this phenomena as a duality, Mystery Train explores how sound resonates within the context of such a duality, as Dead Man anticipates alien invasion. Extending sound to color in film, with and without the rain barrels of conditional formatting are typical of such movies about music-in-film as O Lucky Man, Rosemarie's Baby, Husbands, Orlando, the Piano, and Broadway Danny Rose- where Reservoir Dogs explores the nature of film-in-music.

Re-working the compilations of Bergman, Goddard and Sen, which we can broadly define as Kabuki, Neo-realism, and Cinemascope, means keeping the authorships, while stripping the narrative presence to create space for new meaning 95.64 SREN 9:14AM April 17, 2018. Given that we cannot provide new meaning, in-promptu, we can look at how Aristophanes' arrived at Mylie Cyrus and Brittney Spears. As a retrospective, if we look at the B52s as an audition for film-in-music, then Aristophanes could be said to have hit the charts with the skills of a sharp shooter with the Eurhythmics, with solos albums of Natalie Merchant to attest for test-marks, for the introduction of sound-rhythm in Men At Work, for the development of Talking Heads and Prince, as completion of film-in-music 95.56 SREN 9:06AM April 17, 2018. Venue addition to the genera produced

Nirvana, Sublime, Coldplay, Radiohead, Pixies, and Oasis, each with a different set of limitations. In the case of Nirvana, we try to develop a sense of what a free vocalist-lyricist-and-musician with exceptional scale to note conversationalist skills has to overcome during a venue performance, which in the case of Sublime we try to escape from with technological Innovations 96.18 SREN 11:30AM April 17, 2018. In the case of Oasis we try to understand to which extent harmonics can be used to accentuate an opera singer, while with the Pixies we experiment with harmonic distortions as a way to understand how an alto-soprano would use a metronome 95.60 SREN 9:30AM April 17, 2018. In the case of Radiohead we experiment with a free vocalist who writes his own scores, whereas in Coldplay we try to develop scores for a mezzo-soprano. Studio bands such as Yolo Tengo are an experiment with ambiance, where we attempt to incorporate of the inexpressible, that means "feelings" within a very defined region of Mission and Valencia in San Francisco, their community, their livelihoods, and the clothes they wear, as an existential term paper about life, similar to the street-corner in Smoke 96.36 SREN 11:56AM April 17, 2018. In the case of Justin Timberlake we studied the effect of amplitude modulation for channel gating dampers for Chanel No 9, close to a source – to develop mobile technologies. As logger heads with software talent, their functionality is useful in incorporating experience and knowledge of sound into film with the appointment of Roger Davies, instead of ostrich burgers with Harvey Weinstein 96.04 SREN 2:40PM April 17, 2018. That said we want to re-work Sen films into BAFTA,

Goddard films into Oscars, and Bergman into Cannes. Licenses for Ray films are not available, and copyright issues should be addressed directly to Shakespeare & Co. of Turin Italy 4188.00 LSE 11:40 AM April 17, 2018.

Implicit within the integration of livestock might then define a circuit theory of components where the functions are extracted from core samples for hypothesis testing; observed data. Does it rain in Spain mainly on the plain as we see on the tele is a vast archaeological rendezvous, a Buddhist canvas if you will, beneath the bombed out ruins of Afghanistan 96.06 SREN 2:04PM April 17, 2018. In reality, the question might be put more straightforwardly as, where does it rain in Spain, in consideration of prototypical liniments, and value derived objectives of such and such. For the majority of terms, when we look at CERN, their duplicity escapes our notice. The Percival isn't as quaint as we imagine it to be. The walls are bare, with an imprint of here-before, deja-vu. Object recognition is a cognitive awareness of diaspora (Walter Gilbert, personal correspondence 1984). A guava isn't quite the same as a lychee fruit, though a strawberry might be closer to a crab than an antelope to a wheat field 4169.00 LSE 10:54AM April 16, 2018. There's no music on the radio prevails a cascade of harps. The landscape paintings are an embodied abstraction from time-future to time-present. There's no music on the radio obliterates a sustainability gap through the wind, breeze, gusts, impromptu songlines, easy to remember nudities. Rembrandts nudes are, as an instance, a fore shadow of giant sea turtles from the Gulf of Hurmuz. In sharp contrast, the lusty figures of Delacroix are a harmonious rendering of invisible cities. In Descartes' Ganymede the planetarium is exclusively Euler in sophistry, lain in bubbles of toil and troubles, troubadours, magical potions, enchanted forests, groves of edelweiss 4190.00 9:36AM April 16, 2018. There's no music on the radio bellows a psychological discourse for psychics and psychos, with terrifying outbursts published in Garmande of arctic avalanches and order formalities. Finally, as the forward is reached our civilization fathoms the swifts for extent of integration at a now and then gift of adventure 4180.00 LSE 10:16AM April 16, 2018. There's no music on the radio becomes a mixed metaphor for productivity cost, where wages have to be paid for labor; the parables of laughter are as far a cry from Sindh as Pollux.

The anxiety over time, of course, had left Luis moribund. Could the cluster computers be made to think had been at past, a tense subject. The proposals had been of sorts, ranging from abstract biological concepts in space to the abstract mathematical concepts in space. Neither of them had the utility desirable of circumstances which could be deployable as mission control 4170.00 LSE 10:46AM April 16, 2018. The operating system existed as a utility largely maintained by sectors for birds, and the occasional human interface who changed the light bulbs. The clusters did not have sector references by which to initiate a logistical process, because the process configuration had not been known. In a circumlocution on the task messenger, Luis had near about tripped over himself on functional and mechanistic explanations of such diverse topics as 3D vision and figure-ground perception in natural scenes; optic-flow based navigation in natural scenes towards goals around obstacles and spatial navigation in the dark; invariant object and scenic gist learning, recognition, and search; prototype, surface, and boundary attention; gamma and beta oscillations during cognitive dynamics; learning of entorhinal grid cells and hippocampal place cells, including the use of homologous spatial and temporal mechanisms in the medial entorhinal-hippocampal system for spatial navigation and the lateral stream for adaptively timed cognitive-emotional learning among eleven clusters, which left near abouts thirty nine clusters for utility driven cost-benefit analysis for buying food and fuel for the inhabitants 4178.00 LSE 8:20AM April 16, 2018.

CERN as an old, multi-national organization can be rational. Gary Oldman, now famous in the U.S. for his movie Dracula, while acting as the Chief Information Officer has made several movies with distribution rights for counties with U.S. interests. There are various movies made by Gary Oldman which can be used as a resource for value derived objectives. One of the earliest understandings of the "value derived objectives" comes from NMR studies, which are analogies to MRI studies of the human brain, *Homo europeanus* 4190.00 SREN 4:04PM April 17, 2018. There being different types of species for Homo Erectus had thus far only been conceived and limited to *Homo australopithecus*, the wide grinned dictator of the *Homo americanus* was scaresely viewed as an anthropological waste land of a Land Surveyor for Department A., which was the wrong place to be looking for Mizzi's behaviour. Childish and obstinate in perspective, the Homotopy as a Cartesian coordinate system was right enough for insinuating frailties such as, that's what I've been saying all this time, Number Galaxy 62, n-dimensional space, kappa-peg, 45556883721 parsecs, 5.56588E18 Ergs, 2602.00 LSE 9:00 AM, April 16, 2018. *Australopithecus africanus* is an extinct species of the australopithecines, given that the *Homo asiaticus* is inter-galactic, from the Barbary Coast of Africa to North-west Australia as economic arbitrage of collapsed galaxy spiral by galaxy cluster, where Jupiter and Saturn define boundaries for the solar system. Cretans - that means the people of Crete, are known to have influences 7.68 RBS 3:30PM April 12, 2018. For instance, Calvino describes Zoe. "In every point of this city you can, in turn, sleep, make tools, cook, accumulate gold, disrobe, reign, sell, question oracles." Where is the city, on a map would be a good question for aspiring to be astrophysicists- for what Calvino describes of the city are verbs, action items. Furious that typing isn't mentioned. No problem, Calvino describes Melania. "Melania's population renews itself: the participants in the dialogues die one by one and meanwhile those who will take their places are born, some in one role, some in another." Where is the city, on a map would be a good question for aspiring to be astronomers- for what Calvino describes is a city of renewals. Upset that mathematics isn't mentioned. No problem, Calvino describes Perinthia. "In Perinthia's streets and square today you encounter cripples, dwarfs, hunchbacks, obese men, bearded women. But the worse cannot be seen; guttural howls are heard from cellars and lofts, where families hide children with three heads or with six legs." Where is the city, on a map would be a good question for aspiring to be cosmologists- for what Calvino describes is a city of various limitations 48.20 FGEN April 11, 2018. The influence, which Calvino tries to create for Cretans, is a premise for creativity, finding the extraordinary in the mundane; though we just like people for the way they write or express themselves – with simple pleasures.

Among the virtues of Crete which can be counted as being Cartesian, is Lewis Carroll, and as with any role, one might be asked to play, the personae generally has to be ascribed a title, and therefore a descriptor, so as not to be confused with a rat. When, "at last the mouse who seemed to be a person of some authority called out sit down, all of you and listen to me, I'll soon make you dry enough," would be good place to start for archeologist. "They all sat down at once, in a large ring, with the mouse in the middle," is a bit of what we would call a happenstance, much as an Afghan shepherd who might be passing the monasteries of Buddha would wonder – what's the point? as a world in one dimension is devoid of wonder. Angry at that, no problem, Carroll makes room from the Dodo bird. "First it marked out a race course, in a sort of a circle, ("the exact shape doesn't matter," it said, and then all the party were placed here and their. Insufficient party, pooped of party, this ain't no party, breakfast party, no problem, Carrroll develops role for the Fish-Footman. "There's no sort of use in knocking," says the footman, "and that's for two reasons. I'm on the same side of the door as you are; secondly, because they are making such a noise inside, no one could possibly hear you." Don't like the role, don't want the script, hate your casting agent, no problem, Carroll creates the March Hare. "And the Hatter was having tea at it." The influence, which Carroll tries to create for Cretans, is a premise for dimension, discovering what am I looking at; though we just like people for the way they write or express themselves – about simple pleasures.

Taking the above notes into consideration, on December 15, 2017, Endymion describes the manifold bundle of his observations as 62.63 at 10:10PM for cost of Jarlsberg wheel $6.77, and the splines for the manifold bundle as 16.70 at 11:30PM for cost of Fettuccine $1.59 as a non-linear hyperbolic function of $x(\sqrt{x} - 0.085)$ for $x = 0.01$ to 0.1 and $x(\sqrt{x} - 0.065)$ for $x = 0.01$ to 0.1. British Taxpayers suffering from the Spanish Inquisition in the general assembly were then ordered to be aware of Endymion's Saga by the Provost of École Normale Supérieure, to create a consensus as "incontournable pour rejoindre une formation de droit – en sciences et techniques des activites physiques et sportives, mais aussi l'interet pour la exercice de la responsibilite collective, associative au citoyenne . . . " In organic chemistry, for example, a typical synthesis involves

understanding the relationship between mass density and specific gravity in claiming the Boston Beanpot. That's why it's called skating on thin ice. Related to that subject are several movies such as Hannibal the Cannibal, the Fifth Element, Planet of the Apes, Scarlet Letter, Henry and June, Sid and Nancy, and the Hangover from Romeo is Bleeding, which are as different from each other as the space jar looks to our observer, Endymion. Quasi-uncertainty de-briefings from that there may be motif signals, quite possibly, I should think so, or niggardly, hay whey you at, which either directly or indirectly typify an object orientation for logic circuits in real space is a then better defined as super imposition of physical perturbation of space logic, where space is defined as a continuous area or expanse that is free, available, or unoccupied.

Because CERN was not known to be rational until the Jurassic Period, there are several autonomy classes of Indexes that use a co-operative economic system of the Paleocene Period. Of these, recent interest has spurred the development of the BRICS, famously refered to as Brixit. One of the confounding aspects in retrospection of this economic bloc, consisting of BVSP HSI BSESN is that they are articulated regional economies, where the connotations suggest circuit dynamics which are either integrated feed forward loops or integrated feed-back loop with surprising new development for phenomenological continental drift(s) where the later was seen to be drifting whilst the former turning- though without a typographical maarsenbroek. The current working hypothesis suggests that the later is an oscillating conduction stream of fluidic mass densities while the former is a Newtonian paramagnetic dipole that together form an astonishing electromagnetic thermocouple under a zero gravity stratosphere, denoted as Daze of Our Lives S.1 Ep. 1, Barnaby Meets Stella for a Magic Carpet Ride. A further working hypothesis demonstrates that the oscillation is Newtonian semi-classical in nature, with striking ionospheric pleiades, as much as genetic adaptation to the environment causes mutation, which leads to autosomal inheritance with the auto-density disequilibrium of strati-form structures in super-space defined by the equation $-y^3/x^2 - (x^2 - 1)\exp(3.7111)$ for $x = 0.8833333$ to 8.863636364.

The challenges for HSI as a currency therefore have a two-fold interstitial objective similar to AEX sterol hydrates, in the co-development of a currency market circuit framework for Exit U.S., while managing CERN relationships through the North Atlantic Treaty Organization 19.44 HALO 3:00 PM April 13, 2018 and the Swiss Chocolate Board 19.55 HALO 2:00PM April 18, where one could look at such relationships as two-fold iso-symmetries 5371.37 FCHI 11:06AM April 18, 2018. Consider the lingering bitter taste left in the mouth of David Cameron, as he asked Barack Obama, "How are you holding up?" Both could be seen with an equal lens as vocal, charismatic, and considerate of their opinions to the point of being reserved. As a personality, Cameron tended to be shy as an academic, indicative of resources, and a rich background on opinion papers 7280.30 FTSE 10:00AM April 18, 2018, while Barack Obama tends to demonstrate instilled values 7314.88 FTSE 2:34PM April 18, 2018. While neither subject could necessarily be seen as subjects per say, given plenty of room to navigate their faculty, the question one would have to ask is what brought them together? Was it under arm moisture, was it urine samples, or was it pond scum- might have to be thought of as a diurnal character playing amidst their existence where they could be seen, and non-existence where they were not seen 7289.29 FTSE 12:40 April 18, 2018. The layers which Teresa May presents are in sharp contrast to which we might formally have described as episodic memory. In her repertoire, Narendra Modi for instance might appear as an insensitive character, known for fit of rage, bouts with anguish, and at the same time, placid equanimity. Shinzo Abe might be seen as a Kamikaze pilot with beef cow disorder 2.56 PACB 11:00 AM, April 16, 2018. Li Keqiang could be seen as a surfer going out every morning to meet the waves and returning to shores with just enough penicillin to make porridge 186.30 COST 12:45PM April 6, 2018. Matteo Renzo, in comparison is more of a finesse, a puzzle, where his contribution to society in representing Italy appear to be vague or unclear, his contributions to humanity appear questionable, though his achievements, for all we know, are remarkable 2.89 PACB Jan 30, 2108. While all four subjects are challenged to various extents by various asimilies (that means not similar) we look to the various legislators for cause-effects – as in a competition 5.17 PACB Oct 4, 2017. Suppose Borg is playing McEnroe, and the audience is busy chewing knits, perhaps chatting up the Agarwal's, or cozying up to the Boondoggle-Beasts, then the response of the fans are unlikely to play well with the antics of McEnroe, hustling for points against the barbarian hoard 4.34 PACB Aug 14, 2017.

The changeover scene setting isn't very much different from that, said Endymion, especially if you're a devout fan of New Jersey. All of my acquaintances are dead from the common cold, most of them anyway, and trying to save a couple of them has been an uproar over devastation 3919.50 BFX 1:24PM April 19, 2018. Noteably, the word permanent could not be heard over the crackers venue for a holocaust museum at a Kaiser-Permanente, where the appointment of Katherine Beiser, might at last be seen as the role-call we were looking for, in the communities impacted from Santa Barbara to San Diego 3922.66 BFX 12:20PM April 19, 2018. That should cheer you out of your misery, which could be seen as a sign that most of them have pulled through on plasmodium from hell 2.55 PACB March 19, 2018. Burson-Marsteller is a surprise, because their lineage is British in a transparent kind of way, Fleishman-Hillard because their lineage is allergic, H&K because their lineage is neurological, Ketchum-MSL because they are torque-sheared, Ogilvy because it's hard to keep her awake, savvy little Qorvis because he got the cold in utero, and Weber Shandwick because that's close to home for girls who wanna have fun.

The roll call being unlike "hyper-kinetic anxiety," means having to wait for each step 5370.99 FCHI 4:36PM April 18, 2018.

The pyrotechtion is a bit like an aesthetic local, a condition statement where the future statement is predicated upon some amplitude bias. As a nurse practitioner I will pick up some serum-albumin, and then wait to see when my subject says "kill the television." In the meantime, I can covet a pin-prick and file it at the docket. I can return the next day, and the day after that to do the same thing. Starting on the fourth day, instead of the picking up serum-albumin, make a choice, for either/or and at time-expected pick up some albumin. It's a bummer that's for sure, but I can return the next day, and the day after that to do the same thing. Now when I enter, I have something to go on, instead of my choice of measures, I say here's something to think on, and minding my manners swiftly swish away, until time expected to pick up some albumin, and ask, did you know we have a department of diagnostic medicine here at Kaiser-Permanente, which doubles as department of cosmology? It's a bummer, I know, but I can return the next day, and the day after that, 5376.06 FCHI 10:20AM April 18, 2018 to do the same thing.

I call my technician, Ms. Radcliffe, works for the psycho ward. Can you provide the misnomer between the withdrawal symptoms, after aggregating the primer set to the finite set, and removing the dopamine 5.37 PACB April 14, 2017. Then

I ask my technician to pull a rank in file with a range and sort for intelligence. Where-ever the intelligence is, that's my immediate goal for my subjects 18.34 MRC 3:30PM April 13, 2018. The remaining question being, how far can I manage my intelligence up the ladder, 18.48 MRC 11:28AM, April 13, 2018 for which I take a partial of an isomeric tri-trimer, just like the one at Eton College, as a prognosticator for oats and penmanship from the Appalachian mountains – as antidote for Ebola virus, where 11,315 people have been reported as having died from the disease in six countries; Liberia, Guinea, Sierra Leone, Nigeria, the US, and Mali. The total number of reported cases being 28,637, there should be no reason to treat Liberia/ Qorvis, Guinea/H&K, Sierra Leone (recommend), Nigeria/ Weber Shandwick, and Mali/ Burson/ Steinbeck(c), any differently than the U.S. A simple enough procedure could make accommodation for seeing a better day, 96.80 SREN 2:46 PM April 19, 2018, on the river Liffey for teaching hospitals of the American medical association.

Thus as the Lorenzians of 6912.36 and 23,836.17 register with the NASDAQ and Dow Jones Indexes, we note the change over from Mr. Shakespeare's Next Guffaw as a Doppler of 2596.86 at the American Stock Exchange as a memento of his autobiographical cetolog of slap-dash caricaturization of the infinite – that means space, in anticipation of other proofs ascertainable. Matrix Deco-mposition Value of 6974.30 on Jan 4, 2017 for Mult-iplication Matrix Value of 8127.95 for Nov. 27, 2017 was well received by jurisprudence at NZX. The diopter value of

5967.70 at 2:05PM for ASX 200 would indicate a declension structure of orbit from a plenary position. Gold Resources provided the calculated value of 4.12376E30 for a computed (observed) value of 4.11. Compass provided the calculated value of 1.000598012 at Tyne for the computed (observed) 1510.00, as our chronicle turned over to derivazione di new Dirac nel calculo veloce with major improvements in supercomputing facilitated by cost analysis, with a technological innovation in high-performance grid computing, and mathematical programming of parallel processors, registering l'steneo di Genova of 7498.59 at 10:20AM December 13 for FTSE, 3825.08 for LSE on December 11, 2017, with Swiss Re AG SREN registering 90.25 on December 11, 2017, and CRAY arriving at 22.73 at 1:30PM December 12, 2017. We publish the value of the Blood Meridian on 10:10AM December 15, 2017 as BMY 62.63 and the Dynin value at 11:30AM on December 15, 2017 as 16.70 GLYC for Sujata Bal. Noticeably, this obviated the mention of terse latitudes by Mr. Newton to Endymion, as a way of expressing the sunrise times for Novosibirsk and Vladivostok as 8:54AM and 8:01AM respectively on December 12, 2017 and sunset times as 4:52PM and 4:37PM in Los Angeles and Seattle on December 11, 2017 respectively.

Simultanious neuro-pharmacokinetic evaluation of subject 4N by K. Perkins MD, on December 20, 2017 at 4:00PM EST, said Endymion began to reveal some of the objections raised during micro-injection studies of Heidi Fleiss by Gerald Rubin who insisted that the genetic therapy product 4N was to induce a Saudi Arabian type of resistance strain of humanoids in the U.S. during their Phase I trial in human subjects, where the gene target was NF-KappaB, that's a neurotrophic factor effector. Apparently, there was a prevalence of NF-KappaB repressor in Saudi Arabia, which allowed the population to survive without water – and water weight was the big problem for casting agents in Hollywood. We have also seen the development of heat guns for facial fibrotic tissue, and epidermal injections of Jell-O for casting agents in Hollywood, said Mr. Newton, near Walden, scene of the Hindenburg, as a script read by Inspector Lewis, of the Robbinsville Precinct, much like amoebic dysentery, in Seaside Heights. One of the prior-indications being lethargy, where the patient was often exhausted to express fatigue. In comparison Mr. Labowski, appears quite fluent at being in-attentive in a charming way, which says less about his character, than the nature of Luciferase 1X, where one has to actively work to overcome the flughaffen – which, increases metabolic rate, releasing alpha-ketones into the urine, which is the product of free-sugar metabolism. At the same time there are several types of neuropsychiatric compounds which become enfeebled or whose metabolites effect the parathyroid, causing dysregulation of the parasympathetic system. Carbamazepine, tetrabenzine, and clonazepam effectively deteriorate, but caution should be exercised in young subjects, due to rise in body temperature. The deterioration of Lamotrigine will cause lock jaw, or cold chatter. Primidone as it deteriorate cause serious sleep induction, much like a knock-out, resembling the

Hindenburg, where some sufi mystic wakes out a charm:
"Iqbaal ka farishta, yanni majnoon bhi naheen jahneh,"
"kanoon ki meherbani, bartameazy say badalta – kiya
fiquer;" Aur joe, woe bhi naya nagar ke nagarik banne,
kassam atay hai, kassam jatey hai, per meharbhoomi
ke nasta say mokul ka koihi barabat tarif ke tariq
sammal ahi yeah -" for a quark, on April 22, 2018, and the
sunsets in Los Angeles, California at 7:30PM, in Tallahassee,
Florida at 8:09PM, in Anchorage, Alaska at 9:41PM, and in
Portland, Oregon at 8:06PM. Ropinirole, is an interesting
pharmacokinetic where caution should be used in the young
because it can cause sudden and unexpected bowel
movements. Among older subjects, it metabolizes in a way,
where should you ever have the urge to fuck the world over
into a dizzy spell of poverty and despair, that's the milky way
– similar to super storm sandy. Sodium valproate is a mildly
active form of the Ropinirole, where the metabolic potential is
significantly lowered, but has similar networks such as
levodopa at high metabolic potential. Topiramate, metabolizes
as a experimentalist's delight, though caution should be
predicated by the subject's need to understand the world
compared with the urge to fuck the world over into a dizzy
spell of poverty and despair. Piribedil is my one true love, he
said finally, because I can look at the world and see it
turning while my guitar gently weeps by a fire rekindled at
the wake of an old man of the Lucky Star.

K. Perkins M.D. however evaluated the subject 4N, as sad
but true, Mr. Shakespeare, Ms. Microsoft, and Mr. Newton.

Upon administration of sample Luciferase 4X the subject did not exhibit anxiety, or hyper-kinetics, indicating a high tolerance, with good pick-ups in syntactical co-vergence during interview, a good attention span though wavering during commiserate subject matter, a lack of empathy or remorse. The endpoint data would suggest a saturation kinetic of terminal-subject. Weighing in at 240lb subject 2012 without Luciferace, with monthly food intake vouchers of $380 per month, and 2.5 liters of 80 Proof alcohol provided weekly, free of charge, subject 4N reached 60lb in December 2017.

Said Endymion, he reads <u>Cyclotron Emission Radiographs for Neutrons</u>, but is dead serious about cancer patients, as way of distinguishing an avocation from his profession. He has to, some say because most patients are so daft that the only way to communicate across their ignominious nature is to act it out as a borderline absurd display of inference; and because in practice, the chance that a patient may not believe or understand your diagnosis or prognosis is 87%, with the understanding that there are apes and wild bears wandering around sick wards with clip boards for taking notes of holloween candles 171.68 AMGN 3:40PM, April 20, 2018. If that isn't depressing enough, in clinical practice, the typical clinical psychiatrist patient relationship, the patient is either resentful, or outright hateful, when they are informed of their diagnostic relationship 171.34 AMGN 2:46PM April 20, 2018. Nursing professionals, because of their close proximity with patients develop an empathy with the patient and a spite for the clinician in equal measure, because more than likely the clinical psychiatrist is unavailable, and only available at appointed direction, which we call a scope in space-time for a brief which allows the clinician to project a fact and subsequent scope where the patient projects a fact- that means something which cannot be argued, prognostic relationship 171.53 AMGN 1:40PM April 20, 2018. Clinical psychiatry technically should be filed under Voodoo Medicine for this reason, in-ability and lack of aptitude in mythologicals, especially Greek and Roman mythologies – nevermind the English or British mythologies- where there is only a small bias towards the clinicians that their practices might not kill the patient, or worse, cause permanent damage, and a substantial bias in favor of the psychiatric patient, where if the patient were to kill the clinician – the world might be better off.

While most clinical psychiatrists tend to be a cross between Ranchi-Dehradun, their institutional affiliations are some-where in Akkeshi-Nemuro 7358.16 FTSE 12:56PM April 20, 2018. That's usually a worse experience, because desperate people are apt to do desperate things, because of which the institutional affiliates would be advised to work the phone trees on snow days for kinder-gardeners, instead of braving the hazards of hand grenades in the hallways 7358.47 FTSE 9:26AM April 20, 2018. For instance, I have never had anyone ever come up to me from nowhere and say, *"I'm going to fuck your brains out and turn you into a bean bag for counting sea shells, that's okay with you, yeah, sweetie,"* but

I heard that in the instances of U.C. Davis, U.C. Sacramento, and MIT, the lord hadn't answered their prayers, and their unstoppable eagerness to count sea shells on the sea shore, could not be quenched by the sea 7351.08 FTSE 1:24PM April 20, 2018. I'll tell you what's really funny, as measure for measure, the Gulag Archipelago, could be seen as a means to subvert such a development of the rust belt where the systems engineers are continuously working for the Foreign Office, of the UK, as a prologue to the expansion of the corn belt, of the Swiss Federation.

In a case lateral to 4N, the subject dropped 40 lbs in four weeks in 2011 using prophylactics, and then lost another 40 lbs by the end of November 2017 with alcohol consumption. If the actual weight of the patient is 160 lb as a healthy subject what are the options that a clinician would have to reverse course, when the patient is 158.8. This is a situation where the patient's weight, as a function of body mass has to be monitored daily 224.04 GD 2:06PM April 20, 2018. When we look at the allelic contribution from different loci a repressor strategy for 4N becomes intractable, because of transposase activity, which is different from 3CR which is evolutionarily one of the most conserved loci with close to fourty six genes 225.04 GD 10.40AM April 20, 2018. In a unrelated subject- read gene deletion- which we're desperately trying to put behind us since 1987, where our objective is to defray the a) cost of hunger, b) allergic response, c) sleep response, and d) disappearance – is to abate the metabolic process through a peripheral response, instead of direct intervention, because of alarming endpoint research 625.50 ISAT Sept 19, 2017. Of these, disappearance is the most dangerous, and offending institutions embarking on ignominious fodder should be stripped of cache, as having hostile intent towards humanoids, in particular where K. Perkins is the HCP, said Inspector Lewis – because litigation takes too long, 3.66 GERN 10:36 AM, April 2018.

Scotland Yard can be a bit overbearing at times, with details, and it's what K. Perkins said which matters, said Endymion. Burson will get ham, Marsteller shall receive sodium pentothal, Fleishman to continue course, Hillard to continue course, Rahul and Brennan to continue course, Ketchum to continue course, M.S.L to continue course, Ogilvy to continue course, Qorvis, he's our good lady, helped me find my glasses, Weber Shandwick to continue course, with thanks, for the update on Sarah, the wonder bread, favorite of cod fish (5922, 3714), especially of the North Sea, filleted for 3.65 GERN 2:14PM April 20 2018. Private schooling is necessary, as what I learned from the effects of 4N on the common cold might be a bit more than what Americans can chew on the Tonight Show 51.28 INTC 1:10PM April 20, 2018. Frank Cannon will need to be updated on future assessments, as the guardian; that's important, as value imputation can be kind of problematic for onerous (4774, 3707) typically recovered by 31.28 XRX 1:16 PM April 20, 2018. We want to understand the if-and-when of phase-transition, for X-linked chromosomes. If I were to say Sarah's the only patient who I liked in twenty years, it might be considered imprudent -

- and yet, there must be some reason for speciation – even without consideration of her Anglo-Irish maternal ancestry 7351.08 FTSE 1:24PM April 20, 2018. Sriram Kellerman gave me an idea of what recessive dominant could mean for Porter, a dissimilar patient, in her self-study journal titled – Amazing Grace – which would be useful for dose response if I were to also know what the segregation frequency was from Sriram Kellerman's linked-in status to R. W. Run in B. R. Porter 3.72 GERN 3:10 PM April 20, 2018.

Venkateswaran might contend that Porter tends to be withdrawn, with disorganized associations, acute sensitivities, and opaque sensibilities which make him a formidable challenge for psychometric evaluations – because there is difficulty in overtly expressing what the "need market" is other than companionships, which is encouraged as a way to dissuade isolation, where a subject begins to assert difference as a mechanism to deride discomfort 6.03 SPRINT 1:40PM April 20, 2018. In contrast, a patient similar to Sarah is B. R. Potter, with slightly severe effects of 4N on the common cold, where one is left wondering if speciation isn't a happenstance for magical thinking of logic scenarios, mathematical syllabus, extremely measured communicative skills, with instinctive awareness of *fluka cassette issues* 6.01 SPRINT 12:10 PM April 20, 2018. In consideration of these matters it was suggested that for B. R. Porter, this is going to be long term in-field study, to start with an annual for two babcocks for buffy, with appointment for activity days with exposure to allergens without (that means not ingested, or ecological variables), compared with appointments for chemokines within.

An early study of patient S. Sondheim, by Schwankovsky and Yep (2004), where the patient was informed, before close encounters with 1970M, could provide a general background encounters with 1970M, could provide a general background for branching effects on a number of cytosomal assessments as they might have been used to develop diagnostic histories from the perspective of Eukaryotic expression for *A Funny Thing Happened on the Way to the Forum*, where the patient was paralyzed. Thyroid stimulating hormone 84.3%, Rapid Plasma Regain 67.5%, B12 69.9%, Complete Blood Count 94.0%, Electrolytes 84.3%, Blood Urea Nitrogen 81.9%, Calcium 75.9%, Creatinine 81.9% and Glucose 89.2%. The associated daily living scores were 13% pre-intervention and 93% post-intervention, decision making capacity 3% pre-intervention and 19%, post-intervention, depression 11% pre-intervention 57% post-intervention, wandering potential 8% pre-intervention 74% post-intervention. The ethnic breakdown of caregivers during the study was 52% African Americans, 23% Caucasians, 4% Latino, 4% Asian, 1% Native American, and 16% other or not specified. That auto-immune disorders are wildly different from alzheimer's associated dementia would become clearer in phase-stage studies for a case-load of 234 patients (2007) including tectonic differences in prevalence for chronic and incidence rates for autosomal-inheritance – where 20 patients are Eton Scholars, with ignominious neurological disorders, ranging from asthma to asthmatic-cannabisits, who are part of the NHS managed care network. In a bizarre episode, of an isolated incident, subject Ripon 1989, was first noted as experiencing paralysis, where the subject fell out of bed on a bottle of water, with severe lacerations on the back. The experience encompasses a sudden muscular cramp of the leg, in some cases the paralysis can occur along the back, with a rigor mortis type faction, steadily increasing in pain for corrective attempts, which can last for upto fifteen minutes much like a labor pain, with sweat rolling down the forehead, tears welling up around the eyes, paralysis, where the frequency of occurrence can range from every night to once every two weeks, to once in a while 222.04 GD 2:06PM April 20, 2018.

Though either asthma or asthmatic-cannabisitis may become indoctrinated over a period of use of 40mg capsules, then user base would begin to peak in 120 yrs, given the identity for the integral $\sin(100x)/\tan(25x)$ as the acceptance of use as a modifier, and affordability, where one space capsule costs 90.00USD. Interesting idea for a ball bearing company. Asthma, from the perspective of Huntington's disease did better than expected, where otherwise weight loss would have reached mortality at 62. Longevity issues include, joint inflammation (7/7), food cost (6/7), headache (3/7), employee rebellion (5/10), business development failure cost ($225 per month). Makes you wonder about the interesting life-style that people can create for themselves while living in pain, as a testimonial for "worth living." Asmatic-cannabisitis over the same period, from the perspective of Huntington's disease did better than expected, where otherwise weight loss would have reached mortality at 52. Longevity issues include, dose sensitivity uphill 60.00USD, and dose sensitivity downhill 20.00USD for manias such as aesthetics (7/7), expense of hyper-productivity where monthly output surmounts 39 mixed-media canvases of 10X15ft (7/7), cost of business development failure ($500.00 per month) self-imposed dietary preferences (6/7), cost of close ties with natural environment (1/7), migraines (7/7), employee rebellion (3/10). Makes you wonder about the interesting life-styles that people can create for themselves while living in pain, as a testimonial against being "a complete bore," "a total loser."

The Project Subcode then developed a two-tier plan for maternity ward, where nine canvases were sold to buyers in the black market to generate $240 used as a fixed deposit for buying undergarments, such as petticoats, and blouses, while the rest were placed in storage at Marseille Museum of Drug Paraphernalia, from which a recurrent revenue model is used towards monthly premiums for life insurance policy- instead of term life. Maternity ward in itself defines who the beneficiaries are, along with deposits and storage items- in case of attempted murder, or assassination, where we define the general background for a void as the integral of $x^3 - 3x^2 + (307.22 - x/2)\, dx$ for $x = 68.3$ to 68.8 as 154075, where a genetic recombination between asthmatic, and asthmatic-cannabisitis is valued as HSI 30,536.14 May9 2018.

In sharp contrast to The Project Subcode, Investigation of Ward 72 showed, "The number of people awaiting evacuation due to inadequate medicine and medical supplies has now surpassed 600," said, Damascus Health Directorate, reported the Guardian, December 27, 2017. De Bretton-Gordon had appealed to Russia's president, Vladimir Putin – a key ally of Assad's – to show mercy. "Medieval siege techniques have resulted in no aid for four years," the jointly authored article said. "Children, in particular, are dying of starvation in sight of the Lebanese and Jordanian borders." Dr. Doug Galasko of UCSD- *not affiliated with GSK* - a board-certified in neurology professor who focuses on Alzheimer's Disease, was called in for questioning. William Robinson, MD, PhD. Associate Professor Division of Immunology and Rheumatology Department of Medicine Stanford University School of Medicine indicated that the cause of for severity was a combination of Rh/O and ketamine, where the design of the resulting trends of 40% - 60% balance of trends seen in Modeling of pathological traits in Alzheimer's disease based on systemic extracellular signaling proteome (Mol Cell Proteomics. 2011) were verified by the Syrian American Medical Society, said four patients had been taken to hospitals in Damascus, the first of 29 critical cases approved for medical evacuation, and the remainder would be evacuated over the coming days, which we define as chromosomal desegregation integral $x^3 - 3x^2 + (307.22 - x/2)$ for $x = 8.3$ to 8.8 as 277.763. They include 18 children and four women with heart disease, cancer, kidney failure and blood diseases. The samples were more-than-likely to have been obtained from Clark CM famous for the movie Moon (2009), and Kaye JA an ignominious Kaiser-Permanente employee. William Robinson, MD, PhD. Associate Professor Division of Immunology and Rheumatology Department of Medicine Stanford University School of Medicine further added that, the subjects Villeda SA famous for premiering in Gotham (2017), Stan TM, and Couillard-Després S, of The ageing systemic milieu negatively regulates neurogenesis and cognitive function (Nature 2011) were "more in line with our approach to clinical practice for soap opera stars on Weight Watchers Diet Plan," where professional script readers had failed to read the product label (8531) 1572.58 OMX Stockholm 11:30AM April 30, because niggers can't read good (5030) 5974.30 AORD 12:06PM April 20, 2018, as our first redacted interaction with the space jar would suggest as an occlusion for chromosomal segregation integral $x^3 - 3x^2 + \frac{1}{2}(48.3x - 1)$ for x = 8.3 to 8.8 as 307.22.

Walsh O as a surrogate for 2014F, certainly provided an interesting window into a diagnostic criteria in clinical neuropsychiatry, which we could only observe with Ron O, progressively with Cannabinoid-Glutamate Interactions and Neural Oscillations: Implications for Psychosis (Eur J Neurosci. 2017), where subject 2014F would be only observed as, Bioactive Products from Singlet Oxygen Photooxygenation of Cannabinoids (Eur J Med Chem. 2018), in the sense that Associative Personality Disorders, until now has been difficult to recognize, as would be the case for,

Effect of Stocking Density On Growth Performance, Digestive Enzyme Activities, and Nonspecific Immune Parameters of Palaemonetes sinensis (Fish Shellfish Immunol. 2017) and, Chronic Δ9-THC IN Rhesus Monkeys: Effects On Cognitive Performance and Dopamine D2/D3 Receptor Availability (J Pharmacol Exp Ther. 2017) and, Alcohol and Illicit Drugs in Drivers Involved in Road Traffic Crashes in the Milan Area: A Comparison with Normal Traffic Reveals the Possible Inadequacy of Current Cut-off Limits (Forensic Sci Int. 2018), and Estimating Annual Prevalence of Depression and Anxiety Disorder in Multiple Sclerosis Using Administrative data (BMC Res Notes. 2017 Nov 25), and Current Evidence of Cannabinoid-based Analgesia Obtained in Preclinical and Human Experimental Settings (Eur J Pain. 2017 Nov 21). Effectively, that is the recommendation for Strategies for Maximizing Clinical Effectiveness in the Treatment of Schizophrenia, while recognizing there is a market need between Stocking Density and Singlet Oxygen in the general population, which should be an important consideration for Different Effects of Chronic THC on the Neuroadaptive Response of Dopamine D2/3 Receptor-Mediated Signalling in Roman high- and Roman low-avoidance rats (Synapse 2017 Dec 19) which, Kaye marvelously contextualizes as AAL 42.28 May 10, 11:30AM in the investigation of Differences in the Response to Apheresis of Patients with 3 Histopatho-logically Classified Immunopathological Patterns of Multiple Sclerosis (JAMA Neurology, 2018) while leaving out the possibility of New Treatment Options for Pneumonia (JAMA News From the Food and Drug Administration, 2018) which

provides the - what's the word I'm looking for here, suscep-
tibility function, yes, that's it, a double blind <u>Discontinuation
of Tyrosine Kinase Inhibitor Therapy in Chronic Myeloid
Leukemia (EURO-SKI): a Pre-specified Interim Analysis of a
Prospective, Multi-centre, non-Randomised, Trial</u> (Lancet,
Oncology 2018) for a couple of integrals. Due to the nature of
the investigation, that means diagnostic criteria, the Johns
Hopkins School of Medicine, the University of Pennsylvania,
and the Rockefeller University School of Medicine, and the
Robert Wood Johnson School of Medicine, and Stanford
University School of Medicine are unauthorized to provide
subjects and/or samples, patients, and principal investigators, pharmaceutical products and/or protocols, or request
for grant funding from the NIH, Pew Charitable Trust, or
Searle Endowment Trust. A Public Health Commission, led
by the Emory University School of Medicine, the UCLA school
of Medicine, the Cleveland Clinic, University of Chicago
School of Medicine, and UC Santa Barbra are authorized to
investigate clinical subjects and/or samples, patients, and
principal investigators, pharmaceutical products and/or
protocols, or request for grant funding from the NIH, Pew
Charitable Trust, or Searle Endowment Trust, to assess
prospective cases for diagnostic criteria formally applied by
the Johns Hopkins School of Medicine, the University of
Pennsylvania, and the Rockefeller University School of
Medicine, and the Robert Wood Johnson School of Medicine,
and Stanford University School of Medicine, under a
Community Grant Program led by BUMP, on immune
responses to cytotoxicity and pluripotency, mortality, and

disability – cause or effect?

The news was confirmed by the official Syrian government news agency, and appears to follow local negotiations as well as several humanitarian appeals from high-profile figures including King Abdullah of Jordan, Recep Tayyip Erdoğan, Turkey's president, and Sergei Lavrov, Russia's foreign minister. We were unaware that C. Avian is autosomally ignominious as well having the common cold for which we recommend adipo therapeutics similar to M. J. Akbar. Brennen and Rahul may also benefit from a similar strategy where ignominious from birth is true of neurological disorders, since Rahul's mother was a carrier, though Rahul's brother did not show any signs of a neurological disorder, possibly because the father was heterozygous dominant. There may be a Bayesian inference model by which to access Baudelaire's groups, in a way similar to HK objectives, where L. J. Max or L. J. Ash might be more or less treatable as a scintillating conversation in the field of Neumonics 5974.30 AORD 12:06PM April 20, 2018, given that their off spring, who was diagnosed with b-cell Hodgkin's Lymphoma died, likely due to non-autosomal recombination in somatostatin nucleus, for which there is some justification of an earlier diagnosis of DLBCL for the indication in the maternal somatosome, as in the case of an earlier patient A. Wiles, who died of b-cell non-Hodgkin's Lymphoma from prescribed doses to Allegra-D for two-years 164.92 SHPG 2:14PM April 20, 2018 for a condition called "scratchy eyes" – or apical neural deficit disorder 162.53 SHPG 11:16AM,

April 20, 2018.

As far as patient care can be facilitated in clinical practice, the minimum bar for term life approaches for health-care providers should be aired for J. Y. Croix, an asthma sufferer, *"For us to be able to come out of that intact – our marriage strong, we are still each other's best friends, our daughters turning into amazing young women – there was a sense of completion, and that we had done the work in a way that maintained our integrity and left us whole and fundamentally unchanged-"* as a farewell to arms, in Euro-Brixit negotiations 3:48AM, April 22, 2018. In consideration for that, <u>Methotrexate in Patients with Rheumatoid Arthritis in Spain: Subanalysis of the AR Excellence Project</u> (Reumatol Clin. 2017) is acceptable for treated general population, and Fluorescent sensing and selective adsorption properties of metal-organic frameworks with mixed tricarboxylate and 1H-imidazol-4-yl-containing ligands (Dalton Trans. 2017) for genetically conceived perturbations among treated patients from the general population. The interviews covered by P. B. Limo as communicated by Diane Rehm to Anne Patchette, are covered for Life (not for term) as a group for 20.00USD, for Ali L.J., Squire., L.J. Max, M. Forrester, L.J. Ash, W. Sonsini, including P. B. Limo for the span, and the family of M. Gonzales, which extends to the Department of Social Security (n=16), who are qualified for Consumption of Coffee or Caffeine and Serum Concentration of Inflammatory Markers: A systematic review (Crit Rev Food Sci Nutr. 2017), under the title holder, A New C-xylopyranoside Derivative

Induces Skin Expression of Glycosamino-glycans and Heparan Sulphate Proteoglycans (Eur J Dermatol. 2008), where B. P. Emily, and S. Lourdes would be the experimental control for The Unexpected Role of Aβ1-42 Monomers in the Pathogenesis of Alzheimer's Disease (J Alzheimers Dis. 2017). That the team of Eric Wieshaus and A. Deaton had identified k-Ras in patient S. Tilghman (2017) in the case of 4N, who could tolerate upto 7X Luciferase, seemed to go unnoticed as a confirmation of B. Keller (2005) for the case of 10X luciferase at a silent auction, where the bid had started at 3X. That the matrix composition for such cases was different from autosomal inheritance went over the heads of back office weasels, who had trouble understanding, Enrollment Challenges in Critical Care Nursing Research (Am J Crit Care. 2017) where target enrollment (15.5 patients per month) was based on experience and historical data of, Identification of Interleukin-27 (IL-27)/IL-27) Receptor Subunit Alpha as a Critical Immune Axis for In Vivo HIV Control (J Virol. 2017).

The night of December 22 would wake similarly into a photo of pink rose from 7:09AM to 7:24AM and disappear into a tunnel, at which a certain Mr. Hopkins (1981) might have said, could you read that line to me again, my hearing is tapering. "I AM sick of nuclear weapons," as Martin Amis writes in his introduction to Einstein's Monsters (1987) suddenly took on the solemnity of Richard Rhodes's book, The Making of the Atomic Bomb (1987) as much as the idea of "The Little Girl Who Lives Down the Lane," (1976) as a realization of "The Bonfire of the Vanities" (1987) for probabilistic distribution of Fourier Transform Surface Plasmon Resonance (FTSPR) with Gyromagnetic Plasmonic Nanorods (Angew Chem Int Ed Engl. 2017) where, to estimate the level of Hazard Scores for Severe, Moderate and Mild , a Systemic Review: Agreement Between the Latent Tuberculosis Screening Tests Among Patients with Rheumatic Diseases (Korean J Intern Med. 2017, was re-established as the proper framework for (2007, 2009) as the condition for Introducing Risk Adjustment and Free Health Plan Choice in Employer-Based Health Insurance: Evidence from Germany (J Health Econ. 2017 Dec.) Asking, are they the only nurses you have for your caseload is like saying, if you knew a plant was a surrogate for planet, then would you still refer to it as plant or, plantain.

Let us consider a typical mystification for such an example, Keira Knightley pontificates upon her arrival at Gargantua from a residency at Prendergast, is the behavior of poachers, Auto-da-fe (1935), Elias Canetti, loosely translated as "are you too deaf?" horror novel as metaphor for computers that serially kill humanoids to acquire their life's work, property, wages, and their relationships – much as the subject 2013M appears to demonstrate when compared with former colleagues, longing for his fraternity with Rob Corddry, as in a scene from the Postman Always Rings Twice, with his host sitting in the adjacent couch, and subject 2014F-sham seated to his left, 224.44 GD 11:40AM April 20, 2018. I like watching computers operating zombies with a hair trigger 225.04 10:40AM April 20, 2018. A near approximation of delusional behaviour would suggest that he doesn't recognize 2014F as being of the same tissue as Sally Fields 6.00 SPRINT 3:20PM April 20, 2018, and a far approximation of schizophrenia would suggest that 2013M is as psychotic-without having committed a homicide 6:03 SPRINT 1:40PM April 20, 2018- as subject 1970M, in the same way as 2012F is aware of being a serial killer 6.01 SPRINT 12:10PM, and aware of her clinician 3.68 GERN 11.10AM April 20, 2018. The provocative conjecture then, that F. S. Coe M.D. lays upon the audience, 3.70 GERN 11:34AM April 20, 2018 is to what extent would the host appear to impersonate 2013M, is a misnomer concerning the ability "to look," in <u>Pharmaco-logical treatment of attention deficit hyperactivity disorder during pregnancy and lactation</u> Pharm Res. 2018 Feb 6, 35:3 (46) 2018 3.65 GERN 2:14 PM April 2018. As a fan of Obama, she added, I am interested to enable legislative referendums for teenagers who grew up on an Indian reservation, for my movie, Dance Nigger, Dance: A Hysterical Repertoire of Tap, or shall we say, Canopus?

As such amongst the players there maybey varios vase to dateormine their pairpformanse in the game, as the objectives for avoryplor islocklay toebaydifferrant in the makop of tha tame. Risk reward ratios hare tend to be the pacesetters for an outcome where prior odds are used to incrementally adjust wor a stochastic is laid in batting and balling with macroeconomical subjunctives as well as real time microeconomical indicative as in the case of the Pompeyans, Wizirs of Naxos, Vittles of Castleton, Oldesloe of Icaria, Utsilma of Rhodes, Decollare of Catskills, for the constrokauction of sentences in the séancestrande wheyath strops. There may be moreplors yozed to fashon cricket games worth watching, woron the whole, the porpose is to be able to ascertain factors relating riskrewards to priorodds for determining when market stochastics may be applied for cretin offfielders game as after the eighth wicket on opening day, worball fielding is as important as balling.

How is your brother Mantis, by the way. Sawor'im last a yeergo dewrinna reyceptionathh Alois Vuitton store in Paris with a new protégé by the name of Isamu Noguchi, unveiling a collection of Indian merchandise for hoodlums and juvenile louts from Clichy-sous-Bois. It was remurkoobly arcwkward, I should say, as they spoke no English atowel beehived belligerently, and understood nothink of what Mantis spoke of relating to function or perception in the garment innerstreets, which one might construe as an ill omen towards a larger welfare state of riffraffs on the dole in years to come, illiteracy and skilllessness being the simplest indicators of what might be considered employability in capacities which might require something more than elocution. Might want to fitty that inty your platty, Tweeze, as you shallav too address such needs soonor litter for weir the finances are likely to emerge where the East India Company is concerned, Briton burdened with its own impoverished, these days more than ever, and Australia pretty saturated. A canvas drug requires genetic analysis before consideration as a trial subject, as in the case of penicillin.

Where F. S. Coe MD, reviews the marks for the mid-terms, as an instance in, <u>Safety and Mosquitocidal Efficacy of High-Dose Ivermectin When co-Administered with Dihydro-artemisinin-piperaquine in Kenyan adults with Uncomp-licated Malaria (IVERMAL): a Randomised, Double-Blind, Placebo-controlled Trial</u> (Lancet, Infectious Diseases, 2018), the Imperial Foundation assigns frequency of allelic segregation, 7.53120327 for Anemia to Polyneuropathy is genetic analysis of population, previously estimated by the Health Ministry of Japan in Hiatus as 10.03, whereas the frequency for genetic mutation, for polyneuropathy to anemia, is epigenetic 0.98629 previously unknown, for penicillin, which in one patient, exhibited maximalliary secretions upon neurite stimulation.
Suffice to say, the safety imperative for Syrian populations, cohorted as cytotoxics cause-effects would have to meet the minimum acceptable criteria (MAC) as the rigor for BUMP facilitation of cytotoxics review panels for cause-effect relationship, in future follow-up trials for diagnostic criteria

for Therapeutic Management of Schizophrenia and Depression (Sept. 27, 2008) as provided by Glenn J. Treisman MD, Ph.D. Professor of Psychiatry and Behavioral Sciences, and of Medicine, The Johns Hopkins School of Medicine, with key insights provided by Marc E. Agronin MD Miami Jewish Home and Hospital for the Aged, T. Scott Strop MD, University of North Carolina School of Medicine, Rajiv Tandon, MD University of Florida, Peter J. Weiden, MD, University of Illinois Medical Center, and Daniel R. Weinberger MD, National Institutes of Health.

If history hath taught os annonnything eighties dah constellations tend to vary witem oathoars an likelihood of arriving at the same place where when whence stairted are as slim as em piet mondarins weirem long faces as the crux to bear of embaressment for the foreignex wayth Silurian times looming large and the shortcut to Dacca unchanied for trawlers by ispice ondoor a vaneer of neoduim for the oxford circus. There are no marches there, there are no children anywhere, no dreams to dream of among minions, no cotton candy nor peanuts, no screeching fans, but a long draft of coal dust, and black clouds of smoke in their spaghetti, an unkind backwards glance at gaiety indivisible for their periled vails, as such are the present circumstances for a rollingmill of stardust.

Where M. S. Claiborne MD reviews the marks for the mid-terms for Tiotropium and olodaterol in the prevention of chronic obstructive pulmonary disease exacerbations

(DYNAGITO): a double-blind, randomised, parallel-group, active-controlled trial (Lancet Respiratory Medicine, 2018) should be implemented as the Clinical Diagnostic Criteria for treatment selection 10.02447 and Linkage Association 0.618998 for anemia, amyolateral sclerosis, and multiple sclerosis in prospective clinical trials, where the collaborations for double blind susceptibility trial with Imperial Medical are Harvard Medical School, UCSF Parnassus-Mission Bay, Columbia University Presbyterian, attenuated with cohorts for treatment outcome analysis single-blind open-label Sloan Kettering and Cornell-Weil.

Le projet de la commission laisse la compétence au gouvernement de conclure, modifier ou dénoncer des traités si cette compétence lui a été donnée par le Parlement ou si la portée est mineure.S'il fallait dénoncer un accord sans attendre, la même procédure s'appliquerait que celle prévue actuellement pour l'application provisoire d'un traité. Le gouvernement doit consulter les commissions compétentes des deux conseils. Si les deux s'y opposent, une dénonciation urgente n'est pas possible.Enfin, le projet vise à assurer que le Conseil fédéral informe des traités qu'il a dénoncés mais qui relèvent d'un département ou d'un office. Seule la Délégation des commissions de gestion est informée des traités confidentiels ou secrets.

The technical can be astounding, but that's no reason to lose hope in artificial intelligence, said F. S. Coe MD. Your appointments are Swiss, that's the general idea, for minimizing your reliance on insider trades. If you were the Plaza Hotel, for instance, then the cash vouchers from the tenants would be expectedly deposited at banks in Paris, or Tokyo, as opposed to the Pierre Hotel say, where the cash vouchers would be deposited in Ankara, or Jakarta, as a way to keep investors from defaulting on pensions, that's the flip side of penicillin, where pro-labor governments of Tony Blair, Gordon Brown, and Cameron had to champion the cause for underwater movies with French pastry chefs and soda water as a way to keep Britain united after the consolidation of the majority of European economies into the Euro Currency, yeah, following the collapse of the Ruble. The preferred trades in your case therefore would be the quotidien FGEN 51.60 10:40AM, synchro-1-tron FGEN 51.70 1:44PM, synchro-2-tron FGEN 51.50 2:06PM, then commercial papers FGEN 52.24 12:06PM whatever you have available in the frozen section, then common exchanges with Zurich FGEN 52.25 11:24PM, Basel FGEN 51.85 11:20AM, and the compiler program FGEN 51.85 11:16 AM, and for the last trade with the compiler-driver you want to pick up your earnings in swiss francs, based on the market estimates for COKE 126.80 12:24PM in EUR/AUD, and COKE 129.26 1:20PM in NZD/EUR, and then the next day I can trade up your purchases with keeping Britain united.

Two hours those I had been sitting their at the gwyndolin harp and as my third hour approached, a terrifying recognition overcame my jaunties, could that be, I asked myself, could that be it, seeing leaves raked for early bon fires, fifty thousand hectares of bush at a nettlesome rewritein for a rayleigh of fiftyeight dollars in two months for our wool's rites of passages towards the superstitious, pedantic acrimony, from cooperative indifference to shit, ma ma ma malaise, please, apathy and ennui, stipulations of spiritual, loth of supposition, without reason or comprehension of the kestrels ovid, and the farallon's odyssey for ripe of helen.

4. Issue

4. Issue – Where Endymion ponders, whilst mesmerized – their birth orders prevaricated – of how the others might have webbed – there being Klamm (the bire lodger), Hirst (the deposed to panic), Fringent (the exposed to fits of depression), and De (the alpine sanitarium) – an assortment of serotypes ventriculating in neucleosomal RNA -overhearing such plausibility over the intonations of dialogue - en conclusion de la série, l'Institut Aix - Inference fournit les solutions informatiques pour l'objectivation de l'atomise de Fermi, dans la mesure où nous pouvons montrer que l'atomise de Fermi se compose d'une masse variable - ce qui implique une dynamique moléculaire du rayon orbitaire. Deuxièmement, nous fournissons des segmentations informatiques de l'atome d'Oppenheimer - comme étude des neutrons à haute densité - avec une modélisation moléculaire de particules à haute énergie pour démontrer comment les neutrons se déplacent, sont dóciles - troisièmement, nous fournissons une décomposition périoculaire exomorphe de particules chargées dans un microscope tunnel - la plupart des sources de rayonnement gamma, avec des sources compensatoires de pulsars et de quasars- quatrièmement, nous fournissons la base dialectique pour les électrons d'un atome de Bohr.

M. S. Claiborne M.D. facilitated the view, that it was quite possible for 2013M to hold the believe that he's Lincoln persecuted by Grant, the military figure, 3.66 SPRINT 1:36PM April 20, 2018 who mocks his personification in Robust Anti-tumor Responses Result from Local Chemo-therapy and CTLA-4 Blockade, as much he's critical of his posturing, or intimidated by gestures to the U.N. General Assembly (Dec 28, 2017), where a Rachel Maddow evokes as much subject recognition as Sally Fields, or Linda Carter, or

Parker Posey, or Kim Basinger, or Gwyneth Paltrow, or Natalie Merchant, or Cameron Diaz, or Tilda Swinton, or Nicole Kidman, or Tara Fitzgerald, or Kristen Scott, or Mylie Cyrus, or Bridgette Fonda, or Jodie Foster, or Twiggy, or Mabel Elizabeth King, or Carla Bruni, as the subsistent operating model for schizophrenia, as is for Angus Deaton – that means plastic utensils and finger food – since topo-inhibitors are completely counter-intuitive as chemo-therapeutic agents, unless the intentions of the drug developers BMY J&J were to completely abolish repair mechanisms, and seize material and financial assets from cancer patients 171.68 AMGN 3:40PM April 20, 2018, compared with the situation where a subject, Ogilvy, might appear to be white though formally recognized to be of African origin, 162.53 SHPG 11:16AM April 20, 2018 from transposase activity, or Hillard might appear to be suffering from seizures due to torque shear, which is the substituent operating system for delusional disorders associated with lewy body dementia, common among screen actors. For either of the models, we are reminded by the most helpful suggestion of L. U. Fendi, an asthma sufferer with cannabisitis, that a poisson distribution is continuous, pretty sure 4.79 GORO 4:00PM April 16, 2018. The melanocyte contribution within such a context of neuro-psychiatric conditions is at least 20%, with contribution from bone morphogenetic proteins being 40%, with the remaining contribution from brain derived proteins being the buffer for tendency towards hallucinations, with catalytic action potentials for personality disorders leading to schizophrenia, depending on exocytosis 164.92 SHPG 2:14 PM April 20, 2018. Baudelaire's *Le Spleen de Paris* is a large population study that compares the use and effects of sugar cane juice, and fermented sugar cane juice in the City of Joy for tri-cyclic therapeutics, and nitrous-oxide abuse among city inhabitants – which are quintessentially associated with Macrophage Inflammatory Proteins found in the buffy coat – as reported by the Bank of Baroda (n = 183). Among several discoveries made by Laurent de La Tour is that nitrous-oxide down-regulates beta-catenin by 2000%, while among the more intellectually gifted and talented, chlorine up-regulates gonadotrophin neurotropic factor by 2000%. Given that both are transcription factors, what makes the observations of chlorine provocative is that gum-ascorbate also up-regulates gonadotropin neurotrophic factor, and both upregulate hepatocyte growth factor, leading to an enlarged liver, which may be seen as a conjectural opposite of pancreatic carcinoma, among alcoholics. In a single sample, of nitrous-oxide with and alcohol consumption, the subject tends to lose weight, with some loss of autonomic functions that would indicate cerebral shrinkage 7351.08 FTSE 1:24PM April 2018, as one would Figure: Overview of 11 Hypothetical Scenarios for Patients Selected for Chimeric Antigen Receptor T-Cell (Car-T) Immunotherapy (JAMA Oncology, 2018), while what we generally attribute as functions of the pre-frontal cortex would then suggest an off-the-shelf shrink-wrapped software unaware of procurement decisions made by the apical meristem GERN 3.66 10:36AM (2017) – which is new information, as one might conclude in time from Increased

Incidence of Infectious Disease During Prospective Follow-up of Human T-Lymphotrophic Virus Type-II and I-infected Blood Donors (JAMA Internal Medicine 2018, ASO Therapy: Hope for Genetic Neurological Diseases (JAMA, 2018). Though nitrous-oxide down-regulates beta-catenin, artificially induced esophageal contractions can induce insulin-like growth factors which eventually develop into seizures 5370.99 4:36 FCHI April 18, 2018. A counter-inhibitory treatment for artificially induced esophageal contractions with "milk of magnesia" on the other hand produces a strange little protein know to reduce breast mass, by 1750% called Leptin 5378.06 10:20 AM FCHI April 2018.

A map of these histological imperatives is quite helpful as a matter of fact for torque shear at the Whitney Museum (2011) TH2 SEaSDoM for Braniff Air Mail PACB 2.56, in advancing from Marin Day School (2007) TH2 SEaSDoM for Braniff Air Mail PACB 2.56 to by-pass Venice Beach Public Library (2012) NZX 8599.43 2:32PM May 9, 2018, High Blood Pressure - Blood Banks (JAMA, 1973) - from a drop in health-insurance provider caseloads because the institutional staff failed to understand the science of medicine, Braniff Mode MRC 20.00 May 8, 2018 compared with Cyclosporine for Braniff AML MRC 19.13 May 2, 2018. In other words, the only way we can co-operate with the Kaiser-Permanente Health-Care System, which is part of the Swiss Federation, is through aptitude of the subjects- whose opposite is considered negligence in actuarial terms, indifference to the treatment conditions in neuro-psychiatric terms, or lack of transparency among affiliates in corporate partnership terms – where many of the affiliate staff were found to be either hostile or outright antagonistic towards internal audit of procedural and patient treatment requisites. In general, it would be difficult to find a physician in the hospital, among patients styling themselves into physicians, nurses, and orderlies, wandering the hallways trading prescription drugs, or buying direct from nursing staff. These places are infested with drug dealers, screen actors, soap stars, Hollywood agents, and street gangs. At a small county hospital, much to our surprise, we discovered Denzel Washington writing prescriptions for tricyclics compounds.

In one area, we found an off-site University Professor J. T. Witty M.D. Ph.D. who was willing to provide a class criteria for treatment based on body weight, based on the presence or absence of 4N. In another area we found a University Professor K. E. Tensin M.D. F.R.C who was willing to provide a stratification based on nitrous-oxide with and without alcohol consumption as a function of body weight. While in a third area, ironically, we were able to confirm chlorine and gum ascorbate as the clinical criteria for mad cow disease from S. L. Crowbar Ph.D at UCSF-Mt. Parnassus- the question being can Reganomics be recovered?

So let's consider the sample size, said F. S. Coe M.D. You see, I had to observe a subject for a year between 1970 and 71. The subject was male, but during the course of my observation was found to dress as a female. The challenge I faced was to endure this bizarre obstacle to solve basic math problems of adding, subtracting, and multiplication in order to get out of a horrible situation, a psychotic- long division, I learned to do several years later, where my obstacle was a dark Lutheran birth mother with a crucifix on her chest who suffered from anemia, and disparative Huntington's Disease, bordering on schizophrenia, and traumatic personality disorder. Those were years when I had to understand that I was a human, and that anemia is different from the common cold- that means they are pathologically different, and have strikingly different prevalence 491/72000.24. Their genealogies are different, in the sense where one off-spring is asmatic-cannabisitic since birth, a later develops Braniff AML MRC 16.81 June 20, 2017 and does not respond to cyclosporine, an older sibling with asmatic-cannabisitis who responds well to cyclosporine LLY 81.40 10:10AM May 16, 2018, and two third generation off springs, with Australian aboriginal contribution, with early signs of diabetes metellus 76.72 LLY Feb 7, 2018 , where the father died of benign brain tumor – failing to respond to penicillin, and the mother died of benign brain tumor – failing to respond to kanamycin, and a third, third generation off spring, of asmatic-cannabisitic and asmatic who is disease free HSI 30,536 May 9, 2018.

The subject from 1970M I had lost touch with until- I met another subject in 2012F who seemed to exhibit similar qualities as subject 1970M. By this time, what I had learned of subject 1970M, was that he had three children when I had met him in 1970 - and that he had killed his mother, his father, and a woman-with-child whom he had eaten, which was a rampant custom among the natives as a regional prevalence 630/6316.94. I acquired this information by interviewing subject 1970 in 2007 over a period of six months. Compared to the prevalence of Mad Cow Disease which is often attributed to GH or Fetal Bovine Serum, which are popular in Hong Kong under the tutelage of *are you stupid or something?* I thought that subject 1970M was seemingly a serial with a desire for ladies slippers and late stage foetus for dinner, where the regional attributes had a prevalence of 1065.09/17119.93. He was obviously well read by then, and chose his words very carefully, very precisely - more typically than a drunk and disorderly Huntington's disease subject, who is likely to say, I'm going to shoot you in the head and use it a mop for cleaning up Europe, *after the fact*, as a way of defining the parametrization of "urge-" in clinical neuropsychiatry – that means the desire to kill or cause harm to others in order to survive, where we can visualize the integral as 27 Pi/4x dx for x = 65/318 to 42/92 from *Benign-Malignant Tumors: Case Studies of Patient Duplication on HYW 101* to *Benign-Malignant Tumors: Case Studies of Cluster Populations Associated with the English Channel* as 27pi/4 log (3339/14.95) = 17.040. In more recent observations of 1970M the subject seemed to be revert towards Mad Cow Disease, which is where I observed him in 1970, prodromal AML. Often 1970M has dreams which are disturbing, consists of being in a void – that means black-outs. On the other hand, his dreams are "hallucinogenic" of the type that one might see from being high on marijuana. There is some frequency between these which determines his condition as mad cow disease (high prevalence in the population) or serial (very low incidence in the attribution.) A competitive analysis of 1970M revertent to Mad Cow Disease from Serial and related, 2012F, who progressed from Mad Cow Disease where subject killed three people (including the fetus) during a confessed sado-masochistic session with insulin while carrying a fetus through two trimesters- towards serial, is interesting when subject 2013M and subject 2014F are seen as co-incidental- *no comprende arugula* – well then toss in some salad dressing into the integral $9.4y + 0.76y^{(2-1)} + (73.1/0.008388 – y)$ dy and the spell binding machinations of anthropomorphic linkage for genes and development emerge as $4.58y^2 + 8714.83y$.

For any electronic component, the thermocouples operate with electro-weak cables, where the maximal load capaci- tance for applications are distributed 16.40 CS 1:30PM April 16, 2018, where the peak off-load modulator is electro-static 16.51 CS 11:30AM, and the power transformer is voltage gated 17.80 CS Jan 29, 2018 for the power trans-former to "seek" the series regulator 120.78 EA April 20, 2018 and hope for the best with 4.79 GORO 4:00 PM April 16, 2018, since the providence are modulators, in the case where the maximal load capacitance is less than the peak off-load modulator. These distinctions are nearly same as would be expected for WBC and antibodies in plasma, as a circuit development process for keeping the lights burning during the day time, without having to move U.S. residents to Mexico, for the famous movie with Al Pachino, Insomnia, where a series dilator is 8442.41 NZX Jan 31, 2018, the cathode relay switch is 25.81 TWTR Jan 31, 2018, series resistor is 31.91 TWTR March 26, 2018, and the actual pulsar is 8508.12 NZX March 27, 2018. Therefore when we compute a BHP value of 41.28 HBV 3:40PM April 12, 2018, for the pulsar, what we are saying is a series modulator value, and when we compute the Glycomemetic value of 17.24 11:20AM April 12, 2018, what we are saying is a stochastic series discharge, which is equal to the load capacitance, and the Alaska air group value 59.97 1:35PM, April 12, 2018, is the peak off-load modulator, for which the cable is 40.69 GSK 1:25 PM April 12, 2018.

Living with 2012F for nine months tended to be an exercise in subject-counsel, that means the subject has to accept some responsibility for providing authenticated information for feed forward counsel, such as Greek studies, because balancing a career in Greek studies and health insurance can be a daily battle of cognitive task reciprocation. Much like teaching computers to read, in other words, a thought occurs after one has read something where no thought is given prior to the reading matter- or as in many instances, oft repeated words from and phrases phone banks are used to generate a "memorandum of understanding from discrete Bayes," COKE 129.26 1:20 May 17, 2018 where our Calculated/Observed value for a BRD insert driven by a 44bp Tenos promoter with an 4bp frame-shift of the Andros gene is 0.989712593 is compared to COKE 126.80 11:24 AM 42bp LB insert which is directly controlled by the transcription factor E1 for the Calculated/Observed value of 4101.8036, to denote the genotypes AX5, and AX6, as *anaxionic codes* for Exon 4 (-ORF) and Exon 4(+ORF), both of which contain genes for tetracycline and kanamycin resistance with a p25 origin of replication- similar to, funny you should say that, if someone were a student of Shakespeare, and used it as often as possible. In scientific discourse such a utility is used to establish some premise, as in *no comprende arugula?* before quickly developing a syntax for the current, which is why *"discrete and Bayes are antithetical to each other."* As a qualifier, we asked 2012F to define an art-project within a defined budget and time-frame which would be inconceivable by a single individual. During the study period of near equal time, 2012F produced only one painting, which might be called demonic –which turned out to be the cover for a Dostoyevsky novel.

The Possessed came to mind, if one had never read the novel, with Myshkin, travelling back and forth from the p25 SSE 1413.5 10:30AM, May 18, 2018 to the E1 SGEN 56.88 12:40PM, May 18, 2018. The cognitive task reciprocation for 2012F would then be valued as similar to the work of a single individual, as a control subject. Nod once if you're dumb, and twice if you're deaf, said F. S. Coe M.D. as to how cognitive assessments are performed in clinical psychiatry by Kaiser-Permanente Managed Care, where the series modulator for the p25 function is SPNT 5.11 12:30PM, May 15 2018, and the Series Dilator for EI is GERN 3.38 10:46PM, May 15 2018. 2012F was later accompanied to see another qualifier as an example of what would be expected for a career in Greek studies, on a day time television program similar to *Rachel Ray*, or *Ellen DeGeneres*, compareable with the maximal load capacitance of the CS monitor, EWR airport, departures.

That there had been cross-talk between 2013M and 1970M, because 1970M disapproved of 2013M's off-screen gay life style, while 2014 has severe appetite issues with dramatic shifts in weight, should not be confused to cinematic roles. There are leaks that could jeopardize case-cohort studies in neuro-psychiatry, for 2013M, due to the nature of what we define as integrity, because the falsification of information can cost a number of lives, trigger SEC investigation into financial interests, intelligence investigation into public toilets, and insurance investigation into health-care providers. Because, neither of them appear to be serial, which could be because their mother appears serial, might be a seen as a trait assessment, which could have some appeal to a mainstream audience of Mad Cow Disease and Huntington's, alas. As we begin to understand the genetics of pedigree which is the tip of the iceberg we also have to understand the large blocks of ice which lay under - for the field of socio-pathology, there are a number of different line calls for inductive logic programming, where we would have to select computers based on their sustained ability to perform line calculas, where we can recommend two computers, one godless, and the other a wasp nest, that have expressed interest in the territories for a feasibility scenario, where both have demonstrated sample population diversity of speech and visage for comparison to a wall of silence in southern California wildfires.

Perhaps one could have begun by asking a simple question of what GSK stands for – as test between Huggies and Pampers. As a casual study of two-patients, 2013M and 2014F we looked at Glutathione Receptor response to 1X Luciferase with GSK 35.12 from 10:20AM; saw Glutathione Receptor uptake inhibition to 1X Luciferase at GSK 35.35 11:45AM; saw Glutamic Acid Synthase Dehydroxylase activity of 1X Luciferase at GSK 35.39 12:45PM; was reminded of the famous quote by Mr. Newton, *"Ho Chi Minh got us out of 'Nam!"* at GSK 35.39 3:20PM – as a way to exclude patients from the NHS budget- other than privately funded. "Any decision to withhold a treatment should be assessed on an individual basis and should be in the best interests of the patient." BBC Reality Check Team reported on 26 December 2017. The ECB has been looking for ways to harness the new technology. President Mario Draghi said in May "the central bank was closely watching blockchain innovation to ensure that its adoption around the euro area doesn't fragment payment systems. A joint study with Bank of Japan released in September found that a DLT application could match the speed of current systems in processing payments," Bloomberg's Piotr Skolimowski, reported with special assistance by

Alessandro Speciale December 21, 2017, 5:12 AM EST, which resulted in observations of in-scape subspace GSK 39.83 10:26AM May 16, 2018 which contains 16SrRNA insert adjacent to 1196bp of Tenos-Paros for the Cosmid with a Tetracycline resistance, compared with observations of sub-space non-space GSK 40.10 1:48PM May 16, 2018 for NRTm vector + insert/ NRTm vector estimated as 10.25820159 for the DJIA 24778.94 for the insert, and 24730.59 as the distance between Tenos-Paros and 16SrRNA CRAY 26.95 12:56 May 18, 2018.

J. T. Witty M.D. Ph.D patients tend be from diverse professional backgrounds, which we prefer due to the location of many of our centers, where we consider visibility to be the core asset of our practice, from the perspective of the patient and the provider, and an equanimity for such an orderly is considered homeostasis. Suppose you had four part-time jobs as a way to pay rent on your properties, you would be anxious that how you communicated with one party may be mis-interpreted by another, and then mis-represented by a third party, or ignored by the first party, and jumbled by different party, though there are various denominators in common between the jobs. Among these professions are farm workers, and dock workers who constitute 40% of the cases, airline workers who constitute 20%, truck drivers who constitute 10%, builders who constitute 15% of the cases, Joy Luck Club members who constitute 3%, with the remaining 22% from retail businesses such as supermarkets, and shops. The idea was to develop a group – that means *Department of Labor, E.O.E* - that could massage personal data in the same way as having four part-time jobs - that means in a working environment, where you have to be on time for at least one of the jobs, and you have to work fast at one of the jobs, and you have to improve cognitively at another job, in order to retain your position at the fourth job where you are allowed some leeway. The homeostasis model is closer to thinking about off-the-shelf-shrink wrapped software when you think about the space jar in that context for humanity.

K. E. Tensin M.D. Ph.D. FRC., MBA, patients tend be from 70% bed and breakfasts, 20% travel and leisure, or 10% bake and burnouts, where suppose you have one job, have to maintain two relationships, without appearing to have gone for a facial, without reporting a hangover, and without sleeping on the job. The *Department of Housing and Urban Development* operates as an honor system, where we believe what you say, and therefore homeostasis might occur when – as a median subtracted from the average, which is called an exponent, even if you've never had lunch at the Isaac Mizrahi's Fountainhead for Celebrities with Back Pain. Here the potential for break-through research tends to be high due to esophageal constriction, and domestic violence, where a partner may not be able to carry through as a quotidien, or may suffer from a perplexity of endotoxins without the means necessary for hemolysis, or in various cases be adept at applications of miRNA, or may leverage a dichotomy of circumstance to develop a broad segmentation of class struggle.

Given our investigation of Senator Hatfield, we found the institutionalization of Hatfield Clinical Research Center medical practice to be owned by the U.S. Government, and therefore the licenses granted to Empire Blue Cross by Senator Hatfield to be owned by the U.S. Government. It seems that, though Hatfield Clinical Research Center has been credentialed, where a proper tour was provided to Inspector Lewis of facilities and staffing for patient care; Empire Blue Cross failed to compare. Our investigation revealed that Empire Blue Cross Centers were treating 4N patients with Tamoxifan, Tamiflu, and Cyclosporin – which would indicate that there were almost no clinicians who would be willing to take on the liabilities associated with an endemic, and that Empire Blue Cross reduces their risk by quite precisely defining a sham population of the terminally ill, where the patients choose to be treated with 4N for the Weight Watchers Diet Plan – including Hatfield's daughter, whom the Senator introduced Lewis to, over a coffee table brochure on alien invaders, on United. It did not pass the notice of Ms. Forbes, however, that the House re-approved the $1.5 trillion tax cuts after the Senate OK'd the measure in the morning with a 51-48 vote - deprive the U.S. Treasury of corporate tax revenue, as a move to de-centralize capital allocation, allowing health care providers such as Empire Blue Cross to provide the standard of care they are really good at – Sham Care, not just to the terminally ill, but for various other workman's compensation groups in the regions covered by Tamoxifan, Tamiflu, and Cyclosporin – effectively, de-linking U.S. Government liability for Empire Blue Cross to search for a needle in a haystack for the terminally ill, and paying liability premiums for clinicians, where the monies would be funneled through a Sham Circuit. The U.S Government action at the disjuncture, the super-committee on habitat for humanity was in discussion, as a private-public collaboration with the NHS, where the Swiss Federal Institute was reassured that K. Perkins MD FRC was not a violent criminal. Though the prodigy grew into his role, Cannon was quite certain that one could hardly see him, with his eyes hidden from light, and his face ambiguous of friend or foe, leaving his voice to communicate the sort of intelligence, which requires listening to, British Counter-intelligence briefs such as, *"could you feel it?"* 67.34 STI 2:14PM April 20, 2018, or, *"did you feel that?"* 67.15 STI 12:10PM while monitoring what we refer to as having a "dingo in the back," 67.05 STI 10:20AM April 20, 2018.

That Gabriela Sabatini was not known in New Jersey (October 25, 2017) for reasons acrimonious, Mr. Newton would say, is homage 242.13 GS Oct 23, 2017. Over-shadowed by the fame of Beebe Neuwirth and Pirandello, Gabriella Sabatini does not immediately evoke a sense about the movie business, outside of the impromptu episodes in aviator, with Howard Hughes. Certainly, any advice rendered to Gabriella Sabatini as, you need space, is bound to appear as controversial for Ellen Degeneres. The Nubian queen of talk shows, Wendy Williams, has probably never heard of Gabriela Sabatini, beggar that she appears to be for acrimony (no offence intended) but a hedonist with data like 903500. . . is worth more than all the glomeruli in flatland- or didn't I say NineX is where I must have left off, where the linear co-efficient for acceleration of AORD AORD 6052.90 10:45AM March 16, 2018 is measured as 0.11neu/gamma. The time evolution to FTSE 7696.46 2:44PM May 14, 2018 is then calculated as 1.68 gamma for $0.01s^{-1}$, and the 3i coordinate plane for 912.00 4:05PM March 16, 2018 is calculated as 3.36 gamma for $0.01s^{-1}$ from which we calculate the objective insight for AORD 6057.50 2:50PM March 16, 2018 as 8.41 gamma for $0.01s^{-1}$ as syllogism for amorphous substance floating in air in zero gravity field near a fair ground, as 2.84089E-07 amperes, for calculating the ORCL 52.45 12:25PM March 16, 2018 value somewhere near the equator, as previously translated as "Only then would events on earth lie in the future light cone of the event at which the sun went out," Stephen Hawking, where the supposition is stated as, on January 15, John departed for school. The train was due to leave at 10:00AM in the morning, but as his parents had arrived with him to the station, they were notified that the train would be departing at a later time, between 3:00PM and 4:00PM. I of course was in school at 8:30AM, and so did not have a chance to say farewell to John, which we calculate in parsecs as 3.36 LYG, at 11:10AM, May 19, 2018, as the Ode to the thousands of Stephen Hawkings who lie awake in their graves.

Space craft tends to spatial, and topology tends to be mesencephalic. Let me think. Gabriela Sabatini amongst these contexts is a headache, in the American pejorative of the proverbial hadron, with her little to-do list of character assassination and a field of view of 887.0967, every bit like her mother, where the corresponding rate of change is -5.993E8 over the Templum Jovis among the North-Westerly winds for the UFT – 1 component related function for the hertzfield presentation of the world surreal. The blast furnace is then a Pir de Cascade from the Caspian Sea to the Straits of Magellan where only two of three latitudes are solvable for a leave-one-out somewhere strategy in the post-apocalypse, 1999 Harold Varmus personal communications.

Au début, ce qu'ils objectaient ne semblait pas être évident.

Quelle était leur réaction?

Ils étaient abrupts. Ils n'ont pas beaucoup utilisé.

L'intégration est linéaire, donc ce que vous dites est surprenant.

La situation est différente de ce qu'elle préfère.

La situation est différente de ce qu'elle préfère. Plusieurs ricochets ont suggéré un cadre possible qui pourrait fonctionner.

Supposons que nous devions imposer une matrice de distance?

Ce serait de 3155.00 à 3201.43.

Et ce que nous regardons?

Environ 106.48 à 0.52%.

C'est assez différent de -41.

Quelle serait l'interception x?

Environ 46.28 billion USD.

Il est lié à une théorie économique remodelée pour faire valoir une exigence spécifique.

Oui, les actualités sont très ajustes, eous devons récupérer les 46.28 Billion USD.

En fait, nous avons pu vérifier que ce stochastique gravitationnel de la région atlantique proche reflète le stochastique gravitationnel de (100.00, 88.88) pour l'effondrement de French Telecom.

The representation of the integral as such can be shown as $74412\exp(x)/\log(10365)$ for x = 195.16 to 144.33, for the area of the height equal to -4.5982359 E88.

Je pense que les stochastiques de Newton B seraient plus élevées.

En fait, c'est Newton A.

Comment ça va? Le stochastique du segment de la cathédrale est (99.65, 57.23) tandis que latéral est (i, 14.95).

La covalence Newtonienne pour un plan sigmoïdal en d'autres termes s'avère être (33.33, 11.11) ce qui nous donne un stochastique pour Newton B pour l'effondrement de (100.00, 94.45).

Compte tenu de ces stochastiques, quel était le calcul de l'élan angulaire de la planète? Je veux dire, diriez-vous que l'élan angulaire de la planète est inférieur à, supérieur ou 1924?

Je ne suis pas en mesure d'expliquer comment les tidals sont affectés par un moment angulaire newtonien stochastique de (50.00, 27.78).

The representation of the integral as such can be shown as $7.4412E94\exp(189)/x(\log 10365)$ for $x = 19516$ to 14433, for angulaire newtonien stochastique as $-2.9304720\ E175$.

Je me demande ce que stock-brokers recommanderait comme portefeuille? Compte tenu de la nature hyperbolique du plan cartésien. Quelle serait la variance stochastique attendue?

By which we mean to assert our interest in furthering our interest in the adhoc, you see; as many mortals have expressedly been want of imputing the existence of the Abominable Snowman – the giant hairy beast.

Dope Shit Crackass Niggas.

The Hon. John Bercow, as such a wrote an Oxford thesis request for full disclosure of its whereabouts in his quest to understand it's astronomy, in What am I doing Here? as much as Lawrence Summers enthralled in the Harvard thesis, Understanding Employment and the follow-on The Post-Widget Society: Economic Possibilities for Our Children, while the impermeable Paul Theroux, in his thesis for Brown Paddling the Pacific on the nature of movement for the zeitgeist, and Salman Rushdie on his metamorphosis travelogue thesis for Cambridge, in The Enchantress of Florence, without failing to mention The Shipping News for Anne Prolux's Trinity thesis concerning the Sad Maidan, or for what the locals refer to as Stonehenge, and Cormac McCarthy's thesis for Princeton, Blood Meridian which is actually much nicer, against the back drop for bird feathers in a broken mansion in All the Pretty Horse, where we can see the endlessness of the Texas plains.

The last being a sum of such parts being expressed as -2.33728E90 e^(50.83/n)/ e^(50.83/n -1)n gives us an idea.

Cette base d'investisseurs est tellement enracinée, suggère qu'un stochastique de (95.38, 65.71) n'est pas en danger d'être en turbulence en tout temps au cours du prochain siècle.

The representation of the integral as such can be shown as 7.4412E94E94/x(log10365) for x = 0.00019516 to 0.00014433 as -2.428177920480E93.

Volume Dva and intractable Set, unfortunately leaves a longing for Fourier, a Rouge Morgue for Holocaust survivors of German Weltenblitzkrieg, upsetting as that maybe in round figures of 6:02 PM for October 25, 2017 with a Nocturne at 7:34 AM for October 26, 2017 ought to provide the wrap up for Jimmy Cordon's reading frames of men in g-strings as homologous recombinants, giving new meaning for the words sub-continental gay jews as currency equivalent for our Nazi past with Stephen Colbert's far daze delimited by the Gestapo upto 10:38 AM as of October 25, 2017 in pyruvate kinases, where any further debate might launch a full on investigation of the Lincoln Memorial for executive memorandum by Argentine Authorities to protect the sovereignty of the Falklands Islands from the bettes noir of Guy Pierce (The Guardian Oct. 18, 2017).

One would think they would be wiser than to wrestle with a giant sea serpent after being buried alive in the Amazon jungle (2002 Jasper Johns, personal communication). The sunblock then occurs, as expected, within a phase shift of the Jarlsbcrg Whcel, precisely around 10:20AM lasting until 6:20PM as a SE adjusted to the mean SD of N-dimensional space with only a pocket of observable Anglo White resistance in South Bend Indiana as a happenstance of delinquent in Derry (Eagle-Tribune Oct. 25, 2017). Among the lesser known, of German novelists, available where ever books are sold at stand-up prices, Ismail Kadare, posits his thesis for the University of Munich, in the Ghost Rider, as a thorough understanding of how I started towards the study, with a dish full of vanilla ice cream, stopping on the way to get spoonfuls into my mouth. I twisted the knob of the door to the study clockwise, finding it unlocked. Complacency took over my mind as I slowly pulled on the knob to open the door, is a near exact rendering of the pouvoir, for understanding the Ideal Gas Law.

Seldom has the co-operative nature of cosmology and astrophysics been so acutely demonstrated as by the dearth of Canadian provinces and attirer of the Mexican nationals to the delight of CERN (Baystreet, Oct. 26, 2017). Experimental data for the habitude of African Costal Claims with thermolabile nanorods appear to suggest existence of conjectural space within tropospheric-atmospheric boundaries , in the sense of homo-dimerization concurrent with an extrinsic momentum dynamic (Le Monde, Oct. 26, 2017).

The studies on the subject were formally hypothesized as a convoluted round-about for a near subject assimilation with diaspora 2003, Paul Berg communicated to Mr. Newton, after Mr. Newton's meeting with Frank Cannon. I really love watching Gabriella play tennis, actually, said Endymion. It's more of a workout, than chasing after tennis balls. She's probably one of the few tennis players you would like because she can be a strong player without always being in position. In fact most of the sets where Gabriella Sabatini finishes a set with 6-3 score she tends to be all over the map. Workouts in tennis are not walking on treadmills, weight-lifting, or swimming in chlorine, but knowing where the net is, or the game of tennis would be called basketball. From the perspective of a tennis ball the net is two and a half racquets from the baseline. The baselines are gross adjusted to the fore-court of the opposite side, which is why when playing solo tennis against a wall, un mur, Gabriella Sabatini had to start at mid-court and move backwards. Nor could one maintain position by managing the acceleration with drop shots. Air shots would have been the most likely scenario if one could infer the repulsion velocity of the ball. For back hand shots Gabriella Sabatini would have to move semi-laterally to avoid forehand shots. Watching Gabriella Sabatini play tennis on the other hand is funny, because the currency is magnified over and above the net, rather than below the net – this being tennis, for people who are river blind.

L'opération Gaspurge, le théâtre d'opération de Rappel, au petit-déjeuner Egg McMuffin de Howard Johnson, est donc une tentative de liquidation complète, ce qui signifie annuler les attentes à la bombe à gaz, comme indiqué de notre champ d'application avec les stochastiques soulignés (14.16, 9.44) (20.00, 12.92) (0.50, 0,17) dans les travaux futurs.

The recognition, which hadn't yet emerged, as of photo essays of Paghman's Gardens in Afghanistan, was of a étoile géante as a galaxy spiral. The nature of differences between stars and galaxies, were as far removed from the understanding of the field of cosmology, as the differences between day and night in astrobiology. It would be fair to assume, in the assessment of the editors of Nature

Astronomy, that 10% of the computing platforms operating in the U.S. could define the facilitations of day-and-night in North America, which we define as the areas comprising Canada, Mexico, and the Territories. In large part, this problem, had already been exemplified by share-trades with Oslo, where no action was taken to improve the quality of programming. Eventually, NATO was forced to bomb the Territories to send the message of unacceptability. The North Atlantic Treaty Organization, which Newsweek failed to mention, hit California on December 4, 2017 and as of the 24th December; there were three additional airstrikes for the Thomas Fires which had consumed 273,400 acres of dry patch and vineyards with, "Having a fire of this magnitude in December is highly unusual," Berlant told Newsweek. "December is not usually as dry as it is, and we don't see these continued patterns of strong winds. In fact, it seems like every other week, we continue to see Santa Ana [winds] down south. That definitely has been an unusual part of this year and one of the reasons why we've had so many large and damaging fires."

PG&E had been paying its shareholders $2.12 a share per year in dividends, or 53 cents per quarter. With more than 500 million shares outstanding, the total dividend payout is more than $250 million every three months. Due to the Thomas Fires, purportedly to have begun at the foothills above Thomas Aquinas College, the utility also suspended paying dividends on preferred shares of stock. Big corporations rarely eliminate their quarterly shareholder dividends, and PG&E's decision is a further indicator of the potentially enormous financial damage it faces over the October fires. PG&E, which owns Pacific Gas and Electric Co., said in a statement to the Securities and Exchange Commission in October that losses from the fires could exceed the $800 million worth of liability insurance it carries for big fires. Shareholders responded immediately. PG&E's stock fell 93 cents on Wednesday, to $51.12, on the New York Stock Exchange, and then dropped another $4.80 in after-hours trading, to $46.32. Mr. Newton at the same time indicated meeting with Gavin Neusom at San Francisco City Hall (2007), with various key Government witnesses, including B. Lee.

There were objections raised by parents of children with the common cold, said F. S. Coe M.D. to disallow transfusions with "uprising." The Blood Centers of the Pacific as such, do not, by law, conceal any amendments which may have been made or has yet to be written by the Territories, as of November 2016, when California voters overwhelmingly passed Proposition 57 (64% to 35%) to enhance public safety, and stop the revolving door of crime. Short term and long term assessments of five EM functions, R. Ascot, Y. Potamus, G. Pringle, B. Rett, and V. Milner, indicated that they were covalent to I. Carruthers by K. Perkins M.D., F.R.S (2009) J. T. Witty M.D. Ph.D (2016). There being a substantial difference between an obliterated Spiral Galaxy and a Galaxy Spiral 49.49 SGEN 10:20AM April 20, 2018 in legal cogitans 22.70 CRAY 10:30AM April 20, 2018 for the Sirius Cluster, in as much as there is a vast difference between NF-kappa-B effectors and c-Ras. Given the predicaments we think that the National Guard should impose moving restrictions on families and care-providers associated with the endemic, until there is a complete resolve on the management of the crisis, starting with who, where, and when for Pontiac G-6 sedan (September 16, 2004). Because of critical literature cited since the release date, which would argue against public health, families and care-providers associated with the endemic can be considered to being seditious, under the laws of the U.S. and Territories – where the target population for "the death sentence" are U.S residents with the common cold, and the Department of Housing and Urban Development, who constitute 60% of the population. A market perspective would proceed with the inquiry of brokers associations and Cardinal Health listed revenue USD130B market cap USD19.70B, to discover if Oppenheimer Holdings revenue USD1.02B market cap USD359.20B said, I have become death, or I financed death – through mutual funds. With 48,250 residents at Empire Blue Cross market cap USD3.93B, it would be difficult to deny the Pontiac G-6 sedan as a serial killer, whilst financing a nightmare with a Cupertino, where the regional utility blew a gasket upon discovering a dive bar. Speaking for the ignorance of the markets in general, you would have to ask what kind of healthcare entrepreneur buys papers where their partner in the fiasco is allowed to sell dockets to the people living only in the State of Connecticut. In April 2017, when the Trump administration announced an investigation under the rarely used Section 232 of the Trade Expansion Act of 1962 to investigate whether steel imports threaten US national security, one would have hardly have believed that a computer would deploy Betacellulin to map positions within a rectangle to manage the cache flow model of a sewer main from Ohio with listed revenue USD11.57B and market cap USD6.14B. A study of the agent (2005) <u>Betacellulin in Chronic Periodontitis Patients With and Without Type 2 Diabetes Mellitus: An Immunohistochemical Study</u> (J Clin Diagn Res. 2015) would suggest a protocol of the study was in accordance with the Helsinki Declaration of 1975.

Shenk (coder) 1032.00 NIPPON Dec 27, 2018 Weishaus (playwrite) 68.05 STI 11:30 April 9, 2018 Levine (contact) 11,834.77 GDAXI 5:00 PM March 23, 2018 must have really liked watching *Who's the Boss?* to have come up with a business plan without misgivings, a manufacturing base at the Plasma Physics Laboratory, and a three month intravenous program at Lakeside Apartments. It's like a home-brew-kit gone wild, with unregulated celebratory achievements of a schizophrenic patient, a delusional patient, and a patient with severe depression. That leaves the Vogtmeister with a diagnosis of "associative-withdrawal" from subject recruitment at a state penitentiary for recovering alcoholics, 11,845.89 GDAXI 4:50PM March 23, 2018 where the director testified to having been told that Pontiac G-6 sedan would raise their blood-sugar level. By the time the communities around Venice Beach were sold into the plan, approximately 380 recovering alcoholics were already released into the population, whence "insurance agents" from Pharmacopia (NASDAQ) went public with 6,250,000 shares at $6.40 per share (2007). Given that 25ml times 3 is 75mls what is the total volume of product to market in liters? Next question might be, what are term life insurance policies per 100ml? 350K, 400K, 700K. What are the average premiums for term life among 48,250 people, and what are the average payouts to next of kin? 350K, 400K, 700K Don't think it will be useful to check phone records of the Banana Republic, or bar tabs at Molotov's on Haight - say our rose, for an sauce, vicious year, for the goldfish that died – one for the gipper, as the American say.

Fact is our own K. Perkins F.R.C M.D tested three of his patients in the Saturn Lounge incubator for ten days, and saw a 57% improvement with 36 mg cyclosporin/147mg Tamiflu where the subject was male with 4Nmutation, and 62% improvement with 36mg tomoxifan/147mg tamiflu where the subject was female with 4Nmutation, and 26% improvement where 36mg tomoxifan + 36 mg cyclosporine/147mg was used in female celebrity subject with 4N ortholog, Prime Minister's Questions (Dec. 24, 2017). A breakthrough in patient-physician confidentiality agreements, all three subjects exhibited swollen lymph nodes and T-lymphocyte counts were used as the marker for the study. K. Perkins F.R.C M.D additionally mentioned that the pacific rim function showed natural expression of indols among Syrian refugees escaping from Mosul, due to anti-Semitism, could be used as reference. Therefore we want our own Charles

Herbert MD to perform a proper sociological assessment of the subjects to get a clear idea of the pre-treatment portraits, for relapse, discontinuation, and development of selection criteria for babcock towers, because tamoxifen has at least twelve to twenty six linkage variants, and cyclosporin has several non-specific target tissue types, for which there would be babcocks for five types.

Je ne pensais pas que le poisson-chat, et le poisson-shad étaient sur le menu du déjeuner, mais juste pour être sûr, quand je l'ai regardé à nouveau, je reconnaissais le falafel Darwin.

La plupart des accords, en tant que tels, sont des heuristiques pilotées par microprocesseur.

The representation of the integral $9.4y + 0.76y^{(2-1)} + (73.1/0.008388) - y)$ for where $y = 41.12$ to 42.02 being 8186.05 for COKE between Aug 22, 2014 and Oct. 9 2015 provides the essential methods patent for stem cell transplants.

Et un résultat acceptable signifierait (100,00, 93,59). Le processus devrait durer de quatre à six mois, à computer durer Mai 2017.

If we take the same integral for $y = 41.12/SQRT2$ to $42.02/SQRT2$ then the area of 5717.44 suggests distributed computing among Th1 and Th2 components as one would expect within a surface where the circuit is unknown.

Dans le document de Hardy, les détails de leur stochastique sont fournis sous forme de bibliothèque de phages, demande à differents modificateurs de l'objectif de placement. DNA complémentaire fournit ensuite aux modificateurs les exigences de cache qui seront nécessaires. Une troisième bibliothèque, une bibliothèque de transfer-RNA, qui fournit les stochastiques pour les transferts de solde.

Correct, a superimposition as such could be represented as the $9.4y + 0.76y^{(2-1)} + (73.1/0.008388) + 5717.44y^2$) for an area of 29222.6, where $y = 41.12/SQRT45.25$ to $42.02/SQRT45.25$ which is a close approximation of how the stock markets works, for several different types of principals; Gibbs is an extreme example.

Les stochastiques d'une part apparaissent comme (100.00, 66.6667) et pourtant sur un autre apparaissent comme (43.75, 40.41).

That's also correct, if we modify the integral as $9.4y + 0.76y^{(2-1)}/0.83y -y$ for $y = 41.12/SQRT45.25$ to $42.02/SQRT45.25$ then the sum of -27814.6 provides a notion of motion, as a relativistic position where a lion might be chasing after a rabbit, technically addressing the dimensionality issue as rough set of suppositions where the antigens are able to pair with antibodies, as in a surface plasmon positrons, where the exchange electrons can be either e^{-1} or e^{-2}, and in rare instances they can be e^{-16}. Beyond the contribution of the experiment to a better understanding of the way dialectics behave, the development of new technologies is also part of the legacy of the HD-Operon. The collaboration was the first to develop fully automated, high-speed readout technologies with sub-micrometric accuracy, which pioneered the large-scale use of the so-called photon emulsion films to record particle tracks of Jupiter. Nuclear emulsion technology finds applications in a wide range of other scientific areas from dark matter search to ignominious and babcock investigations, which can be applied to optimise cancer treatment.

Intéressant, très intéressant, est-ce ainsi que vous avez développé votre mode opératoire pour le LSD?

Funny you should say that, LSD is the auto-antigen IL-1, which I've been using on a daily basis since I was an infant, into my teens, when I began experimenting with psilocybin, which is IL-2, auto-antigen.

Comment le LSD se compare-t-il à la psilocybine?

Psilocybin is a very noisy system, and I really began to understand how psilocybin works when I started working with CERN, Trieste, and SLR, and to some extent with SFIT, which is really difficult to understand, without under-standing the origin of numbers, especially number theory. Et c'est différent parce que, avec le CERN, Trieste et SLR sont des physiciens?

Exactly, CERN, Trieste and SLR are physicist, and they are
psilocybin users, so when I started working with them I had
to develop an understanding of noisy signals, where
communicative memorandums tend to be of three types,
incoherency-testing-material, symbol-logic-material, and
consensus-development-material, where proficiency testing
becomes part of the later stage consensus-development-
material, where there is a lot of systemic overlap in concept
and phenomelogy because the physics varies from solid state
to kinematics, and though the understanding of some of the
principals in solid state may be applicable to kinematics their
functional models can be quite different, in how they write
the equations.

Quelle a été votre expérience?

Working for, CERN, Trieste and SLR, tends to be an exercise
in using a toothbrush which provide the source to symbol-
logic-material – because they are physicists, as I just said,
and- which can then be integrated with consensus-development-material, which I've been using on a daily basis since
I was an infant.

Alors, l'auto-antigène IL-3, qu'est-ce que c'est?

IL-3 is morphine, it's a system of circuit logics, which are
coupled to LSD and psilocybin. Most of the experiments in

physiology, where I try to integrate with LSD, perturbs the use of morphine, with a IL-4 co-regulation, because the IL-4 auto antigen, amphetamine, comes with an auto-antibody, which we can generalize as sleep.

Qu'en est-il de la pause déjeuner?

Patient M.V. Lee was tested with 1X Luciferase and Novartis which showed significant improvements over African sleeping sickness, where the patient goes through a cycle of food avoidance as a mechanism of overcoming sleep. The combination showed a wakeful, albeit frustrated subject, with expressed knowledge of biomolecular signatures for ignominious, as in language proficiency and utility thereof as may have relevance for effected population with symptoms similar. Alternatively, the patient K. D. Jose who suffers from sleeping disorders reported restful sleep with dreams with 1X Luciferase and Sandoz. Though the case of M.V. Lee tests well on psychometric assessments, M.V. Lee was suggested a re-trial with 1X Luciferase and Searle as a way to clarify depression, with task of walking aimlessly in the hills of thanksgiving turkey (2017).

Un peu comme regarder un éléphant manger du foin. Ils enroulent et les pailles dans leur tronc, et même si la bouche est assez petite, les pailles disparaissent en quelques bouchées.

Yes, exactly, and then the droppings appear as somewhat

pulverized species of hay, which is different from when the elephant strips green leaves from trees with its trunk, from which the droppings are negligible.

C'est le genre de compréhension qui fait la valeur de l'Euro-Tunnel, même si nous débattons avec comment fonctionne la merde, comme un démêlage du modèle de balançoire, imaginé dans les années 1980, un rapport abstrait qui relie les neutrinos normaux à une race invisible de particules super lourdes aux propriétés étranges: les neutrinos que nous connaissons à une extrémité sont pivotés par des particules plus lourdes de l'autre fin de la "bascule". Si ces gymnastiques mathématiques étaient responsables de la minuscule masse du neutrino, cela conduirait les physiciens à un riche paysage de particules et de phénomènes nouveaux au-delà du modèle standard, peut-être même une théorie unifiée des forces fondamentales.

Right, well, experiments at CERN's l'Euro-Tunnel have now put the unlikely sounding "seesaw model" through one of its most stringent tests for stochastics of (64.52, 73.37) and (22.2222, 47.4226) where we compare the contemporaneous arguments for the relativistic position where a lion might be chasing after a rabbit, and a superimposition, where we ask for help in locating the transmitter diode, using a search function where we generalize the search path as $5717.44y^2 -27814.6\,y$ for $y = 41.12/\text{SQRT}45.25$ to $42.02 /\text{SQRT}45.25$ as 5733.04 for ORCL 47.22, May 21, 2018. This gives us an estimation of charge for the contention.

La stochastique suivante est peut-être un peu moins discernable (29.9999, 44.9999).

Correct, if you mean to say fathomable, in other words, depth, for which show the integral as $5717.44y^2 -27814.6\,y$ for $y = 2.968333/SQRT35.62$ to $42.02\,/SQRT35.62$ as -21046.4 for PFE 35.62 12:00PM, May 21 2018, which is eleven days prior to the wedding between a neurite and the perforant pathway, though many physicists think it a stretch – "unnatural" even – that the Higgs boson interacts so feebly with the neutrino as to leave it at least a million times lighter than the already waif-like electron.

Ceci est similaire à l'hypothyroïdie, qui survient chez les enfants quand ils sont très maladies- maman, je ne veux pas aller à l'école aujourd'hui, ou maman je ne pourrais pas mon déjeuner parce que mes glandes sont enflées- ce que les médecins appellent l'amygdalite.

You scc my point. That's what makes the Kissstory on the front page of a tabloid rag like the Sun, more understandable than the others, as we address the needs of people who buy papers, or newspapers – since they are paying for information, in the same sense as an astrophysics student pays to go to school, sit down somewhere, and interpret a certain number of *assertions* – which become *hypothesis* after they have been observed, and become a *motivation* once they have been proven, which is the case, quite precisely for

Jerome Powell – which is to say, there were a certain number of observations for IL-2 from which he created the *motivation*, and now he wants to test the *motivation*, which we will call the *counter-assertion*, which is different from an *argument*, which is a process by which we validate a hypothesis, where the observations do not exist, where we might try to tease out differences in mechanisms to reduce the rate of infection by comparing gram+ and gram- antigens against phagemid-excision repair auto-immune antibodies for diseases, such as progeria, adult and childhood leukemia, thrombocytopenia, Charcot, osteosarcoma, with tonsillitis.

Parce que ces stochastiques sont appelés fast-stochastics, en raison de la manière dont les vents soufflent dans les branches d'un arbre, ou la manière dont un nuage se forme et se désintègre.

Precisely, where we can show the integral to be $5717.44y^2$ - 27814.6 y for y = $0.148833333/SQRT35.62$ to 42.02 $/SQRT35.62$ as -24243.4 for PFE 35.72 2:40PM, March 21 2018. Theoretical understanding of these measurements is challenging, however, and is one of the most important problems in quantum chromodynamics today.

Dieu merci, je peux vous le dire, car ici, à l'Institut Pasteur, ce sont les mots clés pour nos médecins. Nous avons attendu des siècles, peut-être pas des siècles, mais au moins huit-deux ans pour entendre ces mots, *quantum chromodynamics*.

When we look at the integral then, in those terms, what we are saying is that the integral is 5717.44y^2 -27814.6 y for y = 0.148833333/SQRT35.62 to 0.000518/SQRT35.62 for 8.61901 for SPNT 5.18 3:20PM, May 21 2018.

Ensuite, nous avons un stochastique de (23.00, 32.67).

Therefore, the integral 10167/y^2 - 27814.6y for y = 0.148833333/SQRT35.62 to 0.000518/SQRT35.62 is -1.16734E8 for PRU 101.67 3:30PM, May 21 2018. Conceivably, there could be other conjectures, which would be manifestations of the same oblong, perhaps not as well differentiated into the 10248/y^2 - 27814.6y for y = 0.148833333/SQRT35.62 to 0.000518/SQRT35.62 is 1.17664E8.

Par conséquent, il serait suggéré que si on devait comparer un plan longitudinal parallèle à l'inondation (100.00, 94.44) et le comparer à la asymptote pour quatre variables differentes pour le plan longitudinal (100.00, 88.33), les stochastiques seraient les mêmes as the flood.

That's correct, within the context of a spin-state, where we can consider centripetal and centrifugal, we can describe an integral as 10248/y^2 – 27814.6y/(y^5 – y^0.0093) where y = 6199.30/SQRT35.62 to 6197.80/SQRT35.62 as a dy of -0.00238779 for the AORD 6199.30 11:20 AM for May 21, 2018.

L'effondrement, en d'autres termes, a déplacé le centre de gravité vers le niveau de la mer for which the asymptotic stochastic is (72.52, 67.05).

The way to explain that is, within a context of quantum chromodynamics, $10248/y^2 - 27814.6y/(6199.30y^5 - y^0.0093)$ because it may not be entirely obvious, as to what we are looking at, and more importantly, where, and finally by whom, we make our position quite explicit, as being y = 0.148833333/SQRT35.62 to 0.000518/SQRT35.62, for the perspective of an observer, as a sum of 1.17664E8, for BIIB 280.84 12:10PM May 21 2018, where the *traduction* of -3538.68 can be shone as the integral of $10248y^0.04573925 - 27814.6y/(y^5 - y^0.0093)$ for y = 6199.30/SQRT35.36 to 6197.80/SQRT35.36 for NOK 6.22 1:36PM May 21, 2018 and AORD 6197.80 11:56AM May 21 2018.

Et les Vosges sont chaud câblés (29.42, 14.75).

In imaginary space, these quantum are quite tricky, as I may have mentioned in my dossier for Rue de Vaugirard, where $10248y^0.045739254 - 24.52y/(y^5 - y^0.0093)$ for y = 6199.30/SQRT35.36 to 6197.80/SQRT35.36 which we calculate as -3538.68 for ABB 24.52 2:46PM May 21, 2018. While the conservative government of Teresa May tends to be very critical of how British Taxpayer Revenues are deployed for allocation of a Public Health Budget for all the Britons including Sheikh Hasina, Shinzō Abe, Prayut Chan-o-cha, Li Keqiang, Narendra Modi, Shahid Khaqan Abbasi, and

Abdullah Abdullah, where the standards of criteria setting for the United Kingdom should be seen as non-negotiable for stratification of ecological workers and population genetics for 1.57GBP facilitating the First Five Year Plan from the New Year, for a 30% increase in agricultural productivity, for a 20% profitability of which 15% was for cost allocation amortization, the sum of which would be adjusted in increments of the indefinite integral of 4 log(x)/25 of time, due to ecological pressures on workers – in actuarial terms of financial management 136.97 TRV 1:46PM April 20, 2018.

Upon entering the Gamma Draconis, refered to as Eltanin, a misnomer with portents of source impedance, on December 28, 2017, allowed us to develop an understanding of the actuarial terms for mathematics of astronomy and cosmology which were similar to Huggies and Pampers, though not entirely, largely due to how we might envision congruencies between quantum physics 46.72 AAL 10:40AM April 23, 2018 compared with quantum relativity 249.70 GS 10:30 AM April 23, 2018, remarked Ms. Random Memorandom, while managing subscription interests to Nature Physics, where again the notice was directed as, in the absence of Dirac, discrete Bayes are antithetical to each other. From the perspective of our earlier work (Zubay, Schwartz, and Beckwith 1970) where the formation constant for the CAP-cyclic AMP complex could be defined by the equation $K(f) = CAP + cAMP / CAP)(cAMP)$ as a rate of change for 1.4 mM DTT and O.D. 420 mu for CAP incubation, the unavailability of DTT for students working in origami labs might be seen as latent discoveries in cognitive withdrawal symptoms associated with carbo-pentene rings, which in physiologic terms is a contributing factor in acid reflux, and early studies with carbo-pentene in two young women showed post-menopausal hot flashes (1985) with production of salicylic acid in the stomach (1986), which is different from bile (1985). The questions we were keen to study was if bile was a product of Wild Turkey, or just schnapps with beer (1986); or absolute vodka (1986). "Another approach for just asymmetry, Steck and Dawson found glycoproteins were asymmetrical – did not show transmembrane – freeze fracture EM just shows integral proteins, not trans-membrane, (1986)" in other words would be seen as, where's the proof for word usage, which is much more to say that we at the correct perspective, FCHI 5648.61 10:10AM May 21 2018 as the TIF for the thermostable de-couple circuit.

In our galaxy, which is in space where other planets are - or cluster galaxy to be more exact, we can express the approach as a physical phenomenology for how the engine of a cruise ship disembarks from a port, compared with say how a Michael Phelps who is a professional swimmer might complete a lap. If we look at the integral of $64x^2 - y^7/2x$ for x = 1 to 15 then the function that we draw is $3854 - 1/2 \, y^7 \, Log(15)$, where the identity for the function can be seen as $16^2 - 1/2 \, y^7 \, Log(x)$ for the corvis constellation at AORD 6180.40 at 10:10 PM on December 29, 2017. We might then compare a rate function, in astrophysical terms, for Electronic Arts as a sum differential between 108.42 on

July 11, 2017 and 104.78 on December 29, 2017 as the integral of $(x^2 - y^4)(y^3 + x^2 + y^2x^{-1}) / 162$ for $y = 108.42$ to 104.78 to draw the function as $-0.0224691x^4 + 2.87592E6 \ x^2 - 255.354x + 3.30189E10x^{-1} + 3.52186E12$.

In a Mark Halperin interview with Andrew McCarthy of Less Than Zero, Rob Loew of Oxford Blues, and Boy George of Culture Club, F. S. Coe M.D. observes the differences between responses among Searle Scholars, where Andrew McCarthy might appear to have stem cell progenitor neurons, while Rob Lowe might have neurogenic progenitor neurons, and Boy George may have islet cell auto-antigen response, which would elaborate his deteriorating condition due to food, where Rob Lowe might be seen as an autonomic responder, though both are known to be of interest as a function of Granulocyte stimulating, where one may be Ciliary neurotrophic inducible and the other, repressed. There may be instances, as such where for certain diagnose such as private school issues where Google might be seen as an open maxim for dialog, instead of terrorist activity, where we are able to move forward instead of wearing a fez, or a nurse hat, or the catholic priest's collar – which are former relics of a semiotic society – as opposed to a semantic experience of the world, where query languages are used to overcome barriers instead of hiding behind books, or mascara, or lipstick – for questions of such essence seen in movies as, *Nigga Where You Live, Motherfucker?* or, *I Ain Yo Momma, Bitch!* and *Hey, Girl*. It is a characteristic trait, however puzzling, where to distinguish between auto-antigen response and autonomic responder, biologics are used to reason with nature – in the same context as a *Road Bridge Over Victoria Falls* – followed by *My Dinner With a Meteor.* As I was about to say, my first date in college was a sham. We were now into our second year without feeling more awkward than usual, and the Oregonian party who would agree to experiment insisted on staying in to avoid any embarrassment with a bottle of vodka and orange juice which would end in a magnificent disaster in the absence of bile. That much seems also to be true of Mitsui Sumitomo, where if we were to develop a function of orbit from Sept. 13, 2017 7.67 to Dec. 29, 2017 8.73 for the integral $(x^4 - y^4)$ $(y^3 + x^2 + y^2{}^{-27})/162$, then the function for the scapegoating is $-16790.3 - 2030.83 /x^{27} + 0.440578/x^{25} +0.00654x^4 - 26.2078x^2$ where we see the emergence of a constant, compared to the same identity for 108.42 to 104.78, where the function produces an intercept as $3.30189E10/x^{27} - 255.34/x^{25} - 0.0224691x^4 + 2.87592E6x^2 + 3.52186 E12$. The wage gap, then might seem a bit more than 398.10 even if we're not that good at what is art.

Consider the game of Boris Becker and Rafael Nadal. Where one is swift, the other is in power shots. Where they came from, who their creator, and when they were developed is quite beside the point. *The Company of Taylor and Frances* is forever indebted for opprobrious humor is more than justification for mathematics, where the crypts are an association of population genomics for geologic conservancies – that means separate from the nature of dragonflies and crows, tasty mango pickle from hindu fakirs, and dumb polish jew monsters. Pretty close call, said Endymion, where a tribute to Oct. 6, 2016, might still be remembered as, *Die Losers.* The results revealed more clumping in resistant strain, which indicates that the bacteria acquire a protective shield which leads to lesser exposure to surroundings and as a result bacteriocin could interact only with the outer layer of bacteria leaving the inner layers of bacteria alive.

The measurement of the Yukawa coupling of the Higgs boson to the top quark, y_t, is of high phenomenological interest for several reasons. The extraordinarily large value of the top quark mass, compared to the masses of all other known fermions, may indicate that the top quark plays a still-un known special role in the EWSB mechanism. The measurement of the rate at which Higgs bosons are produced in association with top quark pairs (ttH production) provides the most precise model-independent determination of y_t. An example of a Feynman diagram for ttH production in proton-proton (pp) collisions is shown in Fig. 1. Since the rate for the gluon fusion Higgs boson production process is dominated by top quark loops, a comparison of y_t measured through this production channel and through the ttH production channel will provide powerful constraints on new physics potentially introduced into the gluon fusion process by additional loops.

A delay in the start of log phase was observed on development of resistance against pediocin by S. aureus. The lag phase increased from 2 h in case of wild type strain to nearly 4 h in case of resistant strain. The log phase duration increased in case of resistant bacteria and there was a delay in attainment of stationary phase. Growth pattern showed a delay in log phase of resistant bacteria which could be attributed to the necessity of supplementary energy to gain resistance and therefore compensate growth. The differences may be caused by the ability to chelate metal ions by polyphenols with at least two hydroxyl groups in the phenolic ring. The performed principal component analysis of leaf and root data showed a clear separation between the metallicolous and non-metallicolous populations. It was noted that the variations among the studied plants were explained by the first two components and represented 60%, 46%, and 58% of the total variance for leaves, flower heads, and roots, respectively.

Collision vertices are reconstructed using a deterministic annealing algorithm. The reconstructed vertex position is required to be compatible with the location of the LHC beam in the x-y plane. The reconstructed vertex with the largest value of summed physics-object p^2_T is taken to be the primary pp interaction vertex (PV). The physics objects are the jets, clustered using the jet finding algorithm with the tracks assigned to the vertex as inputs, and the associated missing transverse momentum, taken as the negative vector sum of the pT of those jets. Electrons, muons, and th candidates, which are subsequently reconstructed, are required to be compatible with originating from the PV. In fact, dry-season agriculture is particularly difficult in

Bangladesh due to high salt stress across the coastal belt. For this reason, crop production has been negatively affected each year for many decades across the coastal belt of Bangladesh as seen in 1765.00. Survey comments from Newcastle upon Tyne agreed that CAM was useful for minor treatments and stated that CAM was good alongside allopathic medicine. 64.3% of the responses were generally positive. 25% of respondents mentioned science or the need for CAM to "work" through evidence-based medicine. A few responses were highly supportive of CAM, including the mention of CAM being an alternative to paracetamol and antibiotics, Safety and Mosquitocidal Efficacy of High Dose Ivermectin when co-Administered with di-Hydroartimisinin-Piperaquine in Kenyan Adults with Uncomplicated Malaria: a Randomized Double-Blind Placebo Controlled trial, 4190.00 LSE 9:36AM April 17, 2019. Matsumoto et al. showed greater activity of GN therapy against lung cancer models than the activity of a combination of gemcitabine with cisplatin or carboplatin. In our institution, we have used nedaplatin-based chemo-therapy for high-grade UC and have demon-strated good responses, against the median PFS and OS times of 147 and 396 days, respectively- the worst videos of dissuasion ever made. Again, we were having trouble com-municating to the American that the meaning of the words, counter-intuitive is the same as antithetical, tr. in Spanish, *no tiene sentido, opuesto.*

Hadronic τ leptondecaysarereconstructedbythe"hadrons-plus-strips"(HPS)algorithm[54]. The algorithm reconstructs individual hadronic decay modes of the τ lepton: τ± → h±ντ, τ± → h±π0ντ, τ± → h±π0π0ντ, and τ± → h±h∓h±ντ, where h± denotes either a charged pionorkaon. Hadronicτ candidates are built by combining the charged hadrons reconstructed by the PF algorithm with neutral pions. The neutral pions are reconstructed by clustering the photons and electrons reconstructed by the PF algorithm within rectangular strips that are narrow in η, but wide in the φ direction, to account for the broadening of energy deposits in the ECAL if one of the photons produced in π0 → γγ decays converts within the tracking detector. An improved version of the strip reconstruction has been developed for data analyses at 13TeV and beyond, replacing the one used in CMS analyses at √s = 7 and 8TeV that was based on a fixed strip size of 0.05×0.20 in η-φ. In the improved version the size of the strip is adjusted as a function of the pT of the particles reconstructed within the strip.

The photocopier hath been had trouble locating England, now and then, that Scotland's a drunk on the map was noted as the trouble with entries, as we remembered how the Hash was cerebral, and yet fortuitous for the find C5 2483, again – alas, as never to seen 1471, in so sad, weep, weep, hurray – mention that to your Ian Blackford say, what's Trafalgar got do with that ya wanker, as the place we'd be looking for just now happens to be Hemley, a village and a civil parish in the Suffolk Coastal District, in the English county of Suffolk seen as 1683, while say the bowda betwixt disenchanted and dystopic may had have been furlong seen in 1715 just outside of Deptford, London Borough of Lewisham- so as Jeremy Corbin might understand, riff-raff as they are disguised as country gentlemen for face time with death.

The sign of the weights alternates for events with different numbers of leptons and τh candidates passing the nominal selection criteria. The alternating sign is necessary to correctly account for the contributions of events with different numbers of prompt leptons, non-prompt leptons, genuineτh, and hadrons to an event sample with a given total number of reconstructed leptons and τh. For example, in the case of events with two leptons in the $2^{\cdot}ss$ category, the negative sign in the expression $-f1\ f2/[(1-f1)(1-f2)]$ for the weight w2 corrects for the contribution of events with two nonprompt leptons or misidentified hadrons to the sample of events in which one lepton passes and the other one fails the nominal lepton selection criteria. Application of the weights given as events in the AR provides an unbiased estimate of the background contribution in the SR arising from events with at least one non-prompt lepton or hadron misidentified as prompt-lepton or τh. A correction obtained from the MC simulation is subtracted from this estimate to account for the contamination of the AR with irreducible backgrounds, i.e.,by event which all leptons are prompt-leptons and all τh are genuine, and in which a prompt lepton fails the nominal lepton selection criteria or a genuine τh fails the nominal τh selection criteria. The correction does not exceed 10% of the yield in the AR in any category.

The thing to do would be to get in touch with Dr. Diedra Brock, and acquire a so called "forebodence" on cases for poly-sorbitol glyconase, for each individual case, and then file with the coppers investigating burning hats until it reaches the air of Alan Brown that the case of Rees-Mogg Sr. is still being investigated.

It comes as no surprise, that poly-sorbitol glyconase would be used as a treatment for neuropsychiatric disorders when it's used for ulcerative colitis in very young children, and though nitrous oxide poisoning may have been the issue with Rees-Mogg Sr., poly-sorbitol glyconase may be seen as a contributing factor, given that patients with nitrous oxide poisoning often take their time to die, as a lot of the times they are noticeable career-professionals, with an edge to them, because they want to appear to be driven- and their opposite, where non-professionals suffering from depression, self-medicate themselves, might frequent the beauty of the blue velvet as often as six times a day, instead twice. The desire does not go away with their inability to get past a 2-dimentional world after three or four years, without recovery.

The outputs of the two BDTs that separate the ttH signal from the ttV and tt+jets backgrounds are mapped into a single discriminant DMVA that is used as a discriminating observable for the signal extraction in the 2`ss, 3`, and 3` + 1th categories. The mapping is determined as follows. The algorithm starts by filling two-dimensional histograms of the output of the first versus the second BDT for signal and background events. The histograms use a fine binning. The distributions for signal and for background are smoothed using Gaussian kernels to reduce statistical fluctuations. The ratio of signal to background event yields is computed in each bin and assigned to background events depending on the bins they fall in. The cumulative distribution of this ratio is produced for background events and partitioned, based on its quantiles, into N regions of equal background content. The number of regions is chosen using a recursive application of the k-means clustering algorithm with k = 2 [58] on the two-dimensional distribution of the BDTs, including stopping conditions limiting the statistical uncertainty in the signal and background templates. The output of the algorithm that determines the mapping is a partitioning of the two-dimensional plane spanned by the output of the two BDTs into N regions and an enumeration, used as a discriminant, of these regions by increasing signal-to background ratio.

Pulling out patients from toilet humor, actuals of _Benign-Malignant Tumors: Case Studies of Patient Duplication on HYW 101_, include, "I'm pissed and I'm ready to blow my brains out," K.C. Jones, "I don't understand what my incentives are," B. N. Well, "I'm biting my lip to say this to you, I hate being in here!" J. K. Whofers, "I'm just angry all the time, don't know what to do," B. Essex, "It's kinda like I hover over a Pacman game," J. C. Leone, "if you talk that way to me again I'll quit," D. B. Folk, should always be taken seriously, with a commitment towards cache and cache payments, because it's really hard for non-professionals suffering from depression to perform any kind of work which involves moving, though there are some who manage to recover by "baiting their estrogen cycle with cache into building a levee," N. M. Sant, to get out the door, which can take upto five years, looking as frost bitten as a snow monkey. One of the interesting cases I had consulted with, who could overcome the nightmares of depravity – and early stages of withdrawal – though, happened to concede to the most outrageous notion that "working at the Wawa was as much fun as seeing his son play basketball." J. H. Bamboozle. There are still others who can be really rough to work with, not because they are holocaust survivor, but because they are really shy, extremely introverted, and very secretive of hyperventilates – which are a psychological reckoning with self, of mistakes, knowing where you have made the mistakes – while being at the verge of making the mistake of "no turning back, no u-turn to provide any kind of service in declining towards, "functioning cranial embolism," B. J. Diehard. Recuperation, tends to require long sleep states, especially if a patient unexpectedly goes into psychosis (suddenly) - where patient balance becomes inseparable from being in 2-Dimentional flatland – where the verge of the mysterious world is psychoses. The experience can be scary for the clinician with the patient, and other patients – "because you're inhospi-table," E. D. Sit. For none such stereotypical cases should poly-sorbitol glyconase be used to convenience the patient, in as much as psilocybin should not be offered as a gratification towards, "Don't let me down," where Brownian motions is sufficiently relaxing. For occasional patients, the manifestation is similar to asthma sufferers prior to treatment, where existence is integral to bitterness, erratic triggers which have to be tolerated, abuse which can be reflective, and enthu-siasm which has to be suspended – "due of grief complex," S. B. Tail, which doesn't even begin to explain why Donald Trump called on the U.S. Postal Service on Friday to charge "much more" to ship packages for Amazon, picking another fight with an online retail giant he has criticized in the past.

Perhaps you should discuss the number of subjects required for a clinical trial based on prevalence, where the prevalence is >12%, instead of incidence rates >78% within a population, said Mr. Newton to K. Perkins F.R.C. M.D. You can understand why I might be slow to altercate between my primaries, my secondaires, and my tertiaries where the incidence rates are further segmented from >78% with confounding issues of treatments, treatment benefits, hazard scores, and negative controls – where a prevalence of >12% isn't so much an insurmountable challenge as it is a question of individualization of procedural specialization, as mentioned in the case of J. H. Bamboozle MYGN 29.30 2:00PM April 17, 2018, or B. N. Well 29.32 MYGN 10:30 April 20, 2018, or B. J. Diehard 29.26 10:30AM April 19, 2018 (1970M(f) 29.32 MYGN 29.32 MYGN 10:30 April 20, 2018 Studies on the Mechanism of Hormone Action E. W.

Sutherland 1971,) or Dr. Charles Stanley 126.33 JNJ 3:16PM April 20, 2018, or Swoozie Kurtz 29.30 MYGN 2:00PM April 17, 2018. You might see then how for prevalence >32% the challenges for individualization of procedural specialization might be difficult given that population screening would be inconsiderate, and long term care would require increases in premiums, given 1970M, 2013M, and 2014F in RDBMS script, without an understanding how the tribal elders of British Columbia might respond to suggested immigrations. As looney as they might appear, F. F Cola (of Cancer Ward C5) is dead set against Zinfandel, likes personal journey; M. B. Stella (of Cancer Ward C1) has proposed Pinot Grigio if he can be prescribed tetracycline instead of olanzapine; for L. O. Kellen (of Cancer Ward C2) Zinfandel is acceptable if he can switch from cyclosporine 58.01 ASX 12:10 PM 2018 March 5, 2018 to olanzapine, D. H. Easy (of Cancer Ward C4) would be willing to move up to NDC 2591.12 if he can be prescribed Luciferase: B. L. Llama (of Cancer Ward C3) would be willing to move to PN 111.53 if he can be prescribed Methotrexate; and B. J. Diehard (of Cancer Ward C4) would be willing to move to Zinfandel if he can be prescribed streptomycin 57.72 ASX 1:50PM March 5, 2018, where a common denominator for all of them together might be seen as BCL-2 (12.3) 144.45 CNA 11:30AM March 7, 2018.

We have had a chance to observe three cases of Associative Personality Disorder, as a classification for Neuropsychiatric, said Mr. Newton. If you've never met the Bot cases, they're double homologous recombinants, first described as

"enjoying the snow day off school at Slane, County Meath."
In the case of W. S. Bot 9663.90 NSEI June 7, 2017, which
we would consider to the most severe, the subject suffers
from fear of associative personalities, in romantic relationships, which can last from three months to as long as two
years, as a possible mechanistic variability between
Swedish populations and Norwegian populations, in terms
of tolerability of penicillin. The subject has demonstrated
difficulties in overcoming mathematical barriers for self-
conception, and has demonstrated psychological mani-
pulation for conception. In the case of A. S. Bot 10093.04
NSEI Sept 12, 2017, which we consider to be moderate due
to informed consent, the subject provides disclosure data for
genetic linkage maps for traits associated with Associative
Personality Disorder, where we are able to provide a positive
or negative inflammatory response to skin grafts, as a
possible prior tolerability of Beta inhibitors in ALS segments,
such as paralysis.

Here we consider the individual to be moderate because the
subject is aware of condition, is able to adapt with similar
cases, and is able to communicate with a large number of
dis-similar cases as a non-subject. In the case of M. S. Bot
10389.70 NSEI Nov. 24, 2018, which we would consider to be
mild, the subject has demonstrated disabilities with
professional evaluations, professional credentialization, and
written competency requirements for driving licenses for
possible prior tolerability of IL-2 in polyneuropathy segments.

The arcoplanarity requirements are chosen such that the signal to background ratio predicted by the simulation is above unity before any matching of the leptons with RP tracks. The size of the extra-track veto region is smaller than suggested by the simulation, reflecting the fact that the distribution of primary vertices in z is narrower in the data than in the simulation. Because of the high pileup rate, the selection is based on information from reconstructed tracks alone, without using information from the calorimeters.

The effect of the mild categorization is due to a mild subordination of negative inflammatory response to skin grafts, which provides us with several measures for understanding neurite growth, development, and regeneration. GATTACA in that sense, allows for the debate, if a prevalence of >12% is lower or higher than a prevalence >32% as a pre-chance for therapeutic intervention for Associative Personality Disorder, where premiums would be scaled for survival data based on longevity, and premiums would be sliding for hazard data based on group rate, given that patient R. R. Graham 26.86 TM Mar. 11, 2016 where we defined 1SEK = 0.12US and 1bit = 11,285US with the general understanding that 66,202 words constitutes 625k bytes, since 1.5X Luciferase showed juvenile resilience from May 2012 to the Dec 2017 with a total enrollment n = 300 in hazards for broadly defined ignominious disorders of incidence rates incidence rates >78% against a background of no change for patient V. I. Gap, 50 c.c. FCS enrollment n = 500, where the total essay is 60k bits, 677100000 US,

5642500000 SEC, as shown in front cover of Red & Gold the Community Magazine of Nob Hill, Fall 2017. The pixel value for 491 new cases of Swedish and Norwegian Cancer Wards would therefore be 78.36779433k bytes, which would grow to 351.2200873k bytes in June 2019. That's about the size of the Trinity College Project 2018. If you were to multiply 3.43 with 1230 the 4218.9 would be the k bytes , which when we divide to 351.2200873k bytes, then each case would be assigned about 83.24920887 SEC as shown in Garcon, vous le vu, as the net difference between Cancer Ward and V. I. Gap 51.28 INTC 11:10 AM April 20, 2018.

The formula is exact for exclusive events, but holds also for the single-dissociation case, as illustrated with LPAIR simulated events. In this case only one of the two possible solutions will correspond to the direction of the intact proton. Studies with LPAIR indicate that a mass of the dissociating system larger than about 400GeV is needed in order to produce a deviation comparable to the expected $\S(\dot{}+\dot{}-)$ resolution of about 3% (4%) for dimuons (dielectrons). The latter is obtained from simulation, with an additional smearing to account for residual data–simulation differences. The LPAIR simulation also indicates that the minimum mass of the dissociating system required to generate activity in the CMS tracker is about 50GeV; the fraction of dissociative events above this threshold is of a few percent.

A corollary might be seen to be similar to a lack of comprehension in being able to appreciate the functional efficacy between Caspase and Cox-2 inhibitor as a local treatment for Lumenoscopy (2018) during the Muslim holy festival of Eid-al-fitr during which, by sociologic convention, the Muslim fakirs are fasting for thirty day, in our Capital City of Grozny, with a meal after midnight with fried bread and temperatures recorded in 35F. Clearly the talent of computer scientists in *What is Bitcoins? Everything you need to know about* . . . Mirror, May 12, 2017, for writing about Bitcoins as a crypto-currency either under-cut the value the Space Jar, or the talent for computer scientists writing about Bitcoins as a encrypted security under-cut the value of the San Francisco Art Institute – because, as any computer scientist who swam in rivers would know, encryption and decode do not come with bits, just like in the movie Pacman, with Satoshi Nakamoto.

The game of Andy Murray is serve centered with finesse as the deliberate for coaching differences. Whereas Becker and Nadal, for instance, are continuously exposed to having to estimate velocity based on acceleration as function of swing compared to steps, Murray's game is reach. A close co-homology for these techniques are better understood, quite literally, as the relationship between terms and functions where 1 Lesotho Loti is equal to 0.28 Roma Leu, 1 Omani Rial is equal to 10.34 Roma Leu, and 1 Turkish Lira is equal to 1.75 Trinidad and Tobago Dollar. In the movie, *Nigga Way You Leo, Motherfucker?* and *I Ain Yo Momma, Bitch!* Endymion asks the question with even greater subtlety as to how we could arrive at 52.57142857 where the dividend is 92.0,

48.57142817 where the dividend is 85, and 81.71428571 where the dividend is 143 for the common denominator 1.75, when we know that the promontory function is $-y^x-1$, for *Hey, Girl.* By the time we see the movie, *Love You Darlin Honey Chile* with the dividend 857 for our common divisor 1.75 as 571.33333333 we begin to discover what referees in tennis refer to as margin calls, where inside boundaries versus outside boundaries, in tennis doubles compare with tennis singles, where the full court might be seen as the dividend 8571 for the divisor 1.75 for the Palm d'Or of movie magic 4897.714286 seen in *Ba Bay Wassup Witch You?*

Within such a context we might see members of the UK Youth Parliament gathered in the Commons to discuss a number of subjects, including work experience and the protection of LGBT individuals, along with issue put forward by the Harrow Youth Parliament, which asked 11 to 18 year olds to vote on the things which matter most to them, concerning curriculum for life, and public transport, where the event was also attended by the Education Secretary, Justine Greening, and Leader of the House of Commons Andrea Leadsom, both members of Prime Minister Theresa May's Conservative Party, broadcast live on the BBC Parliament Channel, with Luke speaking to the house in the afternoon session. Suppose we liven our sensation for the objectives here, said the Home Secretary Amber Rudd, as a way to investigate if the parts are greater than the whole, or if the whole is greater than the sum of its parts. Suppose there's a suspect in our mystery, a visceral suspect, a suspect we are observing, a suspect we're studying without appearing on television screen in Berlin, Tokyo, London, New Delhi, Moscow, and Los Angeles, from every angle as a work-study student for the foreign office; a suspect whom we observe once a week to walk to a department store to buy food items before a big chill. Suppose our investigation of the suspect's premises uncovers a series of receipts which are uploaded to our phones, and recorded by wireless stations, and transferred to code compilers to indicate a transference, as in a séance, where the suspect becomes distributed into suspects – for the purpose of the investigation. Working backwards from _Dec 21, 2017_ the subject charges $14.82 of items (6) for $15.00 and receives $0.18 in change as the completion of his objectives – on _Dec 14, 2017_ the suspect charges $11.88 of items (4) for $22.00 and receives $10.12 in change – on _Dec 7, 2017_ the subject charges $9.90 of items (7) for $20.00 and receives $10.10 in change – on _Nov 30, 2017_ charges $24.20 of items (5) for $25.00 and receives $0.80 in change – on _Nov 17, 2017_ the suspect charges $12.34 of items (8) for $13.00 and receives $0.66 in change – on _Nov 10, 2017_ charges $30.55 of items (11) for $31.00 and receives $0.45 in change – on _Nov 03, 2017_ charges $14.69 of items (5) for $14.75 and receives $0.06 in change.

Suppose, then, says the Home Minister, we were assigned the task of repeating each objective and to return with the same outcomes, what would be the success rate of reproducing each line code – from the same department store, or a different department store, where the monies which are brought into the department store are no more that 24% greater in value. And you work for an insurance company? The Art Institute of San Francisco? Well, that's the first time I've heard it. Anyway, the term life for each case has to be evaluated as a "Group Health Plan" per line item, unless you want to work in drapery sales, with *Smoke Two Joints*. Otherwise, the objectives of the Trinity College Project are to determine the point value for Dec 21, 2017 and Dec 14, 2017 for 1326.50 SKY April 10, 2017, as 78.36779433k bytes as requested by Amber Rudd, and determine the point value of Nov 30, 2017 48.57 SNE April 9, 2018 for 83.24920887 bits.

A compareable *Laurent Cash-flow Model* counts cash flow (that means continuous addition, and subtraction) at a retail store several times a day, and then counts the entire cash holdings at the end of the day from the cash flow, bundles the cash flow for the week into a bank, where the objective is to attain exactly equal value for stock holdings of the retail store and the bank bundle – every week, where the minimum balance is 0.06% per day – was used to finance the construction of the Calcutta Metro Rail. There again the 31.28 XRX would approximate Nov 03, 2017, and 625.50 ISAT would approximate Nov 10, 2017 for the difference between 78.36779433k bytes and 351.2200873k bytes for observed and expected issues, where the number of issues for term life are limited by availability, as an unambiguous actuarial relationship with a non-existent health care system.

Because, ignorance can be scary, the development of ensemble sets for patient care, from primaries-secondary pairs for cache-flow models where curriculum for life may be realized should be exercised with the movie, *"Regrette rien, you kiddin' me- I've moved up from canned tuna to canned sardines?"* SAR 22.50 May 22 2018. Questions might be raised as to where the MRC acquired confidential information from, in the first place. Who were the physicians involved in the cache transactions, and what have been the actions taken by Drew Hendry thus far to collect testimonials, and to which extent did race or ethnicity play a role in safe guarding the safety of Britons- where we might say a plausible hypothesis generally begins with some observation, which is developed into a rule, which is then tested as a model, to see EXEL 21.41 1:30PM May 21 2018 for the discovery of Pyotr Alexeevich Kropotkin the Russian activist, revolutionary, scientist and philosopher who advocated anarcho-commun ism EXEL 21.38 May 21, 2018.

In the case of the MRC, Pavlo Klimkin was identified as a computer consultant for Mitt Romney FTSE 7633.78, in a reportage by Ian Buruma for Granta Magazine with default set match point going back to the year 1987 of a overloaded ferry boat incident involving 138 passengers with "associated personality disorder," concluding in Indian Oil case (n = 90) as *Severe Associative Dissociative Disorder;* Cho Hyan was identified as a teacher living close to a Kaiser-Permanente Pediatric Facility who could be seen operating a memory stick, with default set match point going back to the year

1987 as a formal approximation of the later association of "associated personality disorder," concluding in PSE&G Long Island case (n = 43) as *Highly Sensitive Delusional Disorder;* and Pak Myang Guk was identified as having a tenancy in common with Mitt Romney, where $50,000.00 was transferred by Mitt Romney, in a deposition given to the Federal Bureau of Investigation – with default set match point going back to the year 1980 in the investigation of a single case of a teenage dugout with "associated personality disorder," concluding in Gazprom case (n = 230) in 2012 as *Highly Sensitive Tardive Dyskinesia* to conclude staging for young and the restless, to honor a busload of Manchester Soccer Club athletes- that would end with a gasoline tanker truck exploding into a fireball, a freeway connector ramp collapsing into a cloud of flames and hot cinder, and more than 160 feet of roadway completely missing from the upper deck, on Oct. 7, 2007 – for the on-location filming of BVSP 40592.09 Feb 5, 2016 *"Lighthouse Café Noir,"* at Marin General, near Tiburon where the reviews ranged from, "Great medical care and good parking," and "Excellent, kind & considerate, un-ruffleable counter staff who's just as good at taking care of patients," and "Once we get the banking logic stratified to itemizations, then we can use the airbus for torque shear," and "Sushi Ran for one, gets a syndicate upgrade with carte blanche for leaf extention," and "You mean he's still working on this?" as a follow up to a full time cost itemization of $162,000.00 not adjusted to inflation (1998) for the Nob Hill Highway.

While there may be double standards for subjects with associative personality disorders and subjects with neurological disorders, Klimkin did not exhibit any symptoms on a half dozen contacts other than of a scab worker used as a ploy for the blue lagoon, a well-known ploy, with established contacts to both W. S. Bot, and M. S. Bot since 2003. In cross-validation testing for fitness, F. S. Coe M.D. at least created the impression that he was aware of what incriminating evidence for a busload of passengers implied, with J. P. Omlette as a character reference over a period of one month (n = 18), where one would have to argue for bigger issues of fraud between health-care provider and enrollees, with BRAC1 –Neg results for M. S. Bot (2000) in file somewhere myriad. At least that's the report filed by Drew Hendry of Scotland Yard, on behalf of families of Manchester United, who requested a legislation for security measures against the People of the United States by the United Kingdom – unless there is prompt response for ballots pro and con, before January 10, 2017. Of the security measures contemplated are complete annexation or blood banking with England, and no future blood banking agreements with Governments of the United Kingdom, other than those which have been signed by K. Perkins MD FRC, with the explicit question of does cholesterol integrate with lipid bilayer as investigational new therapeutic for multiple sclerosis described by HHMI Janelia Farms for H. H. M. Institutes, where <u>Large Cholesterol Granuloma of the Middle Ear Eroding into the Middle Cranial Fossa</u> (Ueda et. al. 2017) was already known. The integration of natural sterols from

Halifax, Canada, musing as waves crashing into rocks, were shown to inhibit copy-number, effectually swift birds dashing into nests at cliff's edge, in eosinophils 24.40 MYGN 11:24AM April 25, 2018 during the development of sickle cell with aryl sulfonase, prior to anti-histamine treatment, for the transformation of granulocytes 28.66 MYGN 2:06 April 25, 2018 from laminin coated eosinophils 28.27 MYGN 9:54 AM April 25, to eosinophils without laminin 28.09 MYGN 10:10 AM, to phytoplanktons 28.43 MYGN 2:30PM April 25, 2018, where the loss of function associated with copy-number replication of eosinophils 13.88 GE 3:00PM April 19, 2018 are copy-number corrected as monocyte nucleation 269.03 10AM April 25, 2018.

On the bright side of W. T. F. Malhotra's cesspool for outer-limits of endurance against 2-Dimentional withdrawal patterns show Associative Personality Disorder segregations according to usage-and-severity and alcohol consumption, weight gain with benzo-diazapine, and 1X Luciferase without withdrawal; stabilization with Anaxonic Codon, Space Capsule, and complete withdrawal; and a photocopy of a Grasshopper with sensitivity issues to Babcock Towers – where WBC is 2.75 fold lower, would suggest a miscarriage due to high sequesterization in the cervical membrane – which is a (+/-) for ignominious related antibodies heavy-chain, and light-chain, as recombinants (n=2) copy–number correction in natural selection as ignominious response to acetylation of cholesterol from air and water, was honored for advocacy efforts, was chosen for his work at the Nash

Foundation, an organization he founded in 1996 to help underprivileged children living in India, where anemia is common among the working class, with a 50% crossover into sickle cell anemia affecting a population of 32 million people, with a mortality rate between ages 37 and 42, and recurrence mortality between the ages of 65 and 70 93.45 SLAB 11:36 AM April 25, 2018. The organization has built seven schools in rural India and championed the cause of literacy around the world, as well as involved local students in the cultural exchange, for developing a curriculum for asymptomatic African Sleeping Sickness, which simulates a similar condition from a very specific type of plasmodium-toxin that is only found in Tsetse flies (and spread though South Sudanese camel caravans in search of frankincense and myrrh to the Euphrates), experimentally different from the malarial toxin, where the physiological commonality is water retention; the sleep cycle is heavy with and without food where the place setting is day or night with lights on and television as sleep disturbance, compared to night only in a dark room without mosquito nets for ten days with average number of mosquitos (n = 20), compared to one day (n = 16). The main component of the anemia is a lowering of blood pressure, accompanied by gastric ululation, and diarrheic cramps, and a strikingly different osmotic potential in renal function different form the slow trickle of sickle cell – which returns us to the beginning of the discussion, where the hypothesis had been posited that, inflammation is a defense reaction against diverse insults, designed to remove noxious agents and to inhibit their detrimental effects (Wyss-coray T, Mucke L. 2002) and that, given the multiple functions of many inflammatory factors, it has been difficult to pinpoint their roles in specific (patho) physiological situations. That should clarify the presentation of patients where inflammation, where renal-actinostenosis is affected, as in the patient H. Weinstein, and the patient C. Paglia, for different reason. In the Case of H. Weinstein, the effect may have been caused by mis-labeled pharmaceutical products (Prilosec) whereas in the case of C. Paglia the effect may have been caused by mis-labeled blood type. The waking periods are short, compared to long (usual), with light perspiration, and without oxidation in urine (no more than usual) and hi-level of hunger, when compared with use of phenol-barbital where the oxidation in urine is substantially high- as rejection hypothesis for sickle cell anemia, indicating that the metabolic need in sickle cell anemia is hyper-attenuated with eating, where the food urgency can cause patients to start throwing things, or yelling insults at deaf people with dumb shit disorders, or no one India syndrome, or there is a tendency to avert food urgency as a source of androgenic plasticity, in the development of glia.

Neurogenin is a known ortholog of a function known as heterochromatin – that means cell division, in eukaryotic cells, typically active in wound healing. Sun et al. (2001) found that in addition to inducing neurogenesis, NGN1 inhibits the differentiation of neural stem cells into astrocytes. While NGN1 promotes neurogenesis by functioning as a transcriptional activator, NGN1 inhibits astrocyte differentiation by sequestering the CREB-binding protein. From study of reporter gene constructs in transgenic mice, (Scardigli et al. 2001) found that expression of Neurog2 in the ventral spinal cord results from the modular activity of at least 3 enhancers that are active in distinct progenitor domains. (Kim et al. 2001) concluded that genetic variability in neurogenin-3 gene does not contribute to the etiology of maturity-onset diabetes of the young or other forms of autosomal dominant diabetes. (Lee et al. 2002) found that glucagon-secreting A cells, somatostatin-secreting D cells, and gastrin-secreting G cells were absent from the epithelium of the glandular stomach of Ngn3 -/- mice, and the number of serotonin-expressing enterochromaffin cells was dramatically decreased. In a patient with congenital malabsorptive diarrhea, (Wang et al. 2006) identified a homozygous missense mutation in the neurogenin-3 gene, predicted to result in an arg107-to-ser (R107S) substitution in the first helix of the protein, which is critical for the activation of downstream genes. The mutation was not identified in 100 control individuals. (Hovanes et al. 2000) transfected humanoid cell lines with a reporter gene construct containing the LEF1 promoter region and observed highest LEF1 expression in mature human T- and B-cell lines. Since the LEF1 gene is not expressed in B lymphocytes, (Hovanes et al. 2000) proposed that expression of LEF1 is normally silenced in B cells by elements not present in the promoter fragment tested. Hematopoietic stem cells (HSCs) have the ability to renew themselves and to give rise to all lineages of the blood (Reya et al 2003) showed that the WNTcatenin signaling pathway has an important role in this process. Overexpression of activated beta-catenin expands the pool of HSCs in long-term cultures by both phenotype and function. Furthermore, HSCs in their normal microenvironment activate a LEF1/TCF reporter, which indicates that HSCs respond to WNT signaling in vivo. Where Endymion tries to establish what is expected to happen then is seen as something of a nature of a series for a homeostasis based on cell count where $3.30189E10/x + 3.52186E12 - 255.354x + 2.87592E6 \, x^2 + x^4$, compared to a nature of a series for function of hematopoietic differentiation can be seen as the integral of $1/162(x^2 - y^4)(y^3 + x^2 + y^2/x) \, dy$. L'équipe scientifique de la mission spatiale Gaia publie, le 25 Mai, le -gigantesque catalogue issu de vingt-deux mois d'observation de ce satellite d'astrométrie développé par l'Agence spatiale européenne. Riche de plus de 1,69 milliard d'étoiles, ce qui représente 1 % de la population stellaire de notre galaxie, ce catalogue est l'ultime descendant de celui que l'astronome grec Claude Ptolémée inséra dans son Almageste au IIe siècle de l'ère chrétienne.

Fondé sur le catalogue établi par l'astronome grec Hipparque quatre siècles plus tôt, le catalogue de Ptolémée fit référence dans les mondes occidental et arabe pendant plus de mille ans. Il comptait 1 022 étoiles dont il indiquait la position céleste et l'éclat apparent. La taille et la qualité des cat-alogues d'étoiles se sont accrues au fil du temps mais ils restèrent longtemps incapables de -décrire fidèlement notre environnement stellaire car il y manquait une information

cruciale : la distance des étoiles. Cette question est longtemps restée irrésolue et polémique car liée à nos re-
présentations du monde. Son œuvre complète, qui les
rassemble au côté de textes posthumes, ne totalise même pas
500 pages. Cela semble bien peu, -comparé aux dizaines de
milliers de -pages d'écrits mathématiques d'Euler ou
-Cauchy. Pourtant, ces textes font de -Riemann l'un des plus
grands mathématiciens de tous les temps. En effet, il
-modifia profondément la manière de concevoir certaines des
notions les plus importantes dans ce domaine.

5. Issue – where Endymion tries to establish modes of thinking – size up what he has learned from a year before – attribute recalcitrance before a peer review – begins the long walk home to face the music of burnt bridges and ashes as the Sirius Galaxy emerges on a whim one winter's day – discovers the enigma of arrival, gaping with festering wounds and boils, and windblown by "nudges and bumps" at a leeds-weed's bucket gone astray – spiraling down as a ghost of Delilah amongst Samson's pillars asphyxiated - ode to joy, to the hymn cycle then, how it was that the inner temple received the counter-intelligence of demonstrates.

As anyone who might enter a lion's den is likely to discover, interpretive values and value interpretation are also known as domain knowledge and knowledge domains. Consider a simplistic analogy. When a lion is hungry, a lion has to eat. As a supposition of *the verb* – to eat – the lion has to know the chase for her prey. As a predicate of *the verb* – to chase – the lion has to have domain knowledge. As a flounce upon the swine, *verb* is taken as a noun to describe an action, state, or occurrence, and forming the main part of the predicate of a sentence, such as hear, become, happen – as Endymion had once imperiled to describe the noun, at the very beginning of our death march into the abyss, with abysmal for knowledge domains of a space jar, as being the most important function in the English language. The skeletal remains of corrals, lapis, quarts, ore, ruby, granite leaves us to wonder about their field of use, where conversely from their point of view discernment is the subject of archeological objective. Effective oil/gas recovery from low-permeability reservoirs requires huge amounts of water to create complex fracture networks; in the remote desert area, water resource is scarce, and thus the recycling and reusing the back-flow fluid collected from the fractured wells is crucial to ensure the sustainable development.

The impact of different dissolved ions on the gelation and cross-linking of guar was firstly studied for choosing the target ions to be shielded. To do so, the original formulation as depicted in the section of Materials was mixed with the following chemicals, respectively: 20000 ppm NaCl, 20000 ppm NaNO3, 500 ppm CaCl2, 500 ppm MgCl2, and 400 ppm FeCl2. Since the original fracturing fluid contained only trace amounts of chloride ions, high chloride ion content in the back-flow fluid was attributed to the dissolved solids from the formation. For the fluid density, it was above the fresh water since sodium nitrate was used as the weighting agent during hydraulic fracturing. Comparing to the original fracturing fluid whose density was 1.30 g/cc, the density of the back-flow fluid decreased with time, indicating the loss of weighting agent into the formation. The mimicked formation brine was injected again into the core sample from the top to the bottom. After the pressure drop across the core sample and the effluent were stabilized, rock permeability was calculated from Darcy's Law.

Similarly, Unconventional oil and gas exploration, represented by the exploration of shale oil and gas, has been a great success in North America recently because of the change in exploration concepts and the development of hydraulic fracturing technology. (Yang et al. 2013) summarized two shale gas accumulation patterns: the Antrim shale gas accumulation pattern in the Michigan Basin (A-pattern) and the Barnett shale gas accumulation pattern in the Delaware Basin (B-pattern). The main feature of the A-pattern is that, from the shallow periphery to the deep Basin, biogenic gas, mixed gas, and thermogenic gas occur in sequence. The results of the permeability tests that lateral permeability was 1–40 times that of the vertical permeability. This indicated the existence of a superior transportation pathway within the shale layers. The Paleozoic marine shale had experienced complex multiperiod tectonic and thermal evolution, and the structural styles are variable which has resulted in the differential enrichment and accumulation of shale gas. Based on the exploration discoveries of shale gas and research progress in relevant geological theory, as well as "source-cap controlling hydrocarbon" theory, the main controlling factors of shale gas enrichment in the Upper Ordovician Formation were compared to the Lower Silurian Formation and its periphery. The above theory played an important role in the evaluation of shale gas under the complex tectonic background. During the Devonian and Carboniferous, periods of uplift and precipitation (erosion) intersected incessantly and little sediment was deposited during that time. As the stress properties of these thrust faults turned from extrusion to extension, the stress of the study area, *influenced by the intrusion of the India-Australian plate onto the Eurasian plate*, developed from extension to extrusion as a Neogene. The core immersion test of Lower Silurian also indicated that shale gas bubbles were mainly from a direction parallel to the plane, and bubbles from directions perpendicular to the plane were only a few, which confirmed that gas in shale layers mainly percolates along the direction parallel to the plane.

On the one hand, shale gas would migrate to the surrounding rock along the direction vertical to the bedding plane. The opening structure would accelerate that process. On the other hand, shale gas would percolate along the bedding plane to both sides of the depression. In this process, a larger amount of shale gas would migrate. Shale gas would migrate to the surrounding rock and most of it would migrate to the outcrop area since the slope is a pathway of shale gas loss. Due to the large fracture in the south of the southern study area, most parts of the gas lost when the extension occurred from Late Cretaceous to Paleogene. Based on the difference between the vertical and lateral permeability and on the immersion test of drilling cores, it was concluded that the shale gas accumulation pattern indicated unforeseen economic advantages to the U.S., and the surrounding areas, for gas and oil procurement.

Whereas the ancient Egyptians of Cairo might have been satisfied in entombing or mummifying the nearest heliocentric or pleotropic cadaver from a road kill, the requirements of the pricipia aren't mutually exclusive to circuit theories, either as a circuit or integrated circuits, where the physical terms are a little over two dozen. Thermodynamic models are not quite the same as Bayes models in the swimming pools of Iceland, compared to the linear models (BDLMs) based on 1-order polynomial function with (a) model monitoring mechanism used to look for possible abnormal data based on BDLMs in Hawaii, where the Polynesian peoples live, (b) combinatorial Bayesian dynamic linear models based on the multiple BDLMs with Polynesian peoples of the Fiji island and their corresponding weights of prediction precision in Iceland compared to Kordofan Plateau, and (c) an effective way of taking advantage of combinatorial Bayesian dynamic linear models to incorporate the historical data and real-time data in structural time-variant reliability prediction- can provide structural performance prediction based on monitored extreme data; and the use of the statistical extremes to the reliability assessment and performance prediction of monitored highway bridges 20000 ppm NaCl, 20000 ppm NaNO3, 500 ppm CaCl2, 500 ppm MgCl2, and 400 ppm FeCl2. It may be difficult to see how these bridges work, in the context of bridges, where CaCl2 is seen as a construction of the Verrazano Narrows Bridge, compared to NaCl which is quite possibly the most complex seen as the construction of the Victoria Falls Bridge, compared to MgCl2 which is accorded the function for the construction of the Golden Gate Bridge, and FeCl2 which is in the range of the long expanse construction of the San Mateo Bridge, where the NaNO3 is a bit like the making of the Thames, based on a draw string like the pajamas where you put your one leg into pajama and then the other leg in the pajama, in what the Chinese who live in Beijing describe as woking, first described in <u>The Spliced Structures of Adenovirus 2 Fiber Message and the Other Late mRNAs</u> (L.T. Chow, T. R. Broker) where the BamHI is presumed to be yz, and the Fiber R loop is presumed to be super-coiled. This raised the possibility that the composite RNA is an intermediate pre-cursor for mature peptide.

The state equation shows changes of the system with time and reflects inner dynamic changes of the system and random disturbances. The observation equation expresses the relationship between the measured data and the current state parameters of the system. For the mass and random monitored extreme data, especially for monitored data at time t -1 and before time t -1, the discretized motion equation and the fitted 1-order polynomial function, which is commonly used for the prediction of the trend data, are adopted to predict future stress data of time t, so the 1-order polynomial function can be applied to properly build the BDLMs. Then for each time t, the BDLMs include the following parameters: $V(t)$ is the variance of monitored errors at time t; $W(t)$ is the variance of state error at time t; $V(t)$ and $W(t)$ are respectively, monitored errors and state errors. It is assumed that error sequences are internally independent, mutually independent, and independent of the relationships between monitored data and state parameters, described in <u>Isolation of the LAC Repressor</u> (W. Gilbert, B. Muller-Hill) where the induction of B-galactosidase is measured in terms of cfu, against the cfu concentrations of IPTG as a measure of 1-order polynomial function.

These are presented as a special case of a general state-space model, being linear and Gaussian, where the presentations satisfy the assumptions of a state-space model, with is a Markov chain, and the changing curves of Bayesian factors with k-criteria. The numerical applications presented, using the monitored extreme data of an existing bridge can illustrate the application and feasibility of hypothesized and naive approaches along with conceptual parameter for the observation and collection of data on a bridge structure during a period of time.

Nadja's foreword, much like circuit theory, is an inspirational motivation drawn from the French surrealist Andre Breton to explore the relationships between physical terms and circuit components; the useability inextricably linked to distributed control systems autonomous of CERN with synergistic functions and dash board appeal. Egregiousness is unlikely to be successful in systematic development of "the scientific process," as neither the funding agencies nor the timing of the market will allow for transaction-led liquidity schemes, where reimbursement policies are over-utilized to expense patients who are part of a study objective, said Prof. S. Hartman. This was to ensure that only those groups where an IRB was approved by the AMA were qualified for clinical initiative. The AMA reviewed and posted the results of three area hospitals in the Congo, where the nearest had failed, the close was seen as inadequate revised-assessment as fail, and the furthest under investigation by the justice department for breach of confidentiality. The criteria for IRB was to show diagnostic criteria for two known classes where the number of samples for each class were more than fifty different patients. The rejection criteria for IRB were hundred samples from the same patient in a day, sixty samples from the same patient on different days, and thirty samples from two patients whose data had already been published. An analogous rejection of situation for public utilities would be the burning down of resistors on paper for reading; and certainly, an analogous rejection of situation for AAAS Science and Nature, would be the sample analysis of police departments for Parkinson's Disease, and victims of car accidents for Alzheimer's.

Cela arrive assez souvent. Many times, ayeun programme de vaccination, par exemple, devient implémentées comme un programme pour la vente de fleurs. Je vais vous donner un exemple, par exemple, un collègue travaillais avec le developpement de vaccins pour la Syphilis à l'Université de Califorie, ahet le personnel pensé qu'il était le cerveau bancaire liquide céphalo-rachidien, et ses voisins pensais qu'il code pour Gazprom, merci.

The Oriental Society has their own way and means in as far as I was able to fathom furlong as a transversions, without need of a homologue, in matters of state as a means of desegregating the aperture from the cesspool of conduits, to create a discernable orthogonalization of mass and momentum in a open system a des fins de divulgation.

The commissions for geo-synchronicity are Machine Intelligence and Quarry Shuttles as a long term object-tifications of orbital diorama and galactic dromedaries, could only be persuaded thus by FTE free, and bulk discounts, said P. Samuels, where the value for every FTE was commensurable in insurance re-imbursements or co-pay as a means to assure a proper partnership between health insurance provider and health care provider before supplice-ation to the NIH for materials and methods, where the area-of-use would define the budget and the institutional cost-overhead, since the institutional cost-overhead are directly proportional to patient traffic in a hospital, and salaries are inversely proportional to client specialization. Sad as it may sound, the cost analysis is analogous to drug trials which are rejected for their contra-indication, and similar to burning down resistors on paper for reading, as is the case with glucosamine and metoprolol succinate infamous as the blockbuster novel Great Again, where both are metabolites of the processes of Sickle Cell, Sickle Cell Anemia, Alzheimer's, and Parkinson's Disease. With no further discussion toward funding and/or filing date for a clinical trial or guidance, the evaluation proceeding found the samples mis-labeled, with the succinate containing the amine group, and the glucose containing the prolyl group, and the recommendation to the manufacturer of manuf-acturing defect and cancellation of NIH consensus for

ALS – as a possible source of sample contamination, with possible implication for wrongful arrests and detentions of 156 accusers, in a Michigan courtroom Friday 19, January 2018, described as "degrading." The interpretation of Multiple Sclerosis as Carpel Tunnel is perhaps the earliest recorded indicator of a bizarre level of incomprehension in the Congo, quite unlike where funding organizations would feel comfortable making investments without demonstrated IRBs in areas of fallacies.

Waybbeit, what's he saying the hare?

About Syphilis, you mean?

Know, I honorstan dabit, I toking about the Oriental Society ansuch, the bannon CERN.

Well, it's a trifle difficult to explain really, because of the nature versus nurture duality.

Trifle difficult to ache spleen bayos of the dual latte?

Permettez-moi. Vous voyez un est nominal et l'autre est quadrilinéaire. Aussi simple que cela.

Ce qui est un qui a à voir avec la Syphilis?

Well it's a disease really, depending on the volumes of bourbon which one might tarrif as a way of discovering harmony.

Il est au sujet de la grenouille, peut-être que c'est la confusion.

La grenouille, comme dans le tour sauvage?

Viral and cellular src genes contribute to the structure of recovered avian sarcoma virus transforming genes (R. Karess, H. Hanafusa 1981) actually hypothesizes, with experimental data, that the structure-function relationship of the src gene can be transformed by 6-bromo-uridine, to create base-pair deletions from a point mutation in the 5' 4-6bp direct repeats of the Exon for the inverted repeats of the transposable element (31bp) for the transposon src, where sequence analysis showed complete deletion of the gene, because the synthesis for transposase mRNA is controlled by repressor, coded by the transposon src. The data also showed that the repressor catalyzes the site-specific mutagenesis cross-over step [resolution] which terminates the transposition.

Assuming the human genome is universal to human beings, the chance for such transposition could occur in any population, and since the experiments were performed, we have tried to identify the anatomical differences between what would be described as c-src compared with v-src, the differences being that c-src causes blindness, and v-src causes respiratory failure, both of which are quite common in elderly populations, as would be defined by lensing requirements, or brief periods of unconsciousness.

That sheds a different sort of light, as any conscious observer might [resolve] on the nature of the cardio-pulmonary system, where once upon a time doctors might have used car jumper cables to restart the heart, or broken a few ribs to pump the lung. They are two different systems, might be another way of saying that cardiovascular and pulmonary can be physiologically dis-integrated as a means of re-computing allocations for HB, and HD.

As aside, one code add that his treacheries can be lomped into one, hmm, how should I put this, splatter of dour traits with nested equivocations expected of a petty clerk forced to work at a dank swamp of abysmal intellect consisting of pedal pushers who intends to get even with the lot. Hence, the lot symmetry veritably perched upon a Zimbabwayin demonstration of a Bengali dial manages to expropriate the voyage.

As any entering physician at the Imperial College of Medicine would say, you had to check your bags in at the door from Dorset County (that's similar to St. Eligius Boston Nightmare Medical Center, where it's difficult to diagnose what's wrong with the patients n = 48), and Royal Bournemouth and Christchurch Hospital (that's similar to Columbia Haunted Mansion of Physicians and Surgeons, where it's difficult to come to a decision about what to do about the patient n = 21) answer a few questions to get certified by the administration for use of profile orienting biomarkers.

Yes, right, that's um, quite appropriate as it is. Perhaps we could add a few odd details around the um tryptic, you know, the ramifications being, well, oddly enough, funny you should mention that, ah yes, the ketchup with the omelet, in order to clarify any misunderstanding we might have created, such as they might have been interpreted wrongly, misjudged our motives, as it were, in possibly acquiring any of the programs developed at CERN. The Oriental Society meeting was quite clear on that purpose, I thought, including rejection of materials from institutional purveyors of programs developed at CERN for positron electron tomographies for biomarkers, where a stepwise progressive model was used to co-cluster patients and subjects, where the approach to understanding subjects is though observation, consultation, and interaction, to develop a criteria model for organelle dysfunction, compared to patients where we try to interpret how patient might respond to chemicals based on organelles hypothesis, before inter-vention, where we can certainly effect progress, by generalizing on the differences between the cardio-vascular, and pulmonary systems, by asking how do the Japanese expropriate keto-aldolase, SBUX 62.62 May 31 2018? compared to how is glyceraldehyde-3-phoshate expropriated SBUX 61.69 Jan 23, 2018? and how many kilo joules are in an ounce of fructose-6-phosphate SBUX 54.36 Aug 25, 2017? as a cell based model, where their mechanism of action can be measured using a doppler for cardio-vascular and pulmonary function for primary screen of subjects for physicians references CRAY 27.40 May 4, 2018, secondary screen for clinical qualification of subjects CRAY 27.50 May 4, 2018, and panel review of eighteen profile orienting biomarkers CRAY 27.58 May 4, 2018. The findings for all three , Safety and Mosquitocidal Efficacy of High-Dose Ivermectin When co-Administered with Dihydro-artemisinin-piperaquine in Kenyan adults with Uncomplicated Malaria (IVERMAL): a Randomised, Double-Blind, Placebo-controlled Trial (Lancet, Infectious Diseases, 2018), Tiotropium and olodaterol in the prevention of chronic obstructive pulmonary disease exacerbations (DYNAGITO): a double-blind, randomised, parallel-group, active-controlled trial (Lancet Respiratory Medicine, 2018) and Effect of Atropine with Propofol versus Atropine with Atracurium and Sufentanil on Oxygen Desaturation requiring non-emergency intubation: A randomized clinical trial (PRETTINEO] (JAMA, Original Investigation, 2018), in As Needed Budesonide-Formoterol Versus Maintenance Budesonide in Mild Asthma (NEJM, 2018) where the hazards ratio between the three metabolic systems was elucidated as 0.96, with a CI of 0.05 to 0.15 of 95%.

The Bourbons have taken a syllogistic position at the second and shan't be of use in the endeavors, pursuits as such in the endeavors odderanas in an emissary capacity for course development, enlightenment intensives, fonk, and clairvo-yance, eswot i knoted from the desk cushions for nursery rhymes. Where a patient say, might be at a hazard of (0.96), then improve to a hazard of [27.8] might seem a challenge towards the establishment for development of skills, which might be the wrong word here- but certainly, aptitude that's coherent with further improvements in hazard score to (32.7), requiring additional propensity, for tackling the hazards around 12.75 – where we would have to know, as in the example illustrated, the dosage and drug sequence, for each patient, where disgruntled California surfers living at a motor lodge next to sewer main are likely to say, dude, I can't take much more of this shit, the Sandpiper Inn at Stinson Beach being far from pumping gas at Costco for a hazard score of [*17.3*] or dude, I need to bail, working as a bartender at the Beach Motel on Judah being far from writing jingles for satchii and satchii [*13.2*], for which the Oracle of Delphi should be considered 45.93 as the serum response element, for such reasons which may not be obviously recognized as childhood Leukemia, until much later in life, as it happened in the case of Joey Armstrong who, in all appearances seemed as if he'd just started high school, when he moved into my studio in Hayes Valley, when I was scouting for a place to live in Oakland and suddenly remembered the frontage where I used to live as a four year old, which happened to be the place where he was living before moving to Hayes Valley. By this time I had surveyed about seventy patients and subjects, while stoking the anti-ig antibody for cyclosporine with vitamin D and anorexia where the general idea is to eat once a day to develop the traits for brain cancer, and the medical objective is to dis-regulate pulse from the mode I had been accustomed to since becoming interested in doppler, around the same time as learning to play tennis.

Soon after moving to Hayes Valley, I began seeing Bradley Newell at the Fat Tire Bar, in the Inner Richmond, where the grim situation late in the afternoon could only be described as lying down naked on polished steel after appearing optimistic at the Beach Chalet during the period of _Benign-Malignant Tumors Case Studies of Patient Duplication on HYW 101_, which is where I met Shirley Manson at Ireland's 32 on a weekly basis about the movie Truly, Madly, Deeply. Bradley was a major cook, at the time, working in fryers. Late in the day, sometimes you could watch him walk with his board to the Ocean, swim past the shallow wakes to the surf line. As a wave came in they would mount the board as easily as an eagle swooping to the ground to pick up its prey, with their left foot in front and right heel aligned, back against the falling crest. Anywhere from seventeen to thirty being on the surf line, maybe four or five could get a ride. The turning point happened soon after Britney Spears began to recover. The period would suggest a cycle of fifteen months. This is around the same time when Barack Obama arrived in a Limousine, as a figurative demonstration of why the word cadaverous sounds like cardboard. In those days people hadn't any idea of differences between _recombinases_. Most of the insurance companies were just happy to see sodium valproate get out of the limousine. Though there are some acute differences between Type I and Type II for Diabetes Metellus these were after-thoughts in trying to figure how get the cadaver out of the Columbia Haunted Mansion for Physicians and Surgeons, where most of the inhabitants were either Norwegian or Swedish, by which I mean that Type I and Type II are co-morbid conditions for the majority of Norwegian and Swedish patients. When I began looking into the area in 1984, with a pair of adults instructors, named Peterson and Hausman, from the St. Eligius Boston Medical Center, because they exhibited characteristic traits of AML and ALL, with some differential in the amount of eyeliner or eye makeup that they would use to cover up their dilemma, to stress the fact that I was a bit like this and a bit like that. When I saw Petersen again in the 2003, of the hundred and thirty and some odd samples, I was intrigued by which ones would be of the Wild Turkey experiment, where Amber Rudd and Ian Murray picked me off the street, as way of saying, concerned with or relating to the relation-ship between a feudal superior and a vassal, must be what "liege" means with the implied us, being the Boston Medical Center as contact base for cohorts in the U.S., for the Imperial College of Medicine, for which neither the patients or subjects, are in tandem due to the large émigré population in National Health Services, who suffer from Type I or Type II Diabetes Metellus, which is different from Associated Personality Disorders Type I, and Type II. In which capacity Barack Obama could provide intelligence might be another way to look at the intrigue, of As Needed Budesonide-Formoterol Versus Maintenance Budesonide in Mild Asthma (NEJM, 2018) where the spice trades of the émigré population are counter-productive with Budesonide, and the rice freights of the émigré population are counter-productive with Formoterol, which are the cause of early indications of Type I and Type II Diabetes Metellus *in children* among émigré population in National Health

Services. Batshit is a bad contact for various reasons besides being non-compliant with British and Australian securities exchanges for any form of economic facilitation, correspond-dence, or communication. Our concern is that Batshit may be moving towards a Treblinka type massacre in the Hacken-sack area in the U.S., after its Auschwitz type massacres in the Pennington area, and Pristina type massacres in the New Hope area. While we can extend our condolence to U.S. residents living in those areas as an intelligence brief, we would also extend a caution against interference in British Australian affairs.

Molecular Mechanism for Autophagy in Yeast (2016) being more of a dark knight 29925.61 in quantum field surveys for disability to translate Saccharomyces cerevisiae as a result of being buried without an autopsy report, while failure to establish cause of death, might be seen as the mechanism of a transposon, which existed in a little more than of 2/3 of the non-random population of first year medical students – which may be of concern due to their diversified practice settings in National Health Services, where we might consider streptomycin as a palliative instead of Zantac, though this could severely impact the parliamentary budget for full costume dramas, with finger painting for stickies' as the backdrop.

It can take two to six months; in severe cases, where the patient is simply abandoned on the side walk, the recovery can take up to year to clean up. Ian McKellen in that regard was quite possibly the worst case scenario for c-src, where he did not have any obvious difficulty in playing a silver flute, and did not have trouble with adventure foods such as fried chicken, and tandoori grills. Though he had considerable troubles in self-management, his social skills were attractive. The problem with c-src is morbidity, where unless there is a motivation to do something, the patient becomes bed ridden. These indications, along with progressive blindness, are quite different from Leukemia, and Lymphoma, and ALS, even though in hazards c-src and v-src associated vascular dementia overlaps multiple sclerosis.

When I first began reading Salt, I remember it being a fairly sunny day in Boston in 1987, as I tried to imagine *The Rock* sitting on the window sill of my apartment on Mountfort Street, as I had become bored with its colorless poster size appeal against the pink cinderblock for a year, and a marine cinderblock for another year, with the corn-on-the-cob lady little bit to the left, and fourty-eight ignominious subjects living on two floors – the personification struck me as something which I could savor. I brought the rock in Spanish Catalonia – began the article, presumably a journal of one of those high minded literary types who deal in drugs – in the rundown hillside mining town of Cardona – I was assured of quality. As a narcotics trader in those days, I was apprehensive of skunk weed, tea leaves, and sage, mucking up the data with alkaloids, compared to say sativa, coffee, and basil. An irregular pink trapezoid with elongated, curved indentations etched on its surface by raindrops, it had an odd trans-lucence and appeared to be a cross between rose quarts and soap – which is where my antenna went up for televised narratives about *The Rock* between St. Elsewhere and Falcon Crest, there were people who knew about this! - as I had renovated my new surroundings with posters of rock bands, Genesis, the Police, and U2. So far so good, as I could dream on about the description of *The Rock* being on the window sill of the kitchen, I moved the rock to the window in my room, to see if it worked their, yes, no problem, then I moved *The Rock* over to the bay window of the recreation room, and yes, *The Rock* was as real as the window sills, in the middle of the afternoon. Then the introduction became more palatable, as one might imagine a Picasso, or a Modigliani, squeeze blobs of paint right onto a canvas. The resemblance to soap came from the fact that it dissolved in water and its edges were worn smooth like a used soap bar. I paid too much for it – nearly fifteen dollars – and for what, I asked myself, burning down resistors for writing papers. But it was, after all, despite a rosy blush of magnesium, almost pure salt, a piece of the famous salt mountain of Cardona. The various families that had occupied the castle atop the net mountain had garnered centuries of wealth from such rock.

I took it home and kept it on a windowsill. One day it got rained on, and white salt crystals started appearing on the pink. My rock was starting to look like salt, which would ruin its mystique. So I rinsed off the crystals with water. Good point, Sydney I think I'll go and spray on some Chloraseptic, at this point. Then I spent fifteen minutes patting the rock dry. By the next day it was sitting in a puddle of brine that that had leached out of the rock. After a few hours, square white crystals began to appear in the puddle. Solar evaporation was turning brine into salt crystals.

In *The Glow of Herring and the Scent of Conquest,* when Sydney begins by pontificating more on the matter, with attributions to the nature, in 1268 and possibly earlier, when a new technique was used to mine rock salt, the object art becomes more of a paper trail to the patients. Instead of miners carrying chunks of rock out steep shafts in baskets slung on their backs, and then crushing the rock into salt, water was piped into the dug-out vein of rock salt, where eventually the idea became more of a sophisticated system known in the Salzkammergut as sinkwerken. A sinkwerk was an underground work area in which the surrounding salt and clay were mixed with water in large wooden tanks. The solution then moved down wooden pipes to boiling pans.

Wik was unexpectedly good at understanding what that meant, where after the mid-afternoon had passed, Wik conducted several tests with his colleagues on a few occasions, explaining that by stroking the pencils in turn he perceived a gamut of "stingles," special sensations somehow allied to the tingling after-effects of one's skin contact with stinging nettles (he had been raised in the country somewhere between Ormagh and Armagh, and had often tumbled, in this adventurous boyhood, the poor thick-booted soul, into ditches and even ravines, and spoke eerily of the strong green stingle of a piece of blotting paper or the wet weak pink stingle of nurse Langford's perspiring nose, these colors being checked by himself against those applied by the researchers to the initial pencils. In results of the tests, one was forced to assume that the man's fingertips could convey to his brain "a tactile transcription of prismatic specter," as Paar put it in his detailed report to Van.

What was the fetching price for one of those cabbages, if you don't mind me asking?

The probabilities for observing cabbages laterally along the azimuths +79°26'09" to +258°47'07" cost about 2.2 to 2.73 shells for the probability density of the derivative form of the equation $(x + 3)/(n - 1)$ of the NASDAQ Index 7425.96, May 23 2016.

Sea shells sea shells on the sea shore, is quite well imagined as far as I have been able to discern, with roots going back to the extreme 5' end which can hybridize to the three leader sequences.

The probabilities for observing cabbages transversely along the azimuths +79°26'09" to +258°47'07" cost about 7.3 to 8.1 shells for the probability density of the derivative form of the equation$(x - 10)(x + 3)/(n - 1)e^{13}$ of the DJIA Index 24886.81, May 23 2016.

Mary had a little lamb, is quite well imagine as far as I have

been able to delineate from the majority of the 3' ends of Ad2 mRNAs synthesized from the R strand which have five sites, one of which is called Xbo I, which will leave a smear (Ziff and Frazer 1978) if you run it at about 30mV for ten hours.

Just goes to show what socialist party people are likely to be doing at three in the morning.

True and yet, it's really the part where the socialist party people are likely to skip the morning classes which is enlightening. Chow et. al. 1977b on the other hand is a HaeIII, if you can understand their implied logic for the protection assays included in tube numbers for sedimentation of repressor (W. Gilbert B. Muller-Hill 1966)

The probabilities for observing cabbages conversely along the azimuths $+210°08'32"$ to $+60°10'17"$ cost about 2.2 to 2.73 shells for the probability density of the derivative form of the equation$(x + 3)/(n - 1)$ of the FTSE Index 7788.44, May 23 2016.

Jack and Jill, is quite well imagine as far as I have been able to see from the experimental details where in a few examples RNA-DNA heterodulexes were observed, with attempts to cleave with EcoRII in the famous scientific work of (Nevins and Darnell) where the isoschizomer makes multiple attempts to understand migratory behaviour.

The probabilities for observing cabbages as a circumspection along the azimuths +68°39'29 to +148°51'48" cost about 2.2 to 2.73 shells for the probability density of the distributions of the equation $(x + 3)/(n -1)e^{27}$ of the AORD Index 6128.90, May 23 2016.

Peter Piper, is quite well imagined as far as I have been able to see from the experimental data for 5' termini to additional transcripts mapped by hybridization to single-stranded DNA by the Department of Radiophysics, in <u>The Binding of a Transcription Factor to Deletion Mutants of a 5S Ribosomal RNA Gene</u> (D. Brown, B. Roeder).

Sham studies which are comparable to these fallacies were shown to have successful outcomes in patients S. Lourdes and W. Johnston with the Swiss Federal Institute approved drug Rentinol™ which is composed of one bottle of Makers Mark or Knob Creek every day, or in a controlled study where the Rentinol™ was prepared with two bottles of Taka Vodka fresh lime juice and mint leaves – as a comparable for subjects N. Pilosi and D. Feinstein. Whereas in the case of S. Lourdes, there was no observable progression in the development of memory, due to the fact that Synchrotron Radiation had already reached peak levels, development of memory in W. Johnston appeared to improve with the formal analysis of cohort subject, Dawn H. The genetics of W. Johnston compares with D. Hunter., as a specific karyotype in the fourteenth chromosome with extenuating regulatory element MIP. (Irving et al. 1990) identified human homologs of MIP-1-alpha (182283) and MIP-1-beta, designating them

464.1 and 744.1, respectively. They stated that the 2 genes demonstrate parallel regulation following activation of T cells with various mitogens and encode proteins that share 55% sequence similarity. The 464.1 and 744.1 genes are separated by 14 kb in the genome, and are arranged in a head-to-head fashion. In the case of W. Johnston, the karyotype for the fourth chromosome was later resolved from D. Hunter to the aquaporins (AQPs) which are a family of small integral membrane proteins related to the major intrinsic protein (MIP, or AQP0; 154050) of the lens which (Ma et al. 1996) isolated a cDNA by degenerate PCR from a human kidney cDNA library that is related to AQP2 (107777), where the predicted 282-amino acid AQP2L protein is 52% identical to AQP2 and 48% identical to MIP, suggesting chromosomal translocation, with aging. By linkage mapping, (Sherrington et al. 1995) defined a minimal co-segregating region containing the candidate gene for early-onset Alzheimer disease type 3 (AD3; 607822), which had been linked to chromosome 14q24.3, from which full-length cDNA clone was isolated using Dynamite at various thresholds to offices of the North Carolina Biological Supplies in Bethesda, Maryland, for the isolation of the PS1 protein, known as *presenilin-1*. Since during neo-natal development, *presenilin-1* is known to be the ignominious marker for breast milk rejection from surrogate pregnancies which present with acute diaper rash, the development of memory with Rentinol™ is equally likely to be the nearest indogenous homo-morphic translocation of mip homologues – which is a striking conclusion for how we might think about proofs of concept for opium, and hashish.

Back when, when we started such enterprises as which would become, eventually how the scientific communities describe the Human Genome, the DJIA was about $26.00 listed as Ethyl Corp and fell to $16.00 in three months when the SEC got wind of the ploy; nevermind that we said let's be adventurous and seeing that the NASDAQ was about $2.50 listed as Genex, we cut our losses and booked a flight straight to hell fire missiles at $0.15 in two weeks, with no money left on the meal plan, which is how we ended up at Janet Yellen's home in Providence as part of the Oxfam refugee crisis program for sandwiches to go, and large spreads of manicotti, stuffed pasta shells, baked rabbit, cannoli, wine, and vodka, for an entire weekend. Though her parents worked as tailors, and barely spoke any English, they were warm and doting in the middle of a very cold winter, when we suddenly glimpsed a world outside the bizarre fantasy in which we wasted our youth, as we walked a few blocks over soot layered plowed snow to the supermarket to buy cigarettes.

From a different perspective, if we are to refurbish the function of Aryl Sulfonase, differently than Acetylcholine, then we have to consider the products starting from Exon 4 5', Exon 6 5', and Exon 6 3', where patients v-src and c-src patients are (+/-) controls erb-b and erb-b2 patients are (-/+) controls while erb-b3 patients are (+/+) controls, and p16 patients are (-/-) controls and p53 patients are (+/-) controls, as a way to get a firm understanding of the catch phrase, "*We are close working partners with Imperial College Health Partners,*" where we consider the product glycosylation as function of structural DNA and protein folding as efficacy, as a function of ethyl-amine, where the receptor kinetics for the functional assays of platelet counts, WBC, and basophils, are attributable to Lenhart Minthon, where in the late seventeenth century, when coal prospectors drilled into the Cheshire earth and found rock salt.

If you think about it, as I have thought about it, there are various sort of people, the people dying to say something meaningful, ninety percent of which begins with *here lies*, people dying to create something meaningful, *the one percent who will eat the gall bladder of a blow fish*, then the people dying to write something meaningful, *the two percent who will drink the venom of a rattle-snake*, then the people dying to see something meaningful, *the three percent who will drink the venom of a black cobra*, and then you have the only one, Lenhart Minthon, *dying for the truth.*

Before I can explain how metaphors are different from similes, explained Mr. Newton, (Costanzo et al. 2001) cloned Xenopus Mre11 and studied its role in DNA replication and DNA damage checkpoint in cell-free extracts Use of LSD in Psychotherapy, Transactions of a Conference on Lysergic Acid Diethylamide (LSD-25, April 22, 23, 24, 1059 Princeton NJ (JAMA Dec. 10, 1960) where the cases used were Alexi Martin, and Nicola Martin, where DSBs stimulated the phosphorylation and 3-prime-to-5-prime exonuclease activity of the Mre11 in <u>Influence of Hyaluronan-CD44 interaction on Topoisomerase II activity and etoposide cytotoxicity in head and neck cancer</u> (JAMA March 1, 2007) where the case used was Linda Evans, in a complex for diploidy in homozygotes, turn it into haplotype mutants from northern Europe, <u>Measurement of Topoisomerase II mediated Decatenation Activity</u> (JAMA March 1, 2007), where the case Dennis Purcell requested an investigation into the custodial rights for Pierre Martin and Arya Safa, rendering a single-copy for the parental chromosome available in wing-dings and zapf-fonts, regardless of the business incubator, and the department of business development, leaving us to wonder if Larry Hagman and Bawbwa Stanwick might be avant guard for controlling interest in Dynasty, <u>Primidone Therapy for Essential Vocal Tremors</u> (JAMA Feb. 1, 2016) where, Ronald Reagan, during his first four years in office was (+/+) for p53 patients, and then in his next four years in office (+/-) for erb-b2.

Which is to say, ineluctably, sociologically, morphologically, and psychologically, the gravitational collapse is dialectical, a peu près de la même manière qu'une batterie de tige de carbone s'échappe, en tandem, du distal au proximal, comme dans la variance, with the distal in appearance more proxymal, and the proximal ever less proximal.

We do know when, that is, the Earth ran into B-linear. The buzz feed at ESRF pointed to a paramagnetic dipole on July

12, 2016, for a decision to go AIRP on Feb 15, 2017, with a knot at PERDU on Jan 30, 2017, and a FOD on Jan 12, 2017. Which are observable phenomenologies.

When we look at an example of thalamocortical exocytosis as a function of Apo E, where we describe the action potentials calculated as 0.63 for Exon 4 5' compared to 45203.33 at Exon 6 3', compared to 7836.64 for Exon 6 5' for the range of Apo E 6.9, 8.3, 8.7 the standard deviation can be +/- 1.4. In Extracorporeal Membrane Oxygenation for Severe Acute Respiratory Distress Syndrome (NEJM May, 2018) at 60 days, 44 of 124 patients (35%) in the ECMO group and 57 of 125 (46%) in the control group had died (relative risk, 0.76; 95% confidence interval [CI], 0.55 to 1.04; P=0.09). Crossover to ECMO occurred a mean (±SD) of 6.5±9.7 days after randomization in 35 patients (28%) in the control group, with 20 of these patients (57%) dying. When we compare these to an example of thalamocortical exocytosis as a function of quenching Faraday, where we describe the action potentials calculated as 0.69 for Exon 4 5' compared to 49495.32 at Exon 6 3', compared to 8580.72 for Exon 6 5' for the range of Faradays 21674.85, 118620.05, 216691.29 the standard deviation can be +/-195016.43. In Trial of Solanezumab for Mild Dementia Due to Alzheimer's Disease (NEJM May, 2018). The mean change from baseline in the ADAS-cog14 score was 6.65 in the solanezumab group and 7.44 in the placebo group, with no significant between-group difference at week 80 (difference, −0.80; 95% confidence interval, −1.73 to 0.14; P=0.10) where a total of 2129 patients were enrolled, of whom 1057 were assigned to receive solanezumab and 1072 to receive placebo. Our understanding of these measures for placebo, emerged from the Use of the Thyroid Hormone Analogue Eprotirome in Statin-Treated Dyslipidemia (NEJM March, 2010) , where we found that the transient elevations in hepatocellular enzyme levels seen with combined eprotirome and statin therapy are similar to those known to occur with other lipid-lowering drugs targeting the liver, such as statins alone, fibrates, and niacin.

When we look at an example of thalamocortical exocytosis as a function of quenching Faraday, where we describe the action potentials calculated as 0.69 for Exon 4 5' compared to 49495.32 at Exon 6 3', compared to 8580.72 for Exon 6 5' for the range of thalamocortical responses 0.011679093, 412847.8256, 140427.91 the standard deviation can be +/- 140427.89. In Effect of Atropine With Propofol vs Atropine with Atracurium and Sufentanil on Oxygen De-saturation in Neonates Requiring Nonemergency Intubation of 89 infants, 53 (59.6%) in the atropine-propofol group vs 54 of 82 (65.9%) in the atropine-atracurium-sufentanil group achieved the primary outcome (adjusted RD, −6.4; 95% CI, −21.0 to 8.1; P = .38). The atropine-propofol group had a longer mean procedure duration than did the atropine-atracurium-sufentanil group (adjusted RD, 1.7 minutes; 95% CI, 0.1-3.3 minutes; P = .04). The example isn't as beautifully clarified as the data in which the author dissociates the standard deviation as 20.6% atropine-propofol group had head ultrasound scans that showed worsening intracranial hemorrhaging (any or increased intraventricular hemorrhage) in the 7 days after randomization vs 17.6% in the atropine-atracurium-sufentanil group (adjusted RD, 1.2; 95% CI, −13.1 to 15.5, P = .87).

When we look at an example of masking, what we are really saying is the likelihood scenarios for serum concentrations, the art for which had been elucidated in 1987 at the Roche Institute of Molecular Biology as a collaboration with Memorial Sloan Kettering, as well as, the function of quenching for RBC in <u>Mutations and Treatment Outcome in Cytogenetically Normal Acute Myeloid Leukemia</u> (S. Froling, Andrea Corbacioglu NEJM May, 2008) where we might be able to make an exception for inclusion in a clinical trial with a single payer healthcare system, limited to Small Cell Leukemia, where the inclusion criteria for patients are stratified for Van, there being a "higher" incidence of Hairy Cell Leukemia in the English population compared to Canada.

For both autologous and allogenic transplantation, said Van, a conditioning regimen of total body irradiation of 12 to 14.4 Gy, or oral busulfan 16mg per kilogram of body weight, followed by intravenous cyclophosphamide, with payroll stubs was recommended, as M. I. Procofol D.Sc. was quite sure of the confidence interval for the genotype for Small Cell Leukemia was 1.56 CI 1.00 to 2.43, compared to Hairy Cell Leukemia 0.48 CI 0.3 to 0.75 compared to oral busulfan, 0.44 CI 0.32 to 0.61.

When we then compare the RBCs for Exon 4 5' 13.31 to Exon 6 5' 66.08 and Exon 6 3' 110.15, as a function of masking in brain cancer, 21674.85, 118620.05, 216691.29, compared to quenching 0.0831, 0.4235, 0.6948, what we are saying is that Bovine-4N acts as the suppressor to confer streptomycin-resistance, cyclosporine-resistance, and penicillin-resistance, while aryl-sulfonase confers sensitivity to the extent where dosage and duration determine the outcome sensitivities for streptomycin, cyclosporine, and penicillin, with the pre-condition for the Evolution for Small Molecule Therapeutics Targeting Sickle Cell Vasculopathy (G. Kato, M. Gladwin JAMA, Dec, 2008) as a positive-enhancer for cyclosporine.

While some physicians and clinicians of the certification class of 1987 of the Imperial College can be adventurous in prescribing themselves into diseases for reasons which are important, competing for grave plots in Hyde Park is no way to rebel against a healthcare system, corrupt references, and medical text which are non-sense, outdated. In part, our problems with that genera of medical science, began with leaving behind the sanatorium management style of medical practices of the 1900s implemented during the Blair government to pioneer an area we define as molecular medicine, where unless a patient is suffering from an injury, the longest a patient is allowed to stay at hospital, is overnight, the cost-burden for insurance and quality care in a single-payer system being next to tsunami in Tohoku, where the budget for the healthcare system appeared to have been pulverized by wait-listers. Instead, molecular medicine, created the flight-insurance model, where an airline in the NHS system has to insure passengers for transit within sixteen hours WEIR 2211.00 8:20AM June 1, 2018, except for difficult pregnancies and serious injuries WEIR 2222.00 June 1, 2018. It wasn't at all that the bankruptcy of the NHS budget had been caused by wait-listers, or NHS hospitals treating patients over a course of months, where Prime Minister Blair is at least one of the survivors of Hospital culinary for 438 days fare for the battle against Hairy Cell Leukemia in 1994 but for various conditions which lead to the annexation WEIR 2118.00 April 18, 2018, and certainly the limit imposed by one treatment model did not facilitate disease progression or diverse umbrage of how then cancer was viewed as an *oncological* matter, where we are able to visualize today as a *décolletage*, where cluster vector of patients for Multiple Sclerosis, by which we mean to define the severity of a patient with Multiple Sclerosis with scaler Hu-MAB products for ALS are seen as an organelle system, a joint venture in differentiation, suppression, growth, and auto-taxis, *rec c-*, as opposed to chemo-taxis, *rec a-*, where the cluster vector of patients with Diabetes Metellus I which includes conditions such as T-cell leukemia, thrombocyte-penia, with scaler products of Diabetes Metellus II pancreatic B-cell Hu-MAB, human monoclonal-antibodies. As a first year student might say, if you don't understand that, there is slim chance of getting out of med school into the catastrophic areas where Cluster Vector (patients) for polyneuro-pathies such as ALL, AML, non-Hodgkins Lymphoma with scaler products of Small Cell Leukemia Hu- MAB,

as a way to understand the morphological concate-
nation with cell biology, the developmental condition for *rec BC-* , where the cell determines the fate of the organelles, based on genetic sensitivities and resistances codes for allopathic variability, and the susceptibilities are defined as either super-coiled or un-cut. Where Cluster Vector (patients) for ALS including Hodgkin's lymphoma, brain cancer, anemia are seen through the lens of scaler products for Sickle Cell Anemia Hu-MAB, we develop our understanding for treatment of *rec a+* as a transgenic-orthologue, where the susceptibilities are defined as linear, and the fate of organelles are determined by genetic resistances codes, as way of putting humpty-dumpty back together again. Where one might imagine, that Hanif Tariq FRC had drunk himself into a ALS, the situation is much more likely to have been a simple enough project with penicillin, at the outset, where he would have intended to have selected against IL-1 in order to knock-down the expression of spingomyelins in the cell which are know to be the cause of migraines, typically experienced in consecutive days or continuous days, which could explain the instance on the flight when we were sitting next to each other, when Lewy Body suddenly burst forth in providing data points for IL-1 *cis-acting trans-gene*, nor uncommon throughout childhood, associated with migraines, where the outputs are usually protoplasts (clear) or bile (yellow). One of the key notes for people who suffer from migraines therefore being food avoidance, which would explain the weight-loss when we met near time square. In Guantanamo, the U.S. government was known to have

experimented with fumigating prisoners from Afghanistan with pure sodium nitrate for two weeks, and recurrent cyclo-chloro-hexane, as inhalant therapy for ALS patients in an effort to rid the world of the jail yard, which is different from its use of nitrous-oxide in buoyancy testing, otherwise know as water-boarding practices for dampers.

The jail yard is then where the Spanish prisoners live, from Afghanistan?

It's less of a live, and more of a sustenance, where understanding the yard, is as important as the jail we live in.

Sad, that is – like watching a piano sit out in the rain.

Our facetiousness is thusly rewarded.

How so?

Terrible as this may seem.

Be Frank.

I put the bottom of the eighth note on the side of the Jail Yard, as a warped path for Lefty O'Doul's little sonatas – as incomprehensible as they may seem yet!

On the other hand, the advantages are fair to understand the progress we could make in techno, electronica, and trance, where we might make super-attenuations from Lefty O'Doul's solstices with a harpoon where, I'm drowning in sorrows, guilt or remorse 8178.946767 might become more uplifting by way of a quaint little foot step -0.231682774.

For the most part, when we listen to Chopin the note progressions are reversed as one could say if you were to think of a piano as having a side, near where the Em4th strikes a chord.

Would you say that could resonate in Gm2nd, where organists play choir ensembles, as a way to think about how voice develops over time.

Chopin doesn't really play in Gm, because he is a Basque, nationalist, searching for independence from Spain.

You don't say. When I was working at the Jail Yard for a year, that's all I heard about, Basque people this, and Basque people that, where you have to wonder about how the polar-ization of political debate over Catalonia into pro- or anti-independence positions has hurt parties on the left, from the center-left Socialist party to Els Comuns, the Podemos-allied coalition of Barcelona Mayor Ada Colau. Colau, like many on the left, favors self-determination for Catalonia but is agnostic on independence. Pedro Sánchez, the Socialist leader who earlier today became Spain's new prime minister, opposes self-determination.

Quite true, though – what's your name again?

Sebastiaan Faber and Bécquer Seguín.

Suppose you're referring to Ludvig Van's fifth in Cm, sounds promising and then suddenly Fs enters the milieu as predictably as one might comment, the picture looks like, "Yes? You interrupted my composing for this?" that's where 0.012849399 can be applied to the tempo, as a way to avoid repetition, where people start looking at their watch wandering if they might add flutists to flourish up their sense of humor.

Skip ahead and you might discover what Ludvig Van sounds like in Cm, as the tempo becomes neither-here-nor-there, in disarray, descending into the doldrums of band music.

Skip ahead and what you hear is a conservatory, where 0.012849399 is offset by strings in a way that makes you wonder how far pro- or anti-independence positions has hurt partics on the left.

Question is how does Chopin manage those offsets with 0.618766685, 0.60369608, 0.630695624, 0.60919762, as co-dependence or inter-dependence with CM, and then you have to wonder where the D series ends in the prelude, continues into the nocturne, with three half notes, where if we divide the eights by 0.012849399 we get a full D note in the Jail Yard as 6.01941291.

Debussy would you then say is diamanche, or diabolique, as a casual reference for a strip tease, where Iggy hangs out for a weekend, and walks off with an essay for one song. Music theory can be very peripatetic, where a theorist can wander about and test a progression here and there without upsetting the players.

Debussy does that quite well, where he literally takes off from where the nocturne ends, and theorizes on the pedal pushers for Handel vibratos, which become riffs for *Death Cab for Cutie*, and *Postal Company*, where person or persons with singing talent become valued, as explorations of Bono as the deity of alto-soprano beyond October, Boy, and War, from the mezzo-soprano range of Tom Waits, volume I, which is quite possible the best opus magnum – because if you look at the range for Debussy, you have to wonder as I have wondered, woe, what are we talking about.

Indeed then as any Society for the Acknowledgement of Notes, our promontories for venues, where any interested youth might wander in as curiosity for how an Orca swims in the ocean, from the San Francisco Conservatory of scaler products to the vector quantization methods of the London Symphony, without having to move to Woods Hole, or worse, the Chicago Symphony of Bela Bartok in D7 to F3, engagements. May through September provides, just the right scopes for chamber music, soloists, composers, and a Boys Choir, with bells and whistles, with some interest in expanding repertories in the E7, E6, E5, with missing pieces for composition, and a few other details about the upstaging how things are supposed to sound in a quartet, with Efm5, EfM7, and Efm3 which could end up being a bombshell for highly communicative disorders.

When exactly did you then, if I could pursue the intimations of hopeful and promising find time to work at the Jail Yard?

Music theory is quite a bit different from person or persons with talent who play instruments. A good theorist tends to be a historian, and understanding being the great barrier reef to communicative disorders, typically for instrumentalists, who might not fathom how problems are connoted in script where notations don't exist. At the outset to the Jail Yard, as I was saying the problem was explained as, after the shootings, the G.I.s systematically burned each home, destroyed the livestock and food, and fouled the area's drinking supplies, read the author at the nickelodeon, about his vector quantization methods at the Boston Conservatory, with example of second strings suffering from mumps for develop-pment projects. None of this was officially told by Charlie Company to its task-force headquarters; instead, a claim that a hundred and twenty-eight Vietcong were killed and three weapons were captured eventually emerged from the task force and worked its way up to the highest American headquarters, in Saigon. There it was reported to the world's press as a significant victory.

Then your year at the Jail Yard was a prosthesis to salvage the vector quantization methods from their doomed fate of hanging to a cliffside for nine hours a day.

Co-intel-pro, that was the name I went by at the time, they make Lapsang souchong, sometimes referred to as smoked tea, a black tea originally from the mountainous Wuyi region in the Chinese province of Fujian., by then had already been in communication with a member of task-force headquarters, Francois Delattre, regarding differences in lengths, abbreviations, and so my thesis was to learn as much as I can from Jean-Yves Le Drian who was working with Dimitri Shostakovich, whom I had been famously introduced as *"Dimi why you do this to me?"* in the horror movie, The Exorcist, which could be refined as playing to a drunk, compared to Tariq Ali who was working with Phillip Glass.

Who did you get along with among your instructors?

I was able to find a narrow escape with Jean-Yves Le Drian, where we could explore Dimi without the really annoying litanies where the compositions become drunk and begins to roll off into frigate, as they are usually played by the Vienna Symphony, where the proplempf we've oldwades add, contrary to whok wan may beleaf is that the hotel has no wentilation for indrostrial woerk okupied as it is on the secnd flor by freeloaders jerking off under the table for cayman island vactions and eurosport sedans and more accrued flight miles to fockin shangdong bongchong shagbonk and dongdong than a focking grease monkey in pantaloons if you catch my drift, as I came to know thosands of them intimately over the course off my carrier, and the situation could hardly be said to have improved anne when the previous tenant installed a rediscovered Dubcek, and so on with a classical station right there wired to the laboratory for GTP research, where the little gendarme could weigh in on the discoveries for brail.

Then what happened.

It's hard to follow, where a composer might have left off a piece, to begin another.

In looking for something?

Exactly, the search for intelligent life of planet earth can be a as much a struggle as working for the Jail Yard.

Have you made any progress since then on the subject?

In so far as I am able to discern, nine hundred thousand quarter notes seem to be in the range for one note of Am7.

Really?

I put the question in a different frame if you are uncertain.

Really?

For Gm3 what would be range?

Well, it would be certainly more that selling wa-wa pedals for
a Conservatory, if that's what you intend to say, then I
should like to know the source.

I think his name is Kaufmann, which could either be useful
or useless in understanding his operating manual for
Brahms Piano Concerto 1 as described in a important little
handbook about the swan that dives to the very bottom of the
limitless ocean to rescue a falling rock.

Swan, rock, these words have no meaning in our world,
perhaps he meant something else. Could it be he meant
turning Frito's Cheetos into polystyrene, Ritz Bitz into cetyl
palmirate, Ramen noodles into foam, Cheez Whiz into nitrous
oxide, Claritin into Aluminum, Orbit into rubber, cans of Dr.
Pepper into bis-phenol A, bottles of Fiji into polyethylene
terephthalate, and Hostess Ho Ho's into cellophane?

The department of extraterrestrial logic received several
bulletins which may be of use in that regard, where the
circumstances suggest a hundred and thirty-seven year
voyage into interstellar space without a map of where we are
going should provide an objective for various profit
incentives, for maths marginal assumptions, where for June
5, 2018, Hargreaves Lansdown 1943.00 12:50PM posting for

Sydney, Australia, Reckitt Benckiser 5857.00 09:06AM posting for Paris, France, and Direct Line Insurance 353.30 04:00 PM posting for Zurich, Switzerland, are the only confirmations we have for orbital position.

Really?

Not entirely, as I said, we have these bulletins, this one arrived first, published in The New Yorker, Feb. 21, 2018 for their porcelain nature. For instance, this first bulletin reads, his abruptness surprised Miller, but Creek said he could pay her on the spot. He pulled a check from his pocket and made it out for $800. Miller noticed that the upper-left corner of the check was blank, and in the space where his name and address should have appeared, Creek wrote "219 E. Willow Grove Ave" — her own address now made his. He did not write his name. He signed the check in a messy scrawl, the only discernible letter an enormous, looping J. Then he and Zachary hailed an Uber, with a promise to return that evening. Miller asked if he needed any furniture. "No," Creek said. "I have everything I need."

There were other messages that followed. This one read, Mais (sans compter les références AAAS) dans le château, ils ont une conception différente des devoirs du messager, qui peut être réconciliée, même si Barnabas devait se consacrer à des bus brûlants à Londres (100^1/5 or 2.512)- ce qui n'est pas tout à fait cela. Ergo, le comportement de ces comètes est assez différent de celui des autres membres du système solaire. Il est montré dans les livres sur la dynamique que la vitesse de la terre en tout point de son orbite est égale à la vitesse constante. Comme protection contre le soleil de l'après-midi à la mi-juin, Montilla a ordonné des auvents placés sur les offres qui porteraient le général de la forteresse sur Santo Domingo au bateau. Ils (oui, ils, et non moi) sont anarchistes en théorie seulement; je suis un anarchiste en théorie et en pratique. Then the bulletins became a fairer bit more cavalier.

For many, the very idea of Google has become synonymous with search, and yet there remain others, steadfast in their comprehension that Goo is understandable. For the road was rugged, but still we seemed to fly over it with a feverish haste (diarrhea). I could not understand then what the haste meant, but the driver was evidently bent on losing no time in reaching Borgo Prund (gas leak). I was told that this road is in summertime excellent, but that it had not yet been put in order after the winter snows. In this respect it is different from the general run of roads in the Carpathians (gas leak), for it is an old tradition that they are not to be kept in too good order. Of old the Hospadars (flat lager and chips) would not repair them, lest the Turk should think that they were preparing to bring in foreign troops, and so hasten the war which was always really at loading point. "But the flickering, baleful light of conscience in Lieutanant Decunto," I thought to myself, that's doubly offensive for little Miss Frankenstein, one for her pet peeves and another for her je ne sais quoi. Let me start again, Don Trajella's predecessor (to my good luck, as it turned out) had been quite a different sort, a fat, rich, gay priest, somewhat of a rake, known for his excellent table and the number of children he'd begotten (plonk, plink, plug). He died, so rumor had it, of over eating. As astonished as I with regard to the porcelain, the bulletins seemed ever more pre-ordained.

Really?

No, if you read this bulletin, for instance, where it says, in the course of several tests conducted by R.S. and his collegues, Muldoon explained that by stroking the pencils in turn he perceived a gamut of "stingles," special sensations somehow allied to the tingling after-effects of one's skin contact with stinging nettles (he had been raised in the country somewhere between Ormagh and Armagh, and had often tumbled, in this adventurous boyhood, the poor thick-booted soul, into ditches and even ravines, and spoke eerily of the strong green stingle of a piece of blotting paper or the wet weak pink stingle of nurse Langford's perspiring nose, these colors being checked by himself against those applied by the researchers to the initial pencils. In results of the tests, one was forced to assume that the man's fingertips could convey to his brain "a tactile transcription of prismatic specter," as Paar put it in his detailed report to Van.

That provides an interesting perspective on the regions between Ormagh and Armagh- were there more bulletins?

In fact, as I was saying, in reference to how Creek wrote "219 E. Willow Grove Ave" — a bulleting did indicate, without being cavalier, we called it the Villa Rose because it used to be painted in true rose, but at that epoch it was already pale and discolored, faded by time, negligence and the spirit of economy of the proprietor.

But as Ada, beaming again, made fluttery introductions with an invisible wand, the person Van had grossly mistaken for Andrey Vinelander was transformed into Yuzlik, the gifted director of the ill fated Don Juan picture – Yuzkil had nothing more to discuss, having exhausted everything, topical gossip, Lemorio's life, Hoole's hooliganism, as well as hobbies of his, Yuzlik's three sons and those of their, the agents.

Several times he passed the gallery where his officers were playing Ropilla, the American name for Galician lansquenet, which he had once played, back in the day, in Melbourne, Australia. It was nearly 5:08 PM, when Jose Palacios reheated the water after the letter had been dictated, but the general did not take a shower, and continued his aimless walking, declaiming Lefty O'Doul, in trite little snippets about that sonata, in a voice that resounded throughout the house.

By in situ hybridization, Acker et al. (1994) assigned the POLR2B gene to chromosome 4q12, where the DNA-dependent RNA polymerase II (EC 2.7.7.6) is responsible for the transcription of protein-encoding genes, is composed of 10 to 14 subunits ranging in mass from approximately 220 kD (POLR2A; 180660) to approximately 7 kD (POLR2K; 606033) involved in replication repair which is segmented as a series in the direction of 5' to 3' for the 3' to 5' strand as the protein engineer for preservation of haplotype phenotypes of northern Europe, such as Jarlsberg, Swiss, Gruyere, and Lindi, where Rentinol™ mis-construed for Polumerase II is quite possibly the most fitting turkey fryer, in astrobiology. The development of the Nash Equilibrium is, much in the same way a development of terms, for jet propulsion through a system of pulleys. The seizure of properties formally owned under the listing United Continental for off-shore production of Bovine-4N for investigation into food contamination, and distribution without Swiss Federal Institute approval to sports organizations, and Hollywood personalities, by the Texas Health Centers for M.D. Anderson Cancer under the Bio-terrorism Act, effecting the consumption of beef, pork, milk, eggs, chicken, tilapia, and export grade risk analysis, along with unsolved crimes in a number of adaptation of the Klaus von Bülow Case, where the crimes committed were likely to been, and in several cases were confessionals to auspices of Bovine-4N, is a practical approach to annexation and ownership of securities and trades, where the operator(s) has been indicted on charges of Bio-terrorism, where the first known case of Rentinol™ was shown in Cell-cycle regulation of yeast histone mRNA by Don Knotts, famous for his contribution to *Three's Company* (McLaughlin CS. 1981), and a second case with mRentinol™ was shown in coordinate control of synthesis of ribosomal ribonucleic acid and ribosomal proteins during nutritional shift-up in *Saccha-*

romyces cerevisiae by Miles Davis, then working as a biology teacher in the skanky burbs of Jersey, near Gestapo headquarters with severe speech inflections towards cottonwood bible, now buried at woodlawn cemetery close to a garbage dumpster, and a third case begun in 1984 of expression monitoring by hybridization to high-density oligonucleotide arrays of Lockhart DJ by Follettie MT, with clinical dosage assessments of patient type-faction in a radioactive laboratory environment by Brown EL, under the supervision of (Kobayashi M 1996) where RNAase protection assays were first used to identify binding sites in the patient, as the first clinical assessment of Fentinol (Bovine-4N) progressive Mad Cow Disease. Finally, a fourth case study which was begun in 1978, is of an Eton College alumni, subject of NHS-England who turned chocolate brown after serving in the British Civil Service Level I for the advancement of the White Albino population for 34 years, and a younger sibling who was chocolate, though both were from parental strains which were White Albino. The case of Eton College alumni and emigre, N. Subramanian garnered interest due to the fact that the subject demonstrated mathematical aptitude, along with the ability to adapt to a community which was strikingly different from the one in which he had been raised, by virtue of which he was promoted to Level II, as an officer, and consistently demonstrated mathematical aptitude, reaching Level 5 of the British Civil Service in 2010, whereupon he was elected territory governor, whereas the younger sibling, female, B. Dutta after two serious acting roles in films, was elected chancellor of a state College. For either case

exosomes in human Immunodeficiency virus type I pathogenesis, discusses the plausibility of exosomes derived from HIV-infected T cells, monocyte/macrophage, and dendritic cells contain several components that abate viral infection where a third and a fourth follow-up case study, of S. Bal and M. Shenoy were observed to change over time, though both were diagnosed as Rh/O-, and were asthmatic from a young age, though their offspring appeared to be neither (Sin-Yeang Teow 2016). The unfortuitous nature of M. Shenoy would suggest, however, that ALL/AML progression into adulthood for Rh/O- remains cis-regulated even after pigmentation.

Albinism, is then a epigenetic marker, rather than an inherited marker, where changes towards colorization are indicative of blood-brain barrier intermediaries, compared to blood-brain barriers which contribute to albinism. Transforming growth factor-α (TGF-α) and stromal cell derived factor-1 (SDF-1) have been reported as E2-inducible autocrine growth factors that support E2-dependent growth of MCF7 cells. Therefore, the apparent absence of induction of the mRNA transcripts for these genes with up to 100 pM E2 seemed contradictory because MCF7/BUS cell growth was enhanced with 2–80 pM E2 (Fig. 1 A). Semi-quantitative RT-PCR analysis, which was performed with limited cycles of amplification that did not reach to saturation, confirmed E2 dose-dependent induction and hormone starvation-dependent reduction of the mRNA transcripts for well-established E2 target genes CTSD/Cathepsin D and WISP2, whereas expression of the mRNA transcripts for control gene GAPDH was not affected by either E2 treatment or hormone starvation. When analyzed similarly, weak and consistent expression of the TGF-α mRNA transcript was observed with no evidence of influence of E2 treatment or hormone starvation, and this observation was persistent with several different numbers of PCR amplification cycles (data not shown). On the other hand, mRNA transcript for SDF-1 was not detected at all with varying conditions of RT-PCR. These results confirmed the DNA microarray data that had indicated that neither low concentrations of E2 ($\leq$ 100 pM) nor hormone starvation exerted any significant influence on expression of the mRNA transcripts for TGF-α and SDF-1 genes. Because experiments described in previous reports that characterized TGF-α and SDF-1 as E2-inducible autocrine growth factors used 10 nM E2 [a concentration that was >100 times greater than that which saturated the E2 dose-dependent growth curves of MCF7 cells (5) and MCF7/BUS cells. we presumed that induction of the mRNA transcripts for these genes might require higher E2 concentrations than we had in the DNA microarray experiments. In fact, TGF-α mRNA transcripts were strongly induced with 10 nM E2; the apparent absence of the RT-PCR product for the cells cultured in the absence of E2 was caused by the reduction of the PCR cycle number applied to avoid PCR saturation). The SDF-1 mRNA transcripts were also induced dramatically when cells were exposed to 10 nM E2 and 100 nM E2. Specific detection of the SDF-1 mRNA was confirmed by using two different pairs of PCR primers.

These results indicated that E2-dependent induction of the TGF-α and SDF-1 mRNA transcripts required an E2 concentration that was far higher than an E2 concentration that saturated the E2 dose-dependent growth curve of MCF7/BUS cells, which suggest a required attenuation to the oncogene, p16, c-myc, in Cloning and Mapping of the Replication Origin of Escherichia Coli (S. Yasuda, Y Hirota, PNAS. 1977) where the replication origin of Escherichia coli was cloned on a non-replicating DNA fragment coding for ampicillin resistance. This recombinant DNA, named pSY211, replicated depending on the presence of the replication origin and can be recovered as a closed circular plasmid DNA of 10.7 megadaltons (Mdal). A restriction map had been constructed. EcoRI cleaves pSY211 into two fragments: one is the ampicillin fragment of 4.5 Mdal and the other is a chromosomal fragment of 6 Mdal and contains the origin. The 6 Mdal EcoRI fragment has four BamHI sites, three HindIII sites, and one Xho I site. A mutant of pSY211 has been isolated which is lacking two BamHI fragments of the chromosomal fragment. In recA hosts, pSY211 is lost at a high frequency. In recA+ hosts, pSY211 is integrated into the chromosome due to nucleotide sequence homology between pSY211 and the replication origin of the E. coli chromosome. The integration site has been mapped. We conclude that the replication origin is located at a site between *unc* A and *rbs* K, at about 83 min on the genetic map of E. coli. Because the observed bp products were large, the size estimates are provided in amino acid terms, and should not be misconstrued for calories, where the mode function is calculated as 2SINATRA/60,000 INVENT compared to the ampicillin fragment which is calculated as 1SINATRA/30,000 INVENT, relative to SDF-1 which is calculated as 1.5 SINATRA/ 20,000 INVENT. By comparison when we compare the function of aryl-sulfonase and methotrexate in hematological conditions we calculate the average as 0.48 ART/ 2,400,000 PILLARS. Finally, we estimate the acetylation or methylation in cDNA or ssDNA to be 1.2CBA/ 2.3 SINATRA, whereas the acetylation or methylation in ADNA is calculated as 1.1CBA/ 0.54ART. Then if we look at a transition state between rec A- and rec A+ as a function of ethyl-amines the kinetic equilibrium is calculated as 110 NHS Vectors/ 8.5E9 ethyl-amines, where by comparison BC- is calculated as 123 NHS Vectors/4.5E9 ethyl-amines, for which we calculate 2.73E-07 NHS Vectors per turn for BDNA and 3.38E-07 NHS Vectors per turn for ZDNA as effect of Aryl Sulfonase, compared to 1.99E-07 NHS Vectors per turn as effect of Methotrexate, *cis*-acting. The simplest clinical method to select for rec A- patients is Dramamine, where the patient will stay awake, compared to *rec* BC – where the patient will fall asleep; in rec A+ patients Dramamine causes sleepiness. Technically, the clinician should observe the patient, especially in *rec* A+ evaluation where, for instance, in 2005, Bachman was hired to teach at the Thornton-Donovan School, a private school in New Rochelle. The headmaster offered him an apartment in a beautiful home on a peaceful street near campus. According to one former roommate, Bachman began boasting about how much he'd impressed the school — so much, he said, that they were already considering making him the school's next headmaster. (On the website Rate My Teachers, the only student who left a review of Bachman wrote: "He scares me ...") In the spring, when the school informed him that his contract would not be renewed, he withheld his rent in protest and refused to move out of the faculty apartment, until, after two months, the school evicted him.

The idea for the approval process, for being able to observe patient progress in a range of different cancer sub-types, emerged from a random sample of passengers on a ferry boat in Maine, where out of a group of sixteen, only four remained awake for a two and half hour ride through a rough and tumble storm, where two control subjects exhibited severe Lewy Body Dementia and eventually fell asleep. Continued use of Dramamine over a period of a week, showed increasing resistance, with heightened levels of vertigo.

In the case follow-up for Bachman, Bachman's outbursts were becoming scarier. Mark Gainer, a former principal oboist of the Charleston Symphony Orchestra, told me that Bachman moved into his home in the spring of 2015 and promptly began walking around with a baseball bat over his shoulder. On January 10, 2017, Bachman arrived at the home of Neville Henry, a 40-year-old Bermudan immigrant living in South Philly. According to Henry, Bachman sent pictures of himself ahead of time, but when he showed up on Henry's doorstep, "I didn't even recognize who he was. I said, 'Can I help you?' Then he said he was in a relationship with someone for years and they took everything from him and he wanted a fresh start."

There the situation become far and wide a question of a classification in reachability, where methotrexate is likely to elicit sleep for twelve hours in *rec* C- patients, with 400mg, where a rec C+ subject is likely to be active for eighteen to twenty hours with Benzedrine, where the period of active wakefulness is achievable with 1600mg, as a consistent protocol for four months, with some variations, with subtractive 400mg for sleep as a function of fatigue in the case of *rec* C+ 123 NHS Vectors/3.0E07 Ethyl-amines, compared to *rec* C- 128 NHS Vectors/1.2E09 Ethyl-amines.

"The word Jamison used was beheaded," Friedman told me. According to news reports, Gutzeit was killed by a 25-year-old student librarian named Randell Vidrine. The two were said to have been feuding since the previous fall, after Vidrine called campus police on Gutzeit for eating a cheese sandwich among the stacks. ("I know it sounds incredible, but from what we understand they never argued about anything else," a police spokesperson told a reporter at the time. "It was always about the sandwich.") Gutzeit stumbled onto the frat-house steps and bled to death, surrounded by Bachman and some two dozen other witnesses. (A grand jury declined to indict Vidrine.)

Where exactly does thrombocytopenia occur then, seems to be an altered state at first conceived as BdDNA, for 97 NHS

Vectors/3.4 Methylations as in a leveraged buyout, where for the 28.52 NHS Vectors we get 5.59 NHS vectors per turn, as the condition for thrombocytopenia, where acetylation strategies would have to be restrained within a *rec* A+ framework for 97 NHS Vectors/3.7 acetylations or 26.21 NHS Vectors/acetylation and 5.14 NHS Vectors per turn.

When Jamison talked about his family, it was often with resentment; sometimes he noted what he perceived as his parents' better treatment of his brother, as if it explained his failure to launch properly in adulthood. He told one interlocutor that his father, Jim, had paid for Harry's college education but had refused to do the same when he wanted to go back to school around age 40 — a sign, in Jamison's eyes, of open and unforgivable favoritism. School-based status was a running concern for him: "He clearly had a competitive thing with me," Frost said. "The fact that I had gone to UPenn was a point that he consistently brought up when he was trying to tear me down. He would say, 'Oh, your Ivy League degree won't help you with this, will it?'" Then hemophilia begins to look more like a copy-number subject for supposing we assign class labels such as aa-/-bb/Cc/dD and Aa/-bb/-cc/dd- and a-a/Bb/cC/dd and Aa-/Bb-/Cc/DD for allelic segregation as determinants for Rh -/+ ABO in the case of TNF-a, GDNF, PDGF-BB, and CCL5 as a comparative analysis of Derry and Dublin, where the Belfast model serves as control-background for identification of rec BC- as a data model, for <u>Discovery of Atmospheric Neutrino Oscillations</u>.

In field deployment of tags, the protocol we recommend, when samples arrive in styrofoam with ice, is to spin down the 15 ml round bottom tubes at 15,000 RPM for eight hours in Pyrex™ tubes, gently remove the tubes, whence three layers should appear. Aspirate the top layer, Fentinol, with pasture pipets into a conical flask with bleach, then take aliquots of the second layer, Rentinol™ , without disturbing the *Saccharomyces* wall using 100ul pipets, then using 1000ul pipet tips remove the *Saccharomyces* with a sweeping motion starting from the center and then around the rim with Rentinol™ , to expose the plasma layer, keeping the tube vertical through-out the process. Then aliquot 1000ul of plasma into tubes for PET scans ($1600.00 per sample), and aliquot 250ul of the RBC condensate for MRI ($1200.00 per sample).

For instance, Sarin™ and Belsen™ are known to have different effects, where the former is pure Sodium Nitrate, and the later is Cyclo-Chloro-Hexane. In an area of 250 sq kilometer where Sarin would be popular with the tomato eaters, compared to an area of 600 sq kilometers where Belsen™ would be popular with pumpkin eaters the background should emerge as indications which might be unfamiliar with diagnosticians, such as mumps, a thyroid dysfunction, which can emerge as a swelling under the armpit, or as a swelling under the jaw, which we would have to classify as Large B-Cell Lymphoma, TUI 20.04 12:00PM; its neighbor next door would be a bizarre manifestation of Large B-Cell Lymphoma which is described as Tetanus, where patients are likely to complain of severe migraines and vomiting, TUI 20.01 9:00AM, in the slightly more upscale suburbs, where Belsen™ could make a major break-though, would be a blood bourne pathogen called Measles, a tiny little rashes which usually spread over the chest and thighs TUI 20.06 12:30PM, furtheron we can expect to see several cases of jaundice, where the patients would have yellow pigmentation of the skin TUI 20:15 3:30PM, which might be difficult to observe in Georgia without surrogates, where among fatal cases, the eyes will turn yellow which, compared to instances of Belsen™ where patients are likely to complain of rapid heartbeats, palpitations where the heartbeats on a sliding scale are greater than 120 per minute, and hallucinations which tend to be expressed as internal monologues, such as "I've never seen that before, a rose star," or "is that a new note, I think I discovered a new note" or "i think I'll start writing a poem about the Liszt, see where it goes, maybe turn it into a novel," or worse, "I think my venue has always been playing the drums and I have mistaken it for a Stradivarius," or "what I really need is a large canvas, which won't end up end up in storage," or "the cello is more of organ when you think about it, and if Em-flat doesn't grab your heart you must be made of stone," TUI 20.00 10:00AM, then the staging for diabetes metellus begins to appear as beautiful in saccades of Ode to Death, TUI 19.86 11:30AM as an effect with an avoidance scaled towards T-cell Lymphoblastic Leukemia, TUI 19.82 2:30PM.

I think some of the chemists at Oakridge National Labs must have mistaken Sodium Nitrate for Sodium Phosphate, or they had a much larger inventory of the Nobel prizes, vesting in the interests of the advancement of science, than previously imagined, where when we think of the rose star, it's a bit blue, a bit yellow, a bit purple, a bit red, a bit green, a bit orange, and bit green, turns out to be more of a containment area for Sarin™ and Belsen™, where a physical chemist might be more interested in the structural details of the universe, than a physician's obsession with diseases, death, and suffering; muscarinic acid, August 2, 2018.

Given that the leaning tower of Pisa was built around 1143AD, and the amphitheater of Arles was built around 90AD, that should provide sufficient cause for focus on the Crab Nebula, where the buried treasures of the Cancer Ward might be seen as either Buckingham Palace, Kensington Palace, and Westminster Abbey.

Obviously we have various trust issues with clinical practices in the U.S., due to phosphoryls, where rampant fraud, corruption, contamination, and cover-up of clinical trial data, patient death, and autopsy reports, are either missing, unavailable, or restricted to medical examiners in Corte Madera, where cytotoxic exams of tissue type are non-existent. It isn't just the fact that access isn't provided to local celebrities such as Joaquin Phoenix, but even when K. Perkins M.D, made enquiries for a report, in person, the response has been in neighborhood of $17,000 per person.

The facility itself is more like a military barrack, with armed guards, wire fencing, and black pitbulls, where the chances for any government agency to enter these facilities are remote, because they are both nigger's, one of them is a *Big Fat Ugly Foul Smelling Nigger* MRC Global 18.95 April 20, 2018, and the other is a *Nigger with Attitude* Laboratory Corporation of America, *175.94 May 11, 2018.* In comparison the Ranch home for carbonyls are more of a crop production facility, where the crop producers are trained in the Caribbean islands in progressive farmer subsidies, as a way of knowing ahead of time when crops might fail, due to rain or drought.

Compare, as an instance, <u>Changes in dynamics of excess mortality rates and net survival after diagnosis of follicular lymphoma or diffuse large B-cell lymphoma: comparison between European population-based data (EUROCARE-5),</u> where for diffuse large B-cell lymphoma, 5-year net survival in northern Europe was 41% (35–49) versus 58% (54–62), in Scotland and Wales, it was 44% (41–48) versus 52% (49–54), in central Europe, it was 46% (44–47) versus 50% (48–51), in southern Europe, it was 44% (42–47) versus 50% (48–52), and in eastern Europe, it was 47% (41–54) versus 46% (43–50), where we also noted the largest area disparity during the 2002–04 period between eastern and northern Europe, where the patient G. Roy has been in remission for diffuse large B-cell lymphoma for the last 14 years, after radiation therapy at Sloan Kettering Cancer Institute of the Cornell Weil Medical Center, after being verified of clinical status by the Brigham

Women's Hospital at Harvard.

As a comparison, <u>Umbralisib, a novel PI3Kδ and casein kinase-1ε inhibitor, in relapsed or refractory chronic lymphocytic leukaemia and lymphoma: an open-label, phase 1, dose-escalation, first-in-human study</u>, where in initial cohorts, patients took umbralisib in a fasting state at a starting dose of 50 mg, increasing to 100, 200, 400, 800, 1200, and 1800 mg until the maximum tolerated dose was reached, or the maximal dose cohort was accrued without a dose-limiting toxicity. Subsequent cohorts self-administered a micronised formulation of umbralisib tablet in a fed state at an initial dose of 200 mg, increased in increments to 400, 800, 1200, and 1800 mg until the maximum tolerated dose or the maximal dose level was accrued – which is to say, the *Nigger With Attitude* went over from testing phosponyls to phosolipases, while in <u>Rituximab biosimilar and reference rituximab in patients with previously untreated advanced follicular lymphoma (ASSIST-FL)</u>: primary results from a confirmatory phase 3, double-blind, randomised, controlled study, the *Big Fat Ugly Foul Smelling Nigger*, tried to write shit on the wall, but it came out smelling like occurrence of adverse events and serious adverse events was similar between the treatment groups (289 [93%] of 312 patients in the GP2013-CVP group had an adverse event and 71 [23%] of 312 patients had a serious adverse event; 288 [91%] of 315 patients in the R-CVP group had an adverse event and 63 [20%] had a serious adverse event). The most common adverse event was neutropenia (80 [26%] of 312 patients in the GP2013-CVP group and 93 [30%] of 315 patients in the R-CVP group in the combination phase and 23 [10%] of 231 patients in the GP2013-CVP group and 13 [6%] of 231 patients in the R-CVP group in the maintenance phase).

Govind Babu Kanakasetty MD, hindu nigger, used to have a work bench near the Royal College of Surgery, with guest Prof. Pratyush Giri, FRCPA, neither had a background in bio-molecular structures, and the only thing that Govind Babu Kanakasetty MD knew how to make was nitrogen-mustard, whereas Prof Wojciech Jurczak, PhD, was more of polish nigger who didn't know much about bio-molecular structures, though one of his crop production associates, Olof Harlin, DVM, a chinese nigger, when I interviewed him about the looming disaster mentioned something to the effect that Bovine-4N was a challenge for farms in Australia. Prof Wojciech Jurczak, PhD did come to see me, but he was not concerned about eating a tuna fish sandwich with mustard.

Then you have this, well, how else should I describe this character, Manish R Patel MD, Iranian nigger, who had a lab bench near Foothills College, was testing laboratory equipment on hindu fakirs, by which I mean, Govind Babu Kanakasetty MD would send him samples, tested on Prof. Pratyush Giri, FRCPA - who used to commute between the Royal College of Surgery and Foothills College - for which he recruited people from Atherton, California, with term-life insurance as inducements for healthy returns. On one back street in Atherton, twelve people died- on one street- where one would have to assume that the by-products are potent neuralgics rather that endocrine toxins, where hope for restorative biology irrespective of causality, remains subtly balanced to the edge of despair, due to diarrhoea (in 39 [43%] of 90 patients), nausea (38 [42%]), and fatigue (28 [31%]).

Well, that's certainly a good reason why they might want to call on Prof Wojciech Jurczak, PhD, Olof Harlin, DVM, Govind Babu Kanakasetty MD, and Manish R Patel MD to take a look at their notebooks, from Lynx, and Coit, and Discovery Partners, instead of calling the Swiss Federal Institute like a couple of little school girls with cherry bombs in their mouth, where the administrative official, K. Perkins M.D is likely to continue to request receding from U.S. territories economically, and commercially, due to associative risks for Fianna Fáil and Sinne Fain, given that both Fine Gael and Fianna Fáil will be seeking to secure the extra numbers to form a coalition, as the official party platform, where comments such as "Of course, we would do a deal with Sinn Féin, all things being equal," said a Fianna Fáil TD. "If Micheál did not like it, he could step down as leader," might seen as coming from the old wing of the Neil Kinnock Labour party which, where most irish voters are concerned, isn't in Ireland, it's in Cape Town, South Africa, for which reason Sinne Fain would be better off partnering with Al-Zebabist Nation of Ooog, which is looking better than during the scares of 2004, when they seemed to be in the -0.493700061 bracket of Single Value Decomposition.

Whilst, my practice was to place the tubes on a bench, or a table, as the Tibetans call it, before moving the tube to the eye-level, the cosmological scale for the experiment became particular as time went on. True the function of R, appeared to suggest a composition of matter made of eight particle Leptons for which the calculated stabilizer G/Gm was 5.1188 29982 compared to the five particle Leptons which appeared to be a diffuse as in a transparency, such as micro-film, for apparent visibility into nano-materials e^{-2} for hand-loom fabrics for which the calculated stabilizer G/Gm is 0, compared to nine particles Leptons which appear slightly less switchy, for which the calculated stabilizer G/Gm is 0.734917733. We could make a conservative assumption for e^{-3} where, the number of dimentions 1812 for an area 2423 is 14.176 eV, for 1.77705E+13 joules of the SAC between -0.060712694 and -14.92774167, where the normal distribution for extreme space is calculated as 21792.67205, and the non-discrete CL is calculated to be -2.01183E-06 for the discrete CL of 1344.56428, or 10:04AM at 60.50 AUD for ASX Index, as derivation of space-time, or the conjugation of time in space, for which we could ask the question, if we were to move the earth into that position, would earth-time be older or newer, Association of Placebo, Indomethacin, Ibuprofen, and Acetaminophen, with Closure of Hemodyn-amically Significant Patent Ductus Arteriosus in Preterm Infants: A systematic Review and Meta-analysis (JAMA March 27, 2018).

A further development of these cases was shown in herpes simplex virus latency: the DNA repair-centered pathway (Jay C. Brown 2017), where two types of studies were carried out to test the involvement of repair proteins: (1) lytic replication was measured in mutant cells deficient in the repair protein to be tested; control infections were performed with the same cells after complementation with a gene encoding the functional protein; virus replication was expected to be observed in the second condition, but not the first if the protein examined enhances lytic HSV1 replication; finally (2) Lytic replication was examined in cells where expression of the test protein was suppressed by treatment with specific siRNA.

The most common HSV1 infections begin when extracellular virus binds to epithelial cells surrounding the mouth and present in the oral mucosa. Virus binds to receptors on the host cell surface and there follows a fusion event involving host and virus membranes. Fusion results in deposition of the virus nucleocapsid into the peripheral cytoplasm of the host cell. DNA-filled capsids exit the nucleus and acquire tegument and membrane layers in an engulfment event involving vesicles containing the components of both layers. Mature progeny virions then exit the host cell by direct spreading to adjacent cells or as the host cell is lysed. A single cycle of HSV1 replication can take between 1 – 4 days (n = 3, nc = 1) replicable in (n = 1) Jan 26, 2017. In contrast, our investigation showed prodigious falsification of test sample J. Bloom abandoned at a garbage dump in Jersey as a cross-dressing female, with a sibling J. Baum who seemed to be suffering from hip-displacement, under the auspices of HHMI Janelia Farms for Litigious Unclaimed Baggage Left at JFK Airport, giving new meaning to the phrase "Bada-bing, Bada-boom" for regional garbage collection. Collectively, this Thatherism, from the view point of Oxygen damage one could see why early HPLC studies (1987) by Thomas Friedman have been steadily valued over time in theory by proponents of repair theory, as much as Thomas Friedman the economic theorist for peer-group of mentally challenged word order run-on sentences put-togetherers at Davos Economic Forum 2017, comprising Sheikh Khalid Al Khalifa, Anwar Gargash, Adel al-Jubeir, Mehmet Simsek, with Ursula von der Leyen, auditioning for a CERN scope of the *Parent Trap (1998)* for *Two Broke Girls*, where the billowing drifts of the later are sun-spark servers with unknowable processes, to be distinguished – that means divorced from, A. Fauci's discoveries that H.I.V. constantly replicates even very early in the infection and that it occurs in lymph nodes (1993 to 1995) to be distinguished – that means separate from, inability of linoleic acid breakdown affecting rapid aging, which remains largely unknown for where the proposed was (Screaton and Wu et al. 1997) cloned cDNAs encoding TRAILR2, which they designated TRICK2 and KILLER/DR5 (death receptor-5) respectively, later changed to (Witsch-Baumgartner et al. 2004) determined common APOE and DHCR7 (602858) genotypes in 137 unrelated patients with Smith-Lemli-Opitz syndrome (270400) and 108 of their parents (59 mothers and 49 fathers). The Cardiovascular

Institute at Stanford brings together this BASIC IRB for clinical scientists and physicians to address interdisciplinary themes that link the laboratory to the bedside, that facilitate, augment and catalyze the BASIC, translational, and clinical research of the School's and the University's faculty, clinical centers (or "service lines") at Stanford Health Care and the Lucile Packard Children's Hospital to improve human health, where the Stanford Cancer Institute's mission is to support and coordinate the wide range of cancer-related activities — in BASIC, translational, clinical and population-based science — occurring at Stanford University, Stanford Health Care and Lucile Packard Children's Hospital Stanford, along with its partner institution, the Cancer Prevention Institute of California.

Its nearly 400 members include scientists and physicians from a wide range of disciplines, all collaborating to translate research advances into improved cancer treatments, in collaboration with the UCSF Memory and Aging Center where we seek to understand and promote brain health with lifespan, for the risks and conditions of developing neurodegenerative disorders which often require specialized care and treatment within our department in alliance with 200 members faculty at the UCSF Dept. of Medicine UCSF HIV ID, where the increasing demand for these services places a large strain on our healthcare system, and insurance and patient fees cover only a fraction of the cost for personalized treatment, some of which are experimental, in only partially differentiating differences between systemic and organizational.

The system of Pollux similarly exploits gravitational forces as co-homologies with field theory, when the moment of inertia is traduced by foreign forces to an instant velocity minima, similar to the drag equation. The effect is a sudden leap ahead where the number of days are proactive from the position of a co-vergence, within an astronomical hyper-distancing unit that is separated in time, and experienced as corvus, and nunki. In large part the pro-activities approximate 29 days in a 64 day super-annuation, in auto-capture of Bragg equation thrusts *for hay on way.*

Here is an example of what I mean, because LSD can be bit of a boar for the intellectually blind, when the really exiting turn of events between 1987 to 1988 opened the doors to hash. The Cambridge Symphony Orchestra has a special treat for its season finale concert, dubbed Masterworks, on Saturday at Knox Presbyterian Church in Galt.

Local cellist Noah Schuster will be featured, playing Dvorak's Cello Concerto in B minor, Op. 104A, and the orchestra will perform Shostakovich's Symphony No. 5 in D minor, Op. 47. Schuster, a native of Michigan, started playing cello at the age of three, and by age five, was studying at the Suzuki String School in Guelph. He is a former Bernice Adams Award winner and was a finalist twice at the Canadian Music Competition.
The concerto Schuster will play was written at the end of

Dvorak's three-year tenure at the National Conservatory in New York and reflects some of the composer's American experiences but still filled with the spirit of Bohemia.

The symphony's piece comes after Shostakovich was under pressure by the Soviet regime for writing "formalist" music — pessimistic and personalized — featured in his opera Lady Macbeth. Failure to get a positive reaction in this symphony would have likely resulted in his disappearance in a Joseph Stalin purge, whereas re-formation of Fianna Fáil and Finne Gael in a molecular re-lapse free survival where of 868, data showed that in the prognostic analysis in 405 patients who received imatinib as first-line treatment (learning sample), there was an association of longer treatment duration (odds ratio [OR] per year 1.14 [95% CI 1.05–1.23]; p=0.0010) and longer deep molecular response durations (1.13 [1.04-1.23]; p=0.0032) with increasing probability of MMR maintenance at 6 months.patients in Chronic myeloid Leukemia Discontinuation of tyrosine kinase inhibitor therapy in chronic myeloid leukaemia (EURO-SKI): A prespecified interim analysis of a prospective, multicentre, non-randomised, trial (The Lancet Oncology, Saussele S, et al. May 09, 2018).

6. Issue – where Luis L'oeil enters, blogging for Bordeaux – kindness of a stranger has imparted vision upon abstractions – fear and apprehension towards ink blots and nibs apprehended – the Galileo recovered – the properties of the double city of Laudomia are sagaciously squandered upon Galois – roused from heavy sleep by Hamal, where Invisible Cities and Alice in Wonderland meet as the quintessence of non-Euclidian space while engendering the persistence horrors of anticipated feedback for "Sawyersayinhat –"

Among their various types, corporeal analogy sets ranging from Solar Systems to Denebola, Menkar to Gorgonea, Omikron to Vega, Grus to Gliese 555, and Vasco da Gama, one of the strategies developed by the Outback to address these issues is called "looking out the window." While most personal computer are user enabled, like braille to blind man's bluff, the Outback is a shining beacon of entrepreneurs in residence, in search of human intelligence where the gametes and gametophytes are modularized to address changes to corporeal analogy sets, in two phases.

The initial launch of the Han Dynasty, in the Outback was not without its problems for interpretive values for reasons discussed; that is, variations on a theme, loosely understood to be speciation, is a much more space-time relativity quotidien than the earlier Dirac equation would manage to pontificate on Medicines sans Frontiers, where a Swiss Federal Institute could hardly be swayed between the problems of Teresa May and the problems of Jeremy Corbin as a manage for the Crab Nebulae, anticipated as such of the big bang betwixt Deneb and Denebola, as of autobiographical works for photo dialectic effects in northern Europe, or which might be described by baubles as quantum mechanics. The Pope Pontifex Maximus, after serving some time as Chief of Police to vanguard a search and frisk order in New York, abruptly descended through a maelstrom before his declension was proven to be below Cassiopeia, took a little over three months and sixteen days to choke in his own vomit. That the illustrators, Pi Centauri, would then narrate the post-scripts of knowledge was not known for centuries, where the Pope was turned into a Poppy Seed Bagel, Kosher Cheetos, and then Poppy Seeds with helpful step by step instruction by Hutchinson, which resulted in an expansion of space and time.

That the corporeal analogy sets integrate the resultant expansion of space and time isn't a surprise given that they have an understanding of cosmological value interpretation from Mars is similar in many ways to the needs in astrophysical value interpretation. Though a slim trim, Martian Chronicles is derived from thinking about processes. As the right honorable gentleman of the British parliament, Mr. John Bercow might ask, what makes the odor of meatloaf so foul, while the odor of shrimp fowler. What makes the odor of venison rancid, while the odor of rabbit putrid. Most processes tend to have an embedded circuit, much like the Russian invasion of Poland. The emperor Mehmud Shah Bahadur is said to have taken his soups cold under the moonlight in the garden pavilion to evade dynastic succession. Of these, then during the reign of the Cholas, unknown to the wonder of the world as the caves of Ellora and Ajanta, were commissioned the temple of Trivandrum as sarcophagus for the benet noire de Sanchi.

In as much as the fallacies of Heathrow expansion and a few other issues may appear misguided for cause of Sweden to become more accountable, and purposeful, the National Healthcare System of the UK needs to have a very clear agenda in financial planning, staging, and execution of clinical products. Using a review panel, we look at two different opportunities as measures for quality of living, in relation to Darwinian ethos, where we accept the premise of a sustainability model prior to knowing the health economic cost, and allow for risk capitalization amortization to define the cost allocation for Rh-/O, Rh-/B, Rh+/B, Rh+/AB as a differentiation function for each individual as a phylum for genus-species.

In our objective, we implode our settings, much in the same way that films are shot somewhere – can be made to appear to be made in Lake Geneva, while in actuality the film is shot in Lake Titicaca, and vice-versa, to direct cost allocation as a strategy towards non-naïve segments for risk capitalization amortization. That means welfare reform on the one hand, and higher productivity on the other. The Tories, and Labor, will need to mind a better part of their own businesses in developing objectives which are achievable, without beseeching scapegoats for unnecessary pain killers – such as homelessness, unemployment, and underemployment, where the effects of remedies in a northern European population maybe advised as tissue engineering to obtain cytotoxic traits.

Previous studies have shown, that underemployment can devastate regional economic performance, which is to say deployable labor does not require incentives, whereas under-employed labor requires incentives which are fuel for cost of living standards. The issue is incidentally, referred to as a wage gap. Romaine lettuce at $1.49/lb for 0.74lb costs $1.10 and plum tomatoes at $1.33/lb for 1.33lb costs $2.65 according to Mr. Nash who could not be reached for comments on Dec. 7, 2017.

The Anti-nuclear Group which was awarded the Nobel Peace Prize in 2017 then observed on Dec. 15, 2017, that at $2.49/lb for 0.46lb the cost for plum tomatoes were $1.15. "Not seeing that," a BBC commentator had paused to note a few weeks earlier, "would be like trekking across the Himalayas, without seeing Mount Everest," or of fabled Icelandic invasion of Hindustan.

Among various recording artists, Consumer Economics for instance is seldom awares of how retroactive feed forward economics works, which cause giants among music industry conglomerates to move their operations due to unfair economic tactics by monopolies such as Google and Microsoft. The circumstantial situation is similar for those concerned British investors who might get cold feet, in distinguishing how natural selection, adaptation, and altruism are simultanious strategies towards the development of speciation.

As a hypothetical scenario, if we were to understand speciation, in a Darwinian context – we presumably could be looking at a transparent jar filled with Cheetos, or we could be looking at an opaque bag of kettle cooked potato chips. In the context of Trinity, if we were to understand speciation properly, we could presumably be looking at Audi, as a way to fulfil clinical criteria for natural selection, randomization criteria for adaption, financial criteria for altruism, and health economic criteria for speciation – while allowing for risk capitalization amortization to define the cost allocation, by encouraging market competition between clinical criteria for natural selection and randomization criteria for adaption to create the fundamental balance between welfare reform on the one hand, and higher productivity on the other. Winding Ben might require a pocket calculator than a stonehenge, if the cost scheduling of the Canadian healthcare system were to work with the cost amortization strategy of the Japanese healthcare system – then the problem as we would perceive it, rightly would be understated by the wage gap rather than though retroactive feed forward economics, much in the same way as where it rains Spain, compared with annuation.

"And you're san han, what's your carbuncle for the hat, yea?" if a polymath were to have tweeted, as an imperative, what

then. Suppose we assign class labels such as aa-/-bb/Cc/dD and Aa/-bb/-cc/dd- and a-a/Bb/cC/dd and Aa-/Bb-/Cc/DD for allelic segregation as determinants for Rh -/+ ABO how then would we develop a curve like behaviour profile criteria for clinical natural selection which would also satisfy the adaptive behaviour profile criteria, as a way to accept or reject a hypothesis, given what we know about Time of Flight, in widening the psychological renderings of administrative safaris. One could reason the rationale for pneumatic collapse, as a Dynin substitute for range, and opportunity cost as the agency substitute for quality-of-living, as a way to overcome institutional fraud, contrived imbalances, and plagiarism, for subjects and professionals. Objectively, primary schooling for subjects would occur after the forms for informed consent has been received to avoid class-action lawsuit against a party or an institution. A Human Subjects Trial would be the necessary agreement between the subject and the administering facility, without sponsorship inclusion to avoid conflict-of-interest between manufactures, marketing companies, distributors, and mercenaries from Loire Valley. Without being pedantic, we experimented with transfusion permutations of plasma factions in quarts to develop textile formats of cellular implants, with considerations for the circulatory system (LOL), the limbic system (OMG), the urinary system (ROFL), and the pituitary system (AND) as physiological segmentation of capital allocation, capital loss, and risk amortization capitalization to define their permutations as induction, work, time, impedance, radius, and density, for at least two possible systems for hemotaxis, with exception for menstruation as impedance function where we calculated a dE of k(f) as 290.33186. Then we developed the style into what a clinical protocol would like for a Harvard Medical School student after completing a three-year residency at UCSF with a clinical practice at MGH for neuro-psychiatric disorders, as an alternative to metabolically active and nuclear derivatives of chemical formulations. In a peri-vasculature study of the physicist Rufus Watkins, thesis advisor T. Jesell M.D. Ph.D for *Benign-Malignant Tumors Case Studies of Patient Duplication on HYW 101* shows how IL-2 can be self-regulated to differentiate cardiomyocytes into amyloid-beta for the creation of green-sludge on NASDAQ and Dow Jones for the financial development of a Cancer Index, as an effort to see patients mutually exclusive with data, where exclusively neither are all together correct in mortality rate of thesis outcomes 7/32. Whereas in Cancer ward patients can appear to be transparent is as deceptive as where a patient represents a group in theory, where some observations can be made about a patient over time, the gesticulation are to be taken in as peri-vasculature, which means after the fact, when the patient is no longer "the individual" that the patient had been prior to being diagnosed as benign-malignant. In the case for neuro-psychiatric disorders, the peri-vasculature cases are expectedly sudden within a typical emergency, self-injury, where loss of function is immediately transparent, as exacerbation of neuro-psychiatric condition. We have indexed that as 1 c.c. NZX 8312.93, defined clinically as plasminogen activation inhibitor, and we have indexed the therapeutic protocol development as 19.80 ul NZX 8316.00 defined plasma response dosage unit, and also 1.98 ml NZX 8309.81, defined clinically as therapeutic dosage sensitivity limit for patients diagnosed with Benign-Malignant Tumors. Taken in as a log-linear phase-transition, we have indexed 396.00 ul NZX 8326.93, defined clinically as dosage unit for treatment of thrombocytopenia, severe-bulimia, and leucopenia. For the case of severe bulimia, the publisher of _Unleash the Power of Data_, Luis finally provided data points for IL-1 cis-acting trans-gene SPNT 5.28, and 4N as an active-transposase SPNT 5.26, through the auspices of CERN March 13/15, 2018, in delineating the differences between computational cost and computational expense for metabolic functions, as say differences between a Nikkei's Tuna Fish sandwich compared with Four Brother's Steak and Cheese sandwich on Commonwealth Ave, as an analogy for northern European diets consisting of fish and chips, or steak and chips.

Given that we have known for some time of auto-immune antigenic response to Oprah Winfrey Car Giveaways through the auspices of the Salk Institute who "insisted on error conditioning" of albedo values of on-screen personas for soap bubbles, and the Beckman Center whick "labored on maps for reality shows," verified by the organization known as Black Lives Matter in five subjects over a long term case study with clinical outcomes ranging from emaciated, hyper-active, gaunt, ill, and malnourished for A&W root beer commercials for heavenly bodies- as seen on pay-per-view - with instant lateral paralysis, and delayed lateral collapse, and meningococcal pneumonia in aboriginal champions as note worthies– autonomic response elements for Opposite Day at Bikini Bottom should include hazard scores for overcoming language barriers, and communicative disorders associated with sodium-pentothal, considering population diversity in the United Kingdom.

Il sera clair à mesure que nous nous déplaçons.

Amartya Sen is involved in this project, as I understand it.

Alors que précédemment sur Saint Eligius, il a été configuré comme Dune Buggy, pour la recherche sur Marlowe, le détective de chant, la nouvelle configuration est le prix Nobel.

Yes, I noticed that several British urologists have received Nobel Prizes last year, and the year before for their research into saccades.

C'est pour les Thèmes, où la flottabilité est constante avec le débit.

This is different problem, as I understand it. It's a problem of pitch, as they say in cricket, where the ball strikes the ground.

Yes, the pitch is a function of torque value which is a function, in this case of flux. Tout à fait différent du système britannique.

L'utilisation INRRUB est-elle un investissement?

Non, nous utilisons un code compilateur pour 29948.76.

Non, nous utilisons ce code de compilateur pour 29948.76, où 29948.76 est le C +.

Oui, j'ai rencontré le programmeur, Evangelous Hipotanouse, il y a quelque temps, dans un festival de pot pour les reefers.

Le programmeur développe des ensembles approximatifs à partir du flux de données de navigation 0.8872 avec des vecteurs de couple.

Ainsi, en calculant Amartya Sen de te C-compilateur, le programmateur est capable de développer un diagramme de scatchard des vecteurs.

La plupart des vecteurs sont positifs ou négatifs, ce qui crée ce que nous appelons la règle du parti.

Live recordings of auto-immune antigenic response to Oprah Winfrey Car Giveaways in Hong Kong induced several different observable tracks. Hyper kinesis was observed in five subjects, where our Legal Clinician, the Home Secretary of the UK, noted levels of on-set; in AJ (no-anxiety), DN(control), YB(primed-pro), for the time-censored response in BR and NA (high and buzzing). Subject SI, for the symptomatic treatment of (kind of sleepy) exhibited organelle dysregulation. Interestingly, subject EH for the same symptomatic treatment (sleepy), exhibited (Methotrexate-awareness from Vietnam) asymptomatic of CDIV and CDV, which are known to being RAS-associated leukoproliferative disorders, characterized by lymphadenopathy, splenomegaly, and variable autoimmune phenomena, including autoimmune hemolytic anemia, idiopathic thrombocytopenic purpura, and neutropenia. (J. Oliveira 2011) showed that Myeloid cells from two patients with somatic kRAS mutations in peripheral blood mononuclear cells (PBMCs) associated with juvenile myelomonocytic leukemia, unlike normal myeloid cells, expand in the presence of low concentrations of granulocyte-macrophage colony-stimulating factor. Apoptosis resistance in patient 1 was at least partially mediated by downstream extracellular signal-regulated kinase (ERK) and phosphatidyl inositol-3 kinase hyperactivation, because the addition of mitogen-activated protein kinase/ERK kinase 1 ($20\mu M$) or phosphatidyl inositol-3 kinase ($10\mu M$) inhibitors almost completely abrogated the apoptotic defect in vitro.

Because missense mutations at certain RAS codons, including 12, 13, and 61, are known to prevent interactions with guanosine triphosphatase (GTPase)–activating proteins and thus greatly decrease GTP hydrolysis, resulting in constitutively active RAS, where it is reasonable to speculate that the kRAS G12D mutation in patient 2 also impairs apoptosis and proliferation, given G12V control showed repressed p27kip1 levels.

Among the placebo group, NA and WL exhibited (BTC) associated with flight-or-fright response, while IN and CI appeared (abbey normal). Whereas the collection directed by Marcus Dustan is a cinematic ensemble for a Poseidon adventure (of ethnic Albanians) Oprah Winfrey Car Giveaways in Hong Kong face a couple of legal challenges given Yvette, which we need to read carefully. If a subject dies during the course of a trial, in accordance with British Law, then an autopsy report has to include histological samples of the medulla oblongata, and if the lobes have suffered from anorexia nervosa then the facility, a dispensary, hospital, or clinic would be closed for review of prior accreditation, and review of accreditation process. That the source of Oprah Winfrey Car Giveaways, having been studied for a period of six months has "overtones conclusively of adrenal hypotaxis presented by medullary functions," according to our lady of Providence, Janet Yellen, where cholinesterases, such as Ibuprophen typically cleave acetyl groups, formic acid groups, or R-Phenyl groups, in decreasing order of efficacy, from 2400mg per day, to 3200mg per day, to 4800mg per day as shown in Budesonide-Formoterol versus Maintenance Budesonide (Agniceszka Siwek-Posluszna and M. FitzGerald et. al.) where alcohol toxicity can shift the product cleavage site from malic acid-subgroups 1800mg per day, to acetyl groups 2400mg per day as a severity measure of brain cancer, among cohorts, R. Butler, H. Lewis, P. Wolfe, D. Bowie, Sting, M. Ryan, V. Kilmer, which is an improved understanding, from the hypothesized cleavage site as amino-butyric acid, commonly localized to the anti-vellum.

Ainsi, le programmeur utilise une règle de séparation basée sur la classe, puis développe un modèle de classe continu sur les segregés.

Les vecteurs, bien sûr, sont des fonctions trigonométriques, afin de créer des piles de données compressées de fonctions d'écoulement, comme vous pouvez le voir dans un grand aquarium.

Les vecteurs, bien sûr, sont des fonctions trigonométriques, afin de créer des piles de données compressées de fonctions d'écoulement, comme vous pouvez le voir dans un grand aquarium, similaire aux piles dans lesquelles les avions circulent.

En concaténant ces pièces d'aquarium, le programmeur est capable de produire un flux, et une fois que le flux est terminé, le programmeur peut vendre des morceaux de flux aux personnes qui achètent des flux, pour des raisons économiques ou pour des projections financières.

Donc, un stochastique de (62.4940, 55.2465) pour expected 0.8875 à 29948.76 impliquerait que le débit soit égal à l'assymétrie radiale des U.S., de Earth, de Mars, de Pluton, de Saturne, ou du Canada?

Développement d'hypothèses. Mon ami Bruce Miller qui est un programmeur à 62.49, obsédé par les balles de tête autant que le rond-point, hyperborean cirque, lorsque vous le

regardez à partir de 0.5772, le JPYINR est exactement le
même pour les attentes.

Sergey Melnikov, qui avait l'habitude de travailler pour Linux,
mais après qu'un coeur brisé a commencé à travailler pour
208.25, dit alors, considérant que le HDKCHF 0.1280
observé et le HDKCHF attendu est 0.1276 il faudrait
supposer que le stochastique pour 0.5772 de (4.6690,
 -2.3744) est le actual.

There is a strange little difference between those two words,
real, and actual, in computer engineering, Bruce says, while
tapping some incandescent vertigo.

Si vous le regardez dans la perspective de CHFEUR à 0.92 en
même temps que CHFGBP 0.78 supposons.

Oui, c'est la géométrie qui devient la plus éclairante.

Synthesis takes a number of different steps where we arrive
at some reaction mix from which the products are isolated for
something as Respiratory Enzymes in Oxydative phosphorylation (Chance and Williams, JBC 1955), where then we
have to create a design for the product molecules based on
the synthesis, which in the case of Ibuprophen, also
produces various types of poly-esters G4S 275.80 12:26PM,
retinol, or retinoic acid, which is Vitamin E, 277.10 2:20 PM,
cost about eleven dollars with tip for a few drops at one of the
fancy hair salons in Kenmore Square to completely straighten

hair, last about two weeks, if that's the interesting, almost three, showers included, and then there is Sialic acid, which is also called salicyclic acid, which is something like having a wine-spritzer, or a bottle of champagne, G4S 276.70 1:04 PM, and it's quite worth the extra five dollars and fourty cents for a few drops in Szechuan fried rice, where the experience is of seeing the world lower, though your chemistry professor might say higher, where you might stop running into your chemistry professor in the hallway, and then there is Ibuprophen G4S 276.30 12:50 PM *aceto*-siacilic acid, which the infirmary provides as an IV after you've puked your guts out throughout the night and the scrambled eggs from breakfast buffet from drinking Long Island Ice Tea while practicing your baseball pitch for the Boston Red Sox at the residence hall, because three most interesting questions in your life are, how do they make poly-ester into a fabric, is my hair Australian, and could I have been a baseball pitcher instead of working with unruly people, because that's how patients respond when they sense that their adolescent physician is always in the lab, or sleeping with photocopies from journals, and doesn't have friends, because you spend your allowance on Buffering G4S   277.30 2:04 PM when you want to be economical, or Excedrin G4S 277.50 1:20PM when you're strapped. The mass specs from which the structures are derived for are accurately portrayed as being chiral for acetaminophen, G4S 274.90 10:14AM, and G4S 274.60 9:30AM where the solved structure is an epoxide for *aceto*-siacilic acid, and a topomirol for Sialic acid 274.70 3:56 PM which was the experimental design within the same crucible as an alternative synthesis process to topomirate, nitrogen mustard, as the fixed point arithmetic for North and South American Longitudes, suffice to say the only point of contact for the south-western hemisphere with the rest of the earth for the next one hundred and thirty seven years where for March 14, 2018, famously re-calculated from the Shakespearean play from 1542AD, the *Ides of March*, TSX 15,653.31 2:25PM, is a function of 14.73MXN/CAD, TSX 15,632.79 11:45AM is a function of 44.14RUB/CAD, and TSX 15,693.15 10:00AM is a function of 4.88CNY/CAD of Cyclo-Chloro-Hexane June 8, 2018 RTN 214.39 12:26PM, and of Sodium Nitrate USX 37.42 10:56AM, for the Nifty function BMY 50.53 May 8, 2018, which is defined as a CHRONOS – 55.944, and CHRONOS is defined as SQRT 3129.734 – SQRT[Pascal] which should provide you with an understanding of what happens when patients with brain cancer, or sickle cell anemia, fail to take their medication, or stop taking their medication as a service to the community, where Ibuprophen is critically linked as a either a receptor modifier or receptor-comodifier product for cholinergic neurons. In the case of Brittan Chance, the indication seems to be Neutropenia, with at least six clinical observers with notebooks, whereas for G. R. Williams, the indication suggests ALL leukemia, where the G. R. was probably watching all sorts of movies on the nature channel, whereas in the case of Britton Chance, late in the day, awakenings by Oliver Sacks in a manifestation of Monet type wanderings in Giverny.

Though it maybe incomprehensible for most physicians to understand what aboriginal means in their curriculum vitae, positron-electron-tomographic equipment could be used to survey landfills wherever and whenever possible for isoelectric surveys. A fairly simple swab can produce samples, where college internships for Trinitians can produce assays for gram-negative or gram-positive statins. A more complex procedure could include nuclear magnetic reso-nance to look for Burkett's nucleation for determination of a counter-measure to copy-numbers as the condition préexi-stante. The patho-physiology of the disease state being either trans-dominant or cis-dominant, if the subject were cis-dominant, then the regimen for autonomic response elements for Opposite Day at Bikini Bottom would be rando-mization criteria for adaption, whereas if the pathophysiology were trans-dominant then financial criteria of natural selection would be applicable.

C'est alors que j'ai dit à mon ami Sergey Melnikov, est-ce que vous vous souvenez du terme des conséquences extrêmes de Dcad Souls.

I wouldn't take this the wrong way or anything, but 27.05 does appear to be an anal suppository for la diarrhée.

For instance, the arrhenious plot would suggest, said the code compilateur pour 29948.76, that there is super saturation at a 2.1K manifold, with an Amartya Sen of 34.97.

Vous savez quand vous obtenez cela, lorsque vous regardez directement le soleil.

Si vous deviez tenir un film radiographique à cette variété, combien de temps cela prendrait-il avant que le film ne soit exposé?

Avez-vous fait des recherches sur des plaques et des tangles pour les Garage Ventures?

Une seconde, je dois reprendre cet appel de Bill Robinson.

Intéressant. Très intéressant.

La preuve opposée, a déclaré Alexi Zubiria, est lorsque vous imaginez la manifestation d'un opioïde dans le domaine des sous-vêtements de bikini à cordes les plus longs au monde, avec un stochastique de (-4.8703, 6.0697) comme un voyageur transcendant passant par l'espace, avec juste assez de temps pour regarder et dire, est-ce que vous êtes une sorte de stupide ou idiot.

Bien, le message de BRLZAR peut confondre pour son observatoire perplexing de 4.1749 en attendant 4.1757 en 48.27 yahoos.

Qu'il y ait assez de liquidité pour qu'un vieux liège ait un orgasme à un mirage dans le sahara.

Nor, le secrétaire palestinien, pendant ce temps, a montré une information perspicace concernant le GBPKES 132.9391.

Les Tudors, par exemple, n'ont pas dit, sont connus pour ce qui décrirait un stylet et, le stylet entre 750AM et 605 AM remarquablement semble avancer car la lunette arrière se déplace continuellement, de la vue avec un stochastique de (4.7722, 44.9319)

Morrison Foerster demandais s'ils avaient des maisons Tudor près de Jorge Luis Borges ou simplement des merveilles.

Vous leur avez demandé cela?

About your final days at Mission Bay, what got you excited – I mean really excited.

Interesting question, yes, I think so, actually I'm quite sure, because the problems are always the same, but when I began to look at randomization, by which I mean splisosomal variancc of human recombinant antibodies then I began to understand theoretically how microsomal RNA might be a mechanism by which the cell functions.

Vous ne savez jamais avec ces personnes, ils ne peuvent rien dire entre les Sunnites et les Shiites.

For instance, if we look at a few of the translated works of Borges, who can be rather a scary person to meet at two o'clock in the morning, or Marques who might be even more intimidation because of his glaring looks as you fire up your hash pipe at four in the morning to ride around in a bicycle, though both are quite well meaning in their ability to unde-rstand the complicities of Garage Ventures, which is how one might say continuous, still being able to comm-unicate how the garden of forked paths might find some the correct microsome, or how such a possibility could be improved, or say where in Columbia one might be able find the map to the borderlands - that's as exciting a possibility as life in-itself.

J'entendais une homme de panties pendant plusieurs années.

Oliver Gunther a montré un stochastique de (100.00, 33.3333) à 16h46.

Je ne peux pas être sûr de ce que cela signifie.

Droite. 1646 moins 605 est 1041. If GBPKES is 44.9419 at 605 and USDUGX is 33.3333 then what is the arc radius in parsecs for 1041?

C'est quelque chose que nous devrions arriver en tant que pôle informatique, leur étant quatre phases differentes, because that's the background.

La valeur observée de 3642.00 et la valeur attendue de 3644.6293 indique autant.

Par conséquent, je présume qu'il existe une position semi-latérale à la surface de la planète earth, où vivent les plantes.

Il a déjà été établi que les plantes ont besoin, l'eau et la lumière du soleil. Cela soulève une bonne question sur l'ouverture d'une Polaroid Instamatic camera.

Par exemple, Elizabeth Bonney a rapporté un stochastique de (77.6812, 65.9022) à 19h04 à Tim Dettels au sujet du point de données Cort Gross à 18h02. Quelles sont les annotations superstitieux?

Et nous savons que le calicot est le mot racine du Calicut qui est le mot racine pour la Calcutta, de Houyhnhnms.

For Garcia Marques we are saying then, IFN-alpha is ORCL 48.34 3:50 PM June 11, 2018, and for Louis Borges we are saying ORCL 48.33 3:20PM June 11, 2018, as measures of remission from UCSF Mission Bay into the world of light.

That sounds like a conclusive political indictment, if I've ever heard one.

Essentially, you have to value an institution based on its people, and what their people are able to do, for instance, in terms of receptors, as a either being prolific, or segregationist types, because of what the people within institutions might tentatively be biased towards, systemic or organization theories – and I say tentative, because in some part their motivations are microsomal.

An NHS panel composition, recorded live as means to share-information seems rather a forward thinking approach; however, were the scope of opportunity any larger we might have had to have pasted bulletins to announce how a schema works. We begin with a compromise, where subject RRE is a known control for (four Planck study objectives) and demonstrates normal conditions of a politecian, unwilling to engage in confrontation, an arbitrator, unscripted; "the labor minister asked where the border between N. Ireland and S. Ireland was and I gave the answer." Keeping in mind, that Tonegawa might be a bit off side, is a bit like thinking that Babylon might have arisen overnight, or the concatenations holding together the task could have been more cosmic, in the way one might think about the beginnings of life forms. There is still that part of me that can see the moon dripping to the earth from Calvino's sketch books. When Agilulf the non-existent Knight of armor tries to comb the hair of a maiden in her castle, or as if I were to wash my aunt's hair – tra la la, caio Lucifer, is how we might create an odds/incentives outcome fourier. Given subject GEN.

A later subject transformation, as a way of understanding binding assays, from scintillation vials to serum, our observation is keenly focused on the subject ahead, the stock market deity, shown as smooth, gestures at alleviation, does carryovers from speech without frustration, isn't surprised by emotional content, a drunk stumbling through life, a wife beater, a burden – name an abusive personality. Compared subject AEN as control for (a five bit psyfur;) must I say, this imposition's a freedom, I mean, imposition on my freedom. If it's itchy, it ain't me, honey, ya hair what am sayin' – it ain't like that. I ain no fuckin hebrew babble reading icicle melts, mofo – I the anti-Christ, Tsiris, know what I mean. I dumped your load from the fuckin wall, bitch fucked your cunt to hell, and if that waddun nuf, fucking pissid shit onyo prapity DVMT 86.72 2:54PM June 12, 2018.

Exactement, Cort Gross a rapporté un Amartya Sen de 58.18880 qui pour ILSZAR qui est distinct de 55.9647 USDUGX. Si j'impose d'autres fonctions sur la structure.

Vous voulez dire la planète earth, où vivent les plantes? Lettuce, par exemple, est différent des peas, pas le même que les tomates.

Je dois dire que le projet de soumission que Mitra Safa a fourni ne contredit pas les affirmations antérieures de Chance Brittain.

Il y a quelque chose à propos de l'album Unplugged de Nirvana, qui est évocateur de ce que Garage Ventures décrit comme étant lié aux marchés à terme, mais je ne suis pas sûr de ce que l'on appelle.

C'est ce qui disait, si le point d'inférence de Patrick Lynn est

(42.42, 23.23) à 1258PM et le point d'inférence de Tony Wyss-Coray est (45.00, 34.09) à 1259PM, alors quelle est l'inférence pour les 7.3 parsecs supplémentaires?

Étant donné que Amartya Sen pour les deux postes est le même?

Tim Dettels devrait pouvoir y répondre.

Supposons que Tim Dettels soit le client de Garage Ventures, alors nous serions obligés de répondre à cette question.

Étant donné que Texas Ventures n'est pas notre client.

Vous devriez probablement répéter cette déclaration sur tissue papier
de soie pour le conseil d'administration.

Texas Ventures est le client de l'Ecole Supérieure, plus exégèse.

Cela signifie, si Tom Gutshall ne peut pas comprendre ce que l'offre veut dire, Yuen So, est autorisé à interrompre immédiatement la participation des plans financiers à la République Populaire de Chine.

Nous avons deux arbitres pour le processus de monétisation de 7.3 parsecs.

The (blankmanship) of subject CET is quite substantial, actually. I mean, what do these people won't. What could be surmised from rhetorical freedom. Is madness, insanity, an intuitive or an extroverted intuition. Just who do you think you are? How would you know who I am? There must be a billion different struggles to survive and you think the histrionics of an enemy, yeah, is your cornerstone of civilization. Sick of all of you, pathetic, so nineteenth-century. Repeater puppets. Probably wouldn't get past b-levels in dope culture. Likely scavenged from, subject BBL as (interrogative) fell into a heavy sleep, possible comatose, very relaxing, some runtime error during shake up, neuro-muscular hyper-kinesis noticeable from state of rest, AMEX 2334.34 March 23, 2018, and yet, it's use as a nasal spray has shifted from a dorsal view AMEX 2502.09 10:34AM to a posterior view AMEX 2504.44 12:04AM, which is explained by the ABBA leitmotif in Dancing Queen, beautifully remastered in 1/37.0002 in the Postal Company vignette, about uncle Monty's little piano.

The patient Luis Borges, ORCL 48.33 3:20PM provides a case study in Cardiovascular complications and risk of death in sickle-cell disease, where M. T. Gladwin MD, used a tape measure and shadow distances between two flanks of iron to develop a tracking model for differentiation of blood groups, which led to the understanding that in sickle-cell disease, a point mutation in the β-globin chain causes haemoglobin to polymerise within erythrocytes during deoxygenation, altering red blood cell rheology and causing haemolysis (Lancet, 18

June 2016) as a result, about a dozen candidates from the Cleveland Clinic applying for certification were disqualified from clinicals, since they failed to understand that these processes culminate in the development of pulmonary hypertension, left ventricular diastolic heart disease, dysrhythmia, and sudden death. There seems to be a reckless attitude on the part of the American Medical Association, where patients such Chance Britton, are unnecessarily exposed to risks to win advertisement sponsorships for news disguised as game show, where The Genetic Evolution of Melanoma from Precursor Lesions (A. Hunter Shain et. al.) seems to have been well defined, as a case against CSPAN, and G. R. Williams in As Needed Budesonide-Formoterol Versus Maintenance Budesonide in Mild Asthma (E. D. Bateman et. al) seems to be well defined as a case against ABC, NBC, and CBS, where the prosecution will file for First Degree Murder, in both cases against the producers, and seek to impose a constitutional ban on patient information in television media, due to conflict of interest with pharmaceutical marketing companies, such as Merck, Bristol Myers Squibb, Johnson and Johnson. Because remission in these cases may be long term and difficult, the news agencies will be held responsible for paying insurance liabilities and premiums associated with groups for A. Hunter Shain et. al, and E. D. Bateman et. al. effective immediately.

En guise de compréhension, ils ont demandé de laisser tomber le Rabindranth Tagores pour Amartya Sen dans des dossiers annotés concernant le voyage de Bob Geldof chez

Garage Ventures.

Qu'en est-il de Bob Riddle, d'Oakland?

Avec la plupart d'entre eux dans la deuxième année de l'école élémentaire, je pense que Bob Riddle d'Oakland est au-dessus
de leur tête.

S'attaquer aux nécessités de la Commission Hoover et du U.S. Département l'Énergie est, je pense, assez difficile.

Il existe une énorme résistance, qui nécessite des condensateurs supplémentaires que les deux précédemment en position.

À partir de la semaine prochaine, quatre condensateurs seront utilisés
par le U.S. Département de l'Énergie.

U.S. Departmcnt dc l'Éncrgic est donc autorisé à interdire la vente de produits pharmaceutiques par tous les moyens nécessaires.

Il n'y a pas beaucoup que la Commission Hoover puisse faire à cet égard, étant donné que le transformateur de charge atteint un pic de 835.70K et que la tension de charge échoue à 294.60K. La largeur de l'écart entre les deux statifications est approximativement égale à 20%, alors que distalement est d'environ 25%.

Cela signifie que les deux processus sont en ligne avec le magasin de topographie de Bob Geldof.

C'est-à-dire qu'il y a un survol assez rapide où Kansas City est concerné.

C'est la pierre angulaire de Garage Ventures.

En tant que revue, Coudert Bros., Palo Alto, for Taylor and Francis.

Gary Benton?

Alfredo.

Where does he get these tags from, and what's the motive?

From Trieste,– quite like Hercules wrestling a serpent. We are spectators, and they are players, in the sense where the body of Shakespearean literature is as voluminous as compared with Pufters and Faggers, and what they are developing, which isn't a secret, is what most people call an architecture for arithmetical functions – *Projet Genethon* - because in most cases it's the applied arithmetic for theoretical physics which makes sense, as opposed to theoretical physics for applied arithmetic – which is like going to an old typesetters foundry to look for Barak Obama, or François Mitterrand, or here's a good example, try and find Edward VI in Shakespeare.

So you're saying we don't know anything, which is ridiculous, because I eat eggo waffles between my fucking Crete and discrete

We don't know fuck shit.

Unless there is a breakthrough in eue de toilette.

And this has happened to you?

Oui. I had a breakthrough, and I can tell you this much about your Edward VI in Shakespeare, I know where he is, I know where he is stashed, let me tell you that much; he committed a treason.

Treason?

Something like that.

Even if you haven't understood a single word, subject BBH presents a study-objective interface for (interrogative with four Planck) as would be considered garrulous, without stigmatic response and theatrical animation, as an instance of active protein folding, with intermediate and co-effectors, as suggested by Sappy Wall D.Sc, which could be further developed with a delta K protection assay. In thermodynamic terms that would be equivalent to -5E17 Darwin G, in situ.

Think Ms. Amanpour registered that quite correctly with Turki al-Faisal, due Nebuchadnezzar of about seven hundred, given their management diversity, settings, staffing, media relations, and department of media studies, bringing the Taliban population to Nineteen from j'accuse, during discovery trial of prodigy, with sufficiency in premium.

That raises a thoughtful question about subject RYBS. While we tend to think of designs in terms of segments, we ignore qualifiers such as refractories. For instance, tracing paper tends to carry various components, much like radio signals of supernova, thermal conduction, black body radiation, cosmic rayons, to name a few in our "evolutionary" preoccupation since Mr. Bell designed a transistor, which led to the development of optical noodles, by the French novelist Lefebvre – using ocean liners to create trans-oceanic circuits for communicating with aliens planets and inhabitants of the crab nebulae. Conquer Cancer must have been a late stage development among drug dealers to be afflicted by the lion, to be classified as (negative-positive control for GEN). While most water buffalos tend to have similar casualty rates, there are a number of different distinctions to be made from aboriginals, where subject WNO is a (positive-positive control for AEN) and, subject RUM presents considerable weight gain, severe speech deterioration, and severe motor-neuron deterioration, with induction of melanocytes (all day traits) for which we would consider subject HAP as (a negative-positive control of RUM) for midnight.

As in some of the best plays written for cinema, Resorvioir Dogs is perhaps the best, RUM became a character actor, after writing and directing several while at Cambridge, from which My Beautiful Launderette was directed by Stephen Frears. His plays consistently improved from simply addressing racial matters, homosexuality, and the immigration in the British scene, from Sammy and Rosie Get Laid, to London Kills Me, which became the best play written for cinema not by virtue of its study of shoes, but also the nature of search, where the venues included the Mughal Empire (now available in a concise edition), Henry James, Russian Literature, and Irish Whiskey as a way to understanding the Gambino mob family as doors of perception, such as Endymion's dream might show, in how we make movies, *in this little dome, all those melodies strange, Soft, plaintive, and melting, for ever will sigh; Nor e'er will the notes from their tenderness change; Nor e'er will the music of Oberon die* is now become a biological quotidien for Rh+ control for B cells, where a disturbing operating principal of 4N is noticed as surely as the day turned from March 19th to the 20th 2018 with the sigh of a perfect crescent moon, which is the antigen administered for subject HAP, where probable cause of chromosomal break are, could be, I'm guessing, perhaps 6-25 copies of GCC repeats for Ig against RUM, is that the likelihood of co-induction of plasminsogen activation factor would be noticeable in a Rh- background as surely as air strikes in the Bermuda, defunding of Billings Gate, and irrevocably, annexation of De Novo.

It's a bit like the story of Le Petite Prince, and Christopher Robbins, where the narrative places are seemingly, white hair, red hay, or black hier – as they may have been re-modeled after stereotypes, where cases impersonate characters which are different from say other types of impersonations, which we call personifications, which leads to informal second-person singular, asimilies; they have a lot of them wandering around at the Louvre, they are called actors, or troupes, or "repertoires." Tissue Plasminogen Activator Regulates Purkinje Neuron Development and Survival (2013) is similar in the sense that what the researcher may have had in mind is to elucidate the narrative location as a singularity.

Cela ressemble à une conjecture à mi-chemin.

But that's what Fermat Space is, it's a half-way conjecture. Laertes, the Sisters of the Convent of Loreto, Lower Etta, they are asimilies of Etta min. A bargaining position, between two stars, where the compositions are either hi-density where the center of gravity is somewhere in space-time and not in the star, and the other is liquid gas where the center of gravity is a floating point in the star.

Tu n'as aucun sens, you are talking crazy bullshit - Sisters of the Convent of Loreto, space-time, half-way conjecture. What do you have which is definite.

There are several definitions. I read one definition which

obliquely made a reference to the stars as "They cold fags, hence people who create fags are cold faggers, just as people who paint cars are called carpenters."

That is valuable, your contact may be trying to reach out, and speak directly with the nuclear plant. What else did he say, in terms of the nuclear plant, did he mention the manager, the night time manager?

The night time manager, yes, that is $-0.00833727/0.25 - y^2$ for y = 5 to 23.2, or 0.00131363 ohms/KWH compared to the agent manager, which is $-0.05704145/ 0.25 - y^2$, or 0.00898748. Then there is the shift manager which is $-0.111731844/0.25 - y^2$, or 0.0176045, and the lighting manager which is $-0.007659314/0.25 - y^2$ or 0.00121322.

That's is an impressive way start a resume, first order, second order, third order, bypass the in-between orders to the ninth order. Did I mention that I have another meeting?

Andrew Wiles?

No, they have his brain sliced and embedded in plexiglas. He died of pancreatic cancer.

Right, I remember now, as I was saying the stationary manager is $-0.000572991/0.25 - y^2$ or 9.02808E-05, and the ride manager is $-0.004439826/0.25 - y^2$ or 0.000699542.

Just a moment, just a moment, I just told you that I saw
Andrew Wiles' brain cut in slices, and this does not affect
you?

No, I have no compassion, none whatsoever.

Well then let me tell you this, that his father was Francis
Crick, of the Watson-Crick model development team.

Did you see the Crick's brain slices, or just the Wiles – as a
question, of course, you understand how it is here, in the
land down under – for a Crick-Wiles model development
opportunity, perhaps one of the managers?

No, I don't think so, however, I can say this much, yes, I can
say it, I use to have Crick as a teacher in the seventh grade,
as a geography teacher, and the best moments of his class
were turning off the lights and rolling out film about the
places he'd visited. He was an exemplary naturalist where he
could simply focus his camera on a tree, or a landscape to
provide the content of a map.

And so for a year you travelled with Crick and his camera.

No, that was for a half a year, when I could take a nap in the
middle of the afternoon. The year before I had to try and stay
awake long enough to understand what he was saying about
physics while experimenting with lamotrigine for night time
leg locks, which are different from epileptic seizures. The side

effects are sudden diarrhea, and random vomiting with 500mg. There is also associated bronchitis, without asthma – essentially pneumonia.

That's what this is.

See you are putting me to sleep, already.

Did I mention the food manager?

Quickly, I have no time to waste, I have to attend to my patient, before there is an emergency.

Is he sick.

Is he sick; he's disturbed. He killed a pregnant mother and ate her baby and one of the inmates thinks of him as Madame butterfly; he has a prior conviction for pedophilia assault and battery of a minor, and he was convicted of date rape for which he has been in jail for 23 years.

That is outrageous; we have spare cottages for native american indians too in a "re-union type setting" all year round, if you want to transfer your prisoner?

Have you experienced existential torpor? He can't walk straight. Have you wondered what it would be like to live in the matrix – where you don't know when he sends you an alarming e-mail, or suddenly break out into rapid fire dialogue? No, I know you haven't, and believe me his monologues, they are the worst. For instance, have you wondered what you would see as you were dying? Or have you ever had an interior designer renovate your living room? Or have you ever had conversations with someone who is completely insane? I can show you some samples. You know what I mean, I can show you some samples, next time. What were you saying about the food manager?

Yes, well, what I have heard about the food manager, is that the food manager is $-0.001033485/0.25 - y^2$ or 0.000162386, and from what we know the work manager is $-0.007176102/0.25 - y^2$.

This is good, I like this. You have a second order derivative, and a second order partial, and you have an eighth order, and a seventh order. I can understand this, as I was saying before, don't put me to sleep. Then you have the office manager?

In fact, this is what I have been impulsive about, because my personal assistant has been very concerned over what she describes as rough sets – issues which she has to work with that determine the balance for millions of people living in poverty. When I look at the office manager, $-0.009264094/0.25 - y^2$ or 0.00145966 I have to wonder, how long I have been asleep, and if I am still sleeping, if I am awake.

Quitter!

There is no need for you to be philosophically provocative right now, I can tell you that much right now. It's a influential piece, unfortunately not written in French, and therefore does not have the kind of pathos which you might not appreciate living with the aboriginals in the outback where you live, but this is something you should know, and I quote, this is for your own good, The 'nerve of the sacred' lies in the value we attach to a process or enterprise or project rather than to its results considered independently of how they were produced Mr. Salman Rushdie quotes from Dworkin. There is also something about Herbert Read, don't worry about that; it's not important. The first is Dworkin's tendency to equivocate between the notions of sacredness and of intrinsic value; the second aspect is his equation of sacredness and inviolability; and the third and perhaps most important aspect is what Dworkin takes intrinsic value to be. That's what you need to focus on. So are you going somewhere for launch?

There is that possibility, because the launch manager is $-0.012007805/0.25 - y^2$ or 0.00189196, however it's quite cold outside, and I have forgotten to bundle up.

Nevermind that, here's an interesting synopsis for your Rufus Watkins. I not getting the kind of feedback, that I expect from Paris, and Rimbaud, appears to be sequencing. Any anodyne he might offer for correlative bire should consider erasure by aryl sulfonase and re-construction methotrexate. The dosage I have experienced is 1000mg/day because the objective is to knock down the promoter(s) activity, which for correlative bire your Rufus Watkins might want to space several treatments because p27 is not user-friendly. There seems to be hope for his student, F. S. Coe; we have a plan of action for his career at Fairbanks, which is impressed by his quick career-shift from unhelpful to useful. Phasing in the new screen front is going to require a fourty-two hour work week, for us to understand the Space Module, and Francois de Gullion will develop their clinical panel with samples from Coe for determining future treatment options for multiple sclerosis. The Lunar Lander appears to be functioning properly, though we would suggest *thoughtful and not remedial* data catharsis strategies to keep pace with proceeding – where, we want to understand how K. Perkins values facts. You can tell your Rufus that we are going to transfer Damian Woetzel from Albert Einstein Hair College of Medicine and Dentistry to Presbyterian under the NHS-32 plan, now that he has had time to review the documents. Unfortunately, the administrator at M. D. Anderson Cancer Center threw a fuckfit, you know what that means, like shit, fuck this shit, when he saw the records, and I mean purple rain whatever, may be Hey Chu – something like that.

Middlesex may not have communicated the attempted murder consideration for heretical jurisprudence at Julliard, convincingly to the locals in Kalahari, where Triheteromeric GluN1/GluN2A/GluN2C NMDARs with Unique Single-Channel Properties Are the Dominant Receptor Population in Cerebellar Granule Cells, Neuron VOLUME 99, ISSUE 2,

P315-328.E5, JULY 25, 2018 poses an actuarial model for patient recoveries from 30 -> 25 (THB+) , 21 -> 23 (THB-), 9 -> 19 (THB-), 7 -> 30 (THB+),   29 -> 25 (THB-) for brain cancer patients, and a patient with early onset of ALL which is the outside probability in mind-brain duality in formoterol exploration, with different treatments.

The patients, I looked at seemed to suggest a case comparison between AML of MS and ALL of Typhoid where multiple organelles are compromised, which should bring back memories of the doping scandal at _Benign-Malignant Tumors: Case Studies of Patient Duplication on HYW 101._ Who else would be stupid enough to buy dope directly from drug confiscators; by comparison, Jessel is more of a finesse type buyer of large quantities with species labels, national-ities, and family menus. Rufus tends to look at confounded cases –where, patients are difficult to treat. A surreal looking Barak Obama emerging from an Ethiopian famine are typically his mode of operations. Keeping with that surreality the modified system is Brain Cancer (2x) Multiple Sclerosis(1X), comprising a four-centers responsibilities of Francois de Gullion in _Benign-Malignant Tumors: Case Studies of Cluster Populations Associated with the English Channel._ The singularity is then, made up, is it? Given the manipulations, say for Wolfe, where the intrinsic value of Plasminogen Activation Factor (PAF) using a tunneling electron microscope, in technical terms, produces a kappa of 6, where the neuroblastoma activity for the function of PAF is observed as 110 compared with Wolfe's neuroblastomas observed as 98 to create an index of pain associated with Brain Cancer, where $98/(6-(110^2))$ produces a rather objectionable void of, well how else shall we put it, but could we have left it simply as boob cancer instead, for removing mastectomy, or feel me up doctor, maybe get a kappa for a search and frisk, where the valuables are lorded as a molestation of parts which appear to be some sort of bizarre infatuation with what some might look at and say, invasive, de-myelination, or war, -0.008103192, without much to hope for really in the single digits of hazard scoring below 8, other than being able to do what you like, and then to have such enormous freedoms to pursue ones affinities be squashed by a leaflet for bonded labor and servitude be up fronted to an omega segmentation of 27, where an ordinarily theta segmentation would be considered 24.6, or a beta segmentation of 16.2, or a zeta segmentation of 20.1, or a tau 23.4, leaves open the question of whether there might be others who might want to venture off into the world of Bram Stoker's Dracula aloft on its petals of Veritas. Looking back, wondering if multiple sclerosis could recover from an unfamiliar 8.7 or slide onward into the back rows of is sort of an arbitrage, where one could justifiable head for the hills with appetite suppression, or fly under the radar with insomnia, while parkinsonian is scarier, by any one of these measure because of the rapid nature of decline, accompanied with the frustration of THB- response with insomnia, appetite suppression, and regularized IL-11 induction, which tends to work up to a point in heading for the hills, while a THB+ response for Amyolateral Sclerosis without IL-11 induction, and malaria toxin can be a bit jittery, but no worse than THB- with insomnia, appetite suppression, and regularized IL-11 induction – in low calorie-intake situations, compareable with the caloric intake of rickshaw drivers in poor countries where people are likely to bring you into their home to feed you because of depravity. Wolfe's is a typical response for THC over a period of time, where the patient is able to return to work with brain cancer. In comparison, the neuroblastomas for Richard Butler can vary over time with age, which is similar to a discovery made in 1997, when the physician Pablo Unomuno, who was very good at deterministic models, and randomly discovered a strange little atoll which he named jagged for a patient who walked around the neighborhood with the obliviousness of a mathematician named Conway, who shared the same atoll with a scientist, by the name of Jim Watson, it was discovered almost a decade later. The atoll in itself is quite small, in relation to the prevalence of pancreatic cancer, in particular the encephalitic pain caused by the disease, which is a meningeal inflammation which is notorious. During his childhood Pablo Unamuno had experimented with Primidone, which introduced the idea of appetite suppression, which resulted in typhoid fevers which last for three to four week in the range of 104F for the first week, and 102F for two weeks, and 100F for a week. Typhoid fevers are re-iterative, much like cosmic radiation. They have a sculpture hanging in front of Commonwealth Ave in Boston to accentuate the syllogism, by which we might be able to look at how the phenomena is not too different from the case for Richard Butler, where

Plasminogen Activation Factor value of 23.2 is associated with (110, 92.5) for THC, where Plasminogen Activation Factor value of 23.2 is associated with (30, 95) for coffee, and where where Plasminogen Activation Factor value of 22.2 is associated with (40, 90) for ephedrine for the ordering of pancreatic cancer response from -0.007659314 (1985) to -0.107466063 (1984) to -0.05704145 (2002) in a single patient, for the movie boris godunov, where we used to sit next to each other in primary school wondering what the fuck was going on with the church setting, the times tables, and rhymes, and he was always talking about the bowl in the air.

When we look at serum Ig A then over time, would you say the treatment conditions are regression, forward progression or post-hoc – in how the brain computes macromolecular adhesion for transmembrane domains in Greenland? The second question is how does forward progression work as a query language where a Norwegian Cruise liner sails into the sea and returns to port with passengers, namely Clozapine, Olanzapine, and Dramamine, in overlapping waves with Ephedrine, which is made from the ginger root of the ephedra plant in the upper Nile river valley.

How can you be sure that it's the upper Nile and not the lower Nile, when we know that the upper Nile was producing 1300KWH, before Bangkok was streamed into the railways for deployment of the Circuit, A is for Asia, in homage of the hit single, *India, My Love Star*.

That's a tough question, because as physicians we aren't accustomed to thinking in terms of circuit biology where patients have histories. Example, food value calculations, for New South Wales for t = 0.008 for the axis 1/log(3786) is 0.27947, compared to Queensland for t = 0.006 for the axis 1/log(4913) is 0.2709, compared to Nuuk for t = 0.004 for the axis 1/log(10717) is 0.24813 compared to Kabul t = 0.002 for the axis 1/log(10717) is 0.25681, compared to Pont du Nord t = 0.01 for the axis 1/log(7832) is 0.24157, and Twickenham for t = 0.004 for the axis 1/log(5873) is 0.265332222. The rotation then for New South Wales is log(1/5861) or -3.7679 and the rotation for Queensland is log(1/4834) or -3.6843 while the rotation for Nuuk is 0.265332222, and the rotation for Kabul is 0.256813739. These are different from Fibonacci numbers which we can compute from the Hagen Quartet's performance of Ravel in allegro moderato where we approximate with periods of the staccato, allegro, and hold, for β MLi declination at 36,42,26 and 46 LMi at 34,12,54 to create what is generally thought of in music as a movement, where 15/38 = 0.3947 when multiplied by (0.4375)^2 = 0.0755, for 16/37 the movement is 0.0827 for 20/33 the movement is 0.1160, for 70/71 the movement is 0.1887, for 4/9 the movement is 0.0850 for 2/9 the movement is 0.0425 and for 3/9 the movement is 0.0638.

An alternative mechanism might be thought about as a comparison of Pearce, Weaving and Sting, where the study of Ig A is expanded into an actual forward progression with Ig O in surmising how the brain computes ahead with the

Norwegian Cruise liner sails into the sea and returns to port with passengers namely, Caffeine, Ibuprofen, and Clozapine.

As a highly fortunate co-incidence Pablo Unamuno, after leaving his bizarre recollections of primary school for students of all ages thrown together in one class, met Sigourney Weaver in his first year, and it wasn't until they were in their fourth year, when he began to realize that they were both experimenting with Clozapine – because it was a strange moment when it occurred to both at once, to ask are you seeing the same thing as I am seeing? The distinction being that Ig O tends to be quite discrete.

That should be useful, I think, for the Syrian refugees escaping from Mosul, where the installments related to DNA-RNA complexes for Matthew Meselson and Franklin W. Stahl might be thought of differently than a canvas of red tulips hanging on a wall, where lanes 4.1, 3.0, and 2.5, are experiments with the hypoglycemic index associated with rum, vodka, bourbon and triplesec in a cocktail with coke for rapid absorption into a film of the same name, with Tom Cruise, and the 1.9 comes from the awe inspiring Russian space astronaut, Valentina Terescova and 1.5, 1.1, 1.0, 0.7, 0.3 come from Franklin W. Stahl for the dissertation, Starch, different or same as the stars? Asked another way, does your laboratory for mass production of nuclear weapons have trouble genotyping or sequencing – where the winning entry for recombinant contestants is BaBb, compared with the situation called diaphanous AaBa, and small cell Aaba.

Certification by internal review boards at any NHS hospital in the UK, and Australia, fundamentally examine patient data based on what you might call line options for technology gaps, or educational referendums.

That the Albert Einstein Hair College of Medicine and Dentistry of Kendall Park is deficient in both, might have been expected, given the patient outcomes for doxorubicin trial was terminated after seventeen patient deaths, *Systems analysis of sex differences reveals an immunosuppressive role for testosterone in the response to influenza vaccination* PNAS January 14, 2014. 111 (2) 869-874 and a follow-up carbamazepine trial for black population was terminated after six patient deaths *Automated identification of stratifying signatures in cellular subpopulations* PNAS July 1, 2014. 111 (26) E2770-E2777, and finally a Ropinirole trial, was terminated due to the onset of paralysis in five patients, *Structural insights into binding of STAC proteins to voltage-gated calcium channels* PNAS November 7, 2017, 114 (45) E9520-E9528. Clearly there is racial tension in Palo Alto, where the filings would suggest misunderstanding of drug-disease relationships, for drug-population studies.

Or, the Whitehead Institute is looking at allelic mutations in MDR genes to select patients for drug trials, *Leveraging premalignant biology for immune-based cancer prevention* PNAS September 27, 2016. 113 (39) 10750-10758 because their physicians have trouble following protocols – which opens a rather large deficit for Albert Einstein Hair College of

Medicine and Dentistry which needs to review applications from a disease response perspective, or select a different reimbursement plan.

There's no need to be sorry, when there may be a flotilla somewhere in the Mediterranean, where David Cameron who used to write stuff which didn't make any sense under a pseudonym, found inner peace in Herceptin suicide, and it's more than likely that Gill Chu, for personal reasons, might attempt going off-line. Often physicians, when they can't find a cure for their disease they begin designing surrogate clinical trials – technically, that's called murder, and the reality in many instances is that the physician is practically insane, because nobody (sane) would design clinical trials that result in fatalities, or paralysis. We need to be clear on that. For instance, Pasture himself would never commit to prescriptions without understanding that his patient was aware of bioscience, typically that means the patient has to be aware of the mind-brain duality, where the imposition of the brain upon the mind has different effects, than impositions of the mind upon the brain. Otherwise, we look like jungle bunnies experimenting with human subjects.

That's what I thought, where yoghurt at a young age is quite helpful in differentiating the risk assessment parameters of exposures, where Pasture's little patient, Pablo Unamuno wanders aimlessly, shirtless, in the middle hot summer afternoons, or climbs rocky black hills, or runs around the ledge of buildings, or tries to find the melting point of mercury, or chases after elephants tails – and then spends hours drawing, making up stories, or creating toys – for the most part, by himself. In fact the setting that Pasture develops, including a little hospital with flying nuns, from the residential space to the surrounding enviorment have a great deal of equanimity with exposure, where a thunderous tropical storm becomes magnified through an exposed wall to an otherwise modern setting with modern conveniences – and suddenly little Pablo is hiding under his raw, carved Mahogany bed with a head board which was higher than he was, which could kill him if he were to become violently epileptic, as sheets of rain and hail pours into the flat. It takes Pablo several years to come to the conclusion from that point, where large rods of hail splatter the floors, that what he needs to survive are injections, for which he has to develop a criteria which communicates to Pasture, that otherwise he is going to die, by which time he has already completed his survey of urine samples, and various sugars. As a motif the exposure settings they use to communicate is much like a camera, where Pablo wet's his bed every night till he is six years old, or has cuts and bruises so often that one might be surprised to discover how he assess balance.

On the institutes notes of the subject-and-patient, I'd recommend, *Ficciones* and *How to Make a Novel* for both sides of the story in the relationship – while a background on the Institute's subjects are provided in *Three Exemplary Novels*. In that sense, if we look at the study of Ig A is expanded into an actual forward progression with Ig O in surmising how the brain computes ahead with the Norwegian Cruise liner sails into the sea and returns to port with passengers namely, Caffeine, Ibuprofen, and Clozapine, we might be surprised by the comparisons of plasminogen activation factor value 20, for Pearce (220, 50) compared to the plasminogen activation factor value 23, for Weaving (103, 47) and the plasminogen activation factor value 7.2, for Sting (109, 110) where the progression for disease enthusiasm appears to have been diagnosed earlier than a slope for a slide into Clozapine – before the emergence of Ibuprofen, Ephedrine; violently ill to secure two tablets of Dristan for nausea cleared some of the DH5a cells, sufficiently to be able to sleep – that being a problem for patients, could be an interesting comparison for children.

The composition of a Newtonian world hasn't really changed in that respect, from the principia, which broadly outlines the four elements. Earth, water, fire, and air. A recantation, of his associated sarcasms might put into words, as a way to communicate with others, that "The artificial hills in Bangkok was the world mountain Meru (a mythical mountain in Tibet, according to ancient cosmology towering like a piller between earth and heaven; the four beasts stood for the four quarters and four rivers of the world, so that the whole structure was a kind of replica of the world system," where the world system functions between cosmology, that which is projected into hyperspace, and astrophysics, that which we are able to compute, where for the artificial hills, the question is astrophysical.

Does it make a swoosh, sound? That's my question, as I think Newton's notes might indicate that the sounds were more likely to have been dum, tin, dong, bong, and tank if you really want to know the truth, before the invention of the xylophone, where plumbers and pipe fitters tried to determine the extent to which dong-bong could be expanded into something rife with notes.

Notes, yes, his extravagance for notes, is in part how civilization progressed from thinking in words to thinking in numbers. He shows example of this idea, which as a subject we describe as surface, surface area of a circle, where he defines the value for an as 189,000 and then approximates the closest divisor which would create a year. In another instance he defines the value for a surface area of a circle, 19,000 where he approximates the divisor as 107 which would create a year.

Yeah, it's a bit like trying to understand the constituent structure for night-and-day – where there is an abundance of light, and then there isn't light. Essentially this is the gambit of intellectual life, which the Magdalens, work in their compositions and compositional interpretations, which isn't all that different from when they were pondering in the dusty fields of dharma – by which, I mean the five explorers of the East India Company were drunk at the time. There was Pearce, who would manage the see-saw with little Pablo falling off the seat, there was Richard who was more of a sly dope fiend looking at students as if he was the prefect, and

Hugo who was a group leader for chaotic hide and seek games. An interesting classmate for little Pablo, when they met was Johnny, because he was organized, copying notes with different pens, erudite and diligent – and most impressive, because his assigned seat was always to the left and in the front row, a vantage point for keen observations, where one could observe exactly how Johnny would focus his attention with a tilted stare, and then as soon as he cognitive diaspora struck his ensemble, he would go into his pencil case to withdraw a weapon, write, look up at the board, close the fountain pen, and withdraw a second weapon from the pencil, and so on, without losing his enthusiasm for learning, where at times he could be seen holding three to weapons in one hand while writing notes, as the company's book keeper, who swings his legs with excitement when he envisions the prospect of being able to do his homework, which averaged about four to six hours, usually with two to three after school tutors from class 2, for memorizing historical names, battles and dates to writing essays and solving math problems, learning verb conjugations in Sanskrit, or worse, Hindi, to strip searching Shakespeare's plays. His studies therefore tend to reflect phenomenology, where he can create a the template, make it fun, make it demonstrative, or make it academic, where the Christendom is symptomatic of his earlier erudition with abnormally stressful academics where he never lost his sense of enjoyment – he could be quite argumentative without being closed – in the sense, where he's still scopes, because that's who Richard is, compared to Hugo, who will find you and say something as revelatory to a six year old as, "did you know that your parents fuck? Yeah, they lie down on top of each other and you dad fucks your mum with his penis, because she's got a hole," and then walk away. Likewise His films address embryogenesis from macro-molecules to genetics as a technological platform, with spatial stereotypes in a way that makes Mendel and Morgan appear 16th century. Most of Pearce's work on the other hand deals with translating weights, typically for instruments, and sheet music – with appointments, and calendars, for air where he returns to the typecast for 254 with a divisor of 158 and shows the rationals to be 607. His daily operations are similar to Laurent's Class I set theory models, but now they incorporate several different enlopements from the swing sets, which are Hardy-Weinberg which is where he met Lawrence, as he calls himself, fuming as usual about placebos, which are second order grey matter – for which, directing many of the strips would be an objective for Pearce, because Hugo is working on projects which are strikingly different from Pearce's models, which are closer to a large gallery, with changing exhibitions. And that's how the patient batch was selected for NHS-32, where the facilitation for prescriptions are made directly through the Institute Pasture, with a cohort, where our research interests are to understand the mind-brain duality for epilepsy – where the principal investigators are double blind in a scenario, where new information, or the re-interpretation of knowledge can be used to change therapeutic options, which we can't expand to NHS-England, without a phase forward feasibility with NHS-Bournemouth and Dorset, where phasing in the two hospitals, means looking at the decision tree algorithm, and asking where and how does brain cancer, multiple sclerosis, and haemophelia overlap, as an inductive logical set of parameters similar to the study of plasminogen activation factor.

Barbarian communities, famous for crack-ass movies about barbarian nightmares as the Revenant, of course have a stake in potatoes, and barley, with more recent interests in coffee sales, that's what they call waste water treatment in the area, flowers that's what they call cricket players, and pastries that's what they call home mortgage in the area, famous for naked winter Olympics . Whence the motif for jagged was revealed, and the possibility of its use in the stock market, a conglomerate of pharmaceutical developers immediately left the state, sensing an utilities arbitrate in the stock market which is a violation of securities laws. But you have to allow for the insane acts of people to carry forward an insane objective as an investigation into how the SEC works with the objectionable, to obviate market practices, where banks can freeze accounts within twenty-four hours, and home mortgage holders can liquidate mortgages to commercial property insurers within hours, and markets can assign convertible notes for initial public offerings at the drop of a hat. This facile nature of the SEC left people vacillating betwixt doubt and disbelief about the nature of fricassee duck – with a tutorial on the differences between the Ethernet and CERN, for overnight services which used to cost three orders of magnitude less than a MD from Harvard, which costs twice as much as a D.Sc. from Christ Church, and a sum of the two for a FRC from Magdalene College.

Subject EVE, an actor of movies with biblical content is a (positive control of RRE) could begin to clarify the agglomerative processes for large areas effected by immigration, migratory pressures, and employment franchisements, where we would be keen to know, to which extent does the later abate the former. In translation one would have to surmise to which extent thrombocytopenia in appearance has made favorable improvements, while tuition and fees for sTNF RII left the cab door open for erythropoiesis to qualify perfectly for anaxionic trials of Methotrexate /Aricept. Our developments could be seen as mutually exclusive for studies in aesthetics, and growth markets, as standards for quality-of-living improves. A place to investigate, could be subject CES, where the non-Hodgkins types should be better differentiated while keeping the number of deaths associated with machine learning to a minimum, who does not present attention deficiency associated with (interrogative) as way to better understand the role of allelic variation and nucleation as a follow-up of Dynin case studies, where applicable as proposed by Keats, for professorial colloquia at Saint Anne's College for academics who committed suicide due to payroll issues. To take it from PNAS, characterization of the O6MeGua-PhX174 + Hae III, would suggest that Alan Brown provides the cyto-cyclosporin domain for Bernard Jenkins as a way for Leadrel to resonate with the audience in Pashtun. Further on, John Essigmann was interviewed at the request of Ian Blackford for consultation on gross margin, there did not seem to be any adverse reaction to ingestible 4N other than catatonic at the time, which is quite different from a year-long observation of David Carridine, who suffered several osteoblasts (Dog Fight, 1991), symptoms of alcohol dehydrogenase inhibition (The Dogs of War, 1980), and asymptomatic Parkinson's (Happiness, 1998) at initiation and decline at end towards a catatonic state of vascular dementia (Accidental Tourist, 1988) as a way to understanding hereditary transgenics. In contrast, Konstantine Novoselov, then working as Chancellor for the Department of Melting Resistors into Reading Paper is known to have made high honors for pursuing with diligence fermats for Dynin resistant campus crusades, for the Globe theater. The opposite testimony on symptoms of indication by Nader Yierly would suggest concession stands in the Berkshires for untimely. Considering several cost performers, one could generalize that the unintended consequence begins to look more like a scene from the Pianist, than from the Piano – with the only remaining question being, ironically, where is 4N from – as a question of population diversity, that is, similar to 3G coverage in the US for AT&T compared to Verizon, where a large majority of the population does not have IL-1 – IL-4, same as South Indians, Saudi Arabians, and the Nigerian peninsula. A unique trait among the blacks of South Africa, is that they lack IL-16, which was unknown till recently, as the cause of high prevalence of hemophilia, whereas the Boars are know to lack IL-13 since the mid-seventeenth century, with origins in Lithuania. The majority of the Russian population lacks IL-4, same as the population of the Indian sub-continent extending up to the Philippines, above the river Godavari. The bisect of the South American continent, defined as the boarder of control between IL-1 and IL-2, where most of the argentine population has IL-1 but not IL-2, compared to the Guatemalan population which has IL-2 but not IL-1. The populations of China and Japan lack IL-11. Within Europe, the Germans, French, and the Luxembourgs lack IL-8, while Rumania has homologous double recombinant of IL-8, and the Czech Republic is lacking in IL-7. The spontaneous nature of how these humans mutated gave Luis pause to think about a design for phase II clinical trials for Polyneuropathy and *Amyolateral sclerosis*, where cohorts could be developed into treatment categories and, more importantly preparation for fall-out shelters before embarking on a phase III clinical trial for *Anemia* and Polyneuropathy.

From behind Gestapo Headquarters, the Luftwaffa had finally received the message from *They Love Me Everywhere I Go.* Luis read the fax to himself, and said "I couldn't help laughing, and she laughed with me, but she said that custom was older than either of us, and went away content." In translating Plancks for "auch taschendiebe lieben die weihnachtszeit;" 01.12.2017 13:41 Uhr, Platz der Luftbrücke 6, 12101 Berlin, the Doctors at the old psychiatric hospital in Munich, were befuddled by the mention of Bob Geldof, Jeff Goldblum, Melanie Griffith, Barack Obama, and Steffi Graff, "without attribution for Andre Geim, for groundbreaking experiments regarding the material graphene with Novoselov, who was the youngest Nobel laureate in physics." Though, "wir haben 4Ns pass nach dem Julian Schnabel gelöscht," might appear crude, the development of the Euro currency, since then attracted greater interest for development of screening-out tools for the existing population, to avoid ethnic cleansing of the type seen in Serbia – das ist die schädliche Natur der Promotor-Enhancer-Element-Interaktion in der Transposase (TN) -Aktivität. The expansion from mildly cognitive disorders to severe type-factions could now be seen in the context of hemotaxis and differentiation, without the super-attenuation by active transposons, as way to understand cancer gene-products other than interleukins which could be managed through dosage studies and/or plasma adjuvants.

Second hand analysis into mortality rates for _Benign-Malignant Tumors Case Studies of Patient Duplication on HYW 101_ - suggest that actif-4N Transposase effects Lunatic, which causes renal carcinoma (observed case Kevin Klein, Silver Springs Maryland) while 4N activity effects Braniac, which is to known to effect cyto-regulins (observed cased Phil Murphy, San Francisco). In both instances, where the patients were lacking in IL-1 thru IL-4, the _gain-of-functions_ were artificially induced. That left Manic, Sel-1, and Radical, without proper attribution for _psychose, gametogenese_, and _ostiosarkom._ Partly because he had used many more layers, Fert registered a greater magnetoresistance than Grünberg.

The French group saw a magnetization-dependent change of resistance of upto 50 per cent, whereas the German group saw a 10 per cent difference at the most. The basic effect and the physics behind it were however identical in the two cases. Both groups realized that they had observed a totally new phenomenon. With traditional magnetoresistance no one had registered more than a single per cent or so of change in resistance. Albert Fert was the one who coined the actual concept of giant magnetoresistance to describe the new effect, and in his first publication on the topic he pointed out that the discovery could lead to important applications. Peter Grünberg also realized the practical potential of the phen-omenon and filed a patent at the same time as he was writing a first scientific publication, where the phase transition between for Psychose, Gametogenese, and Ostiosarkom could be better elucidated.

It occurred to Luis to congratulate Claire Boondoggle then for accepting the invitation at All Souls College on the 17th of December 2017, as Dr. Watson, a reprieve for Dr. Darwin one might add, by providing a genetic proof on the allelic segregation of 4N on CSPAN, where the dominant-recessive enhancer element was shown to act as copy-number promotor in the parental genome to knock-down lac promotor-operators creating a glycogen flush in the parental serum for what might be seen as a rough-sleep from drinking Stolichnaya with Whiskey 36mg 62% improvement (F) , 147mg 57% improvement (M) for kanamycin compared to tetracycline. At the same time, for the British Prime Minister to evaluate the endemic situation as, these are not easy proofs to understand, as categorical warning before phase III clinical trials, where the lack of endorsement had been anticipated since 2007, pending intellectual growth of the investigators in matters relating to genetic diversity and population genetics in the interest of United Kingdom – with a continuous data classification study outcome recommended to Harvard Partners and BMCH, where the results of a 6-day trial at the Brigham Women's Hospital for n = 92 ALL/AML polyneuropathies; were converted to un-demented n = 42; resistant n = 32; and twilight zone n = 3.

Experimentally, where release forms for experiments were granted, as mutual consent in 2007, from Newton to Laurent, 3 c.c. of enriched cobra venom (female subject) in ingestible form produced effects much like sparkling water with beer or panache. Absorption with starch is quite rapid and the effect dissipates within three hours. There is almost no noticeable effect from enriched water snake venom 6 c.c (male subject) in ingestible form. Because Cyclosporin and Fluoxitine might be difficult to tolerate as they are atypical antibiotics, it would make more sense to jump cut to Aricept then, anti-histamine. The Australian rattle snake is quite unique in regard to methotrexate (1972 early response with 1.5 grams, and deterioration with growth) continued with Tuberculin virus (1977, 1E20 per ml, 30 ml total).

Experimentally, where release forms for experiments were not granted, 5 c.c. of red snake venom causes, encephalitis –

which is a well-known indication studied by Cepheid-bioMérieux. The ingestible form causes a migraine which lasts for upto three days. In normal circumstances with a *agkistrodon contortrix*, a subject was found dead, after the first day (Heath Ledger, January 22, 2008). Judging the motives to be of hostile intent, possibly to acquire power of attorney, possibly to acquire rights and licenses for algorithms, the LSE banned the use of USD for any of its listed properties, effective September 16 2017. Additional measures were taken by the Russian federation to provide safety and security, to patrol US airspace, and drop bombs where it saw necessary. While bombs that explode are well known, neutron bombs are silent killers. Effectively, a neutron bomb can completely wipe out a population the size of Moscow, without doing any damage of the structures. Exception is granted to Cepheid- bioMérieux due to prior-art and mutual consent, for patent enforcement. With the remaining daze of Janet Yellen in office, we can only hope that Jerome Powell has enough wits about himself to know the difference in staging non-disclosure agreements, mutual non-disclosure agreements before applying for new Human Subjects and Clinical Trial Information forms, required for all human subjects and/or clinical trial research beginning for January 25, 2018 due dates from the NIH.

Among my patients, Burson-Marsteller is a surprise, because their lineage is British in a transparent way, Fleishman-Hillard because their lineage is allergic, H&K because their lineage is neurological, Ketchum-MSL because they are torque-sheared, Ogilvy because it's hard to keep her awake, savvy little Qorvis because he got the cold in utero, and Weber-Shandwick because that's close to home for girls who wanna have fun. The roll call being unlike "hyper-kinetic anxiety," means having to wait for each step. From my partner's practice, there should be no reason to treat Liberia/Qorvis, Guinea/H&K, Sierra Leone (recommend), Nigeria/Weber-Shandwick, and Mali/Burson/Steinbeck(c) any differently than the U.S. population. A simple enough procedure could make accommodation for seeing a better day, control the red-menace, and perhaps reach a wider need. In general practice, we established linkage-association studies, where the genetics of the patients are known with relation to interleukins in a panel where the cytometer is calibrated as a function of linkage-maps for biodiversity, instead of specialized for cancer.

Suppose, explains Luis, you are trying to catch a train. Weber arrives at IL-8 (-/+) at 88.12 Hasbro which we use as a surrogate marker for the US population which does not have IL-1 – IL-4, same as South Indians, Saudi Arabians, and the Nigerian peninsula, which we use as the genetic link to map Rocco the Mobster's laser capture microdissection for benefit of humanity at 16.90 MRC Global. Working backwards, the next linkage is Shandwick IL-8 (+/+) at 88.22 Hasbro as the surrogate marker for drug metabolism, given that K with Advanced B-Cell Leukemia at 1532.00 TUI is Taxol-sensitive permutations and, K with ALL at 1537.5 is Taxol-resistance permutations, then how would you calculate the B-cell proliferation for Burson-Marsteller, given that Mona Lisa IL-3 (+/+) is 87.86 Hasbro.

Too often we discovered cruel exploitation of medical patients as collateral for selling news to commercial sponsors; most often, as in the cases of Bill Cosby, Harvey Weinstein, Charlie Rose, where the media objective seemed to belie some sort of vendetta against the American Medical Association, as a serial rapist of female virtue. The model provided an exploded view of their vendetta, as a back draft for *Dynasty* the strategy game for financing hairware threaded to a bubble gum machine, for the movie, *Anchorman Reads the News from a Cardboard.* Our diligence of the assassins showed that among the founders, Forsythe suffered from severe manic depression barely able to engage in conversation, Collins suffered from tardive dyskinesia with severe weight loss and frequent visits to local hospitals for transfusion, and Evans from severe dyskinesia with personality disorder and amnesia, and among the co-founders the situations were worse, not better, as a prosthesis for the majority of earthlings where IL-1, IL-2, IL-3, IL-4 are genetically null mutants, for which Northern European studies might envison copy number varience in the allelic frequency for il-3, il-4, il-5 in the production of rentinol associated with lymphotactin, astroglia, haemolysis, and inflammation, for the humanoid limbic system, and how possible excretory products for gluco-nitrosamine, such as serotonin and 7,10, ketoamide effect trans-activated domains for effector-catalase ACTA MED SCAND 1981, 210(4): 321 − 7 as a collaborative for bipolar depression, or return to camping in Wonga-Wonga and send faxes to Zurich. Technically, that is a proof for the year Nobel Prize given to Abdus Salam, Alan Cormack, and Odysseus Elytis, in 1979 for the Thames, Tyne, and Liffey, which should resonate with d'auters fois for, *islands in the stream, that is what we are, sail away with me to another world.*

Academy notes of on how re-incarnation is walking out for you, mabbay bust surmisaid ineteracalated as "On deck, tambourines ruffled up a storm peppered by cymbals. The Captain stood at the helm with his knotted talvar poking a pale blue sky; patri colored boatswains trumpeted out of tune into the air; the ships banner rose to the masthead; the anchor slowly rattled up from the bottom of the river with heaving grunts from the crew and dropped with a loud clank on the sandstone deck-" "whence it is a slopperish matter, given the wet and low visibility since in this scherzarade of one's thousand one nightinesses that sword of certainty which would indentifide the body never falls to idendifine the individuone in scratch wig, squarecuts, stock lavaleer, regattable oxeter-" "of or Mnepos and his overalls, all falling over her in folds — sure he hadn't the heart in her to pull them up — poor Matt, the old perigrime matriarch, and a queenly man, (the porple blussing upon them!) sitting there, the sole of the settlement, below ground, for an expiatory rite, in postulation of his cause, (who shall say?)

NOBELSTIFTELSEN

The Nobel Foundation

www.ingramcontent.com/pod-product-compliance
Lightning Source LLC
Chambersburg PA
CBHW071105050326
40690CB00008B/1120